BLACK LEGACY PRESS™
WWW.BLACKLEGACYPRESS.ORG

SLAVE NARRATIVES

VOLUME II
ARKANSAS NARRATIVES
PART 3

By
United States.
Work Projects Administration

Copyright © 2024 by BLACKLEGACYPRESS.ORG

All rights reserved. No part of this publication may be reproduced or transmitted in any form or by any means electronic or mechanical, including information storage and retrieval systems without permission in writing from the publisher, except for student research using the appropriate citations.

ISBN: 978-1-63652-212-8

SLAVE NARRATIVES

A Folk History of Slavery in the United States.
From Interviews with Former Slaves

**UNITED STATES.
WORK PROJECTS ADMINISTRATION**

TYPEWRITTEN RECORDS PREPARED BY
THE FEDERAL WRITERS' PROJECT
1936-1938
ASSEMBLED BY
THE LIBRARY OF CONGRESS PROJECT
WORK PROJECTS ADMINISTRATION
FOR THE DISTRICT OF COLUMBIA
SPONSORED BY THE LIBRARY OF
CONGRESS

WASHINGTON 1941

VOLUME II
ARKANSAS NARRATIVES
PART 3

Prepared by
The Federal Writers' Project of
The Works Progress Administration
For the State of Arkansas

CONTENTS

CHARLIE GADSON	1
DR. D. B. GAINES	3
MARY GAINES	9
WILLIAM GANT	13
MIKE GENES	17
JENNIE WORMLY GIBSON	19
JAMES GILL	21
MRS. CORA GILLAM	29
J. N. GILLESPIE	37
WILL GLASS	41
FRANK WILLIAM GLENN	47
ELLA GLESPIE	49
JOE GOLDEN	53
JAKE GOODRIDGE	59
JOHN GOODSON(GOODRUM)	63
GEORGE GOVAN	65
JULIA GRACE	67
CHARLES GRAHAM	71
JAMES GRAHAM	75
MARTHALA GRANT	77
WESLEY GRAVES	79
AMBUS GRAY	83
GREEN GRAY	87
NEELY GRAY	89

NELY GRAY	91
GREEN NEAR BARTON AND HELENA	95
HENRY GREEN	99
FRANK GREENE	113
GEORGE GREENE	117
ANDREW GREGORY	127
ANNIE GRIEGG	129
WILLIAM AND CHARLOTTE GUESS	133
LEE GUIDON	135
LINLEY HADLEY	143
ANNA HALL	147
ELLIE HAMILTON	149
JOSEPHINE HAMILTON	151
JOSEPHINE HAMILTON	155
PETER HAMILTON	157
LAWRENCE HAMPTON	159
HANNAH HANCOCK	163
HANNAH HANCOCK	169
JULIA E. HANEY	171
RACHEL HANKINS	177
MARY JANE HARDRIDGE	181
MARY JANE HARDRIGE	185
O. C. HARDY	187
ROSA HARDY	189
IDA HARPER	191
ABRAM HARRIS	193
BETTY HARRIS	203

MARY HARRIS	205
RACHEL HARRIS	207
RACHEL HARRIS	211
WILLIAM HARRIS	213
WILLIAM H. HARRISON	215
LAURA HART	221
HATTY HASKELL	225
MATILDA HATCHETT	227
JOHN G. HAWKENS	235
LIZZIE HAWKENS	239
BECKY HAWKINS	243
G. W. HAWKINS	247
ELIZA HAYS	259
TOM HAYNES	265
JOE HAYWOOD	267
MARIE E. HERVEY	271
PHILLIS HICKS	277
WILL HICKS	281
BERT HIGGINS	283
CLARK HILL	291
CLARK HILL	295
ELMIRA HILL	297
GILLIE HILL	301
HARRIETT HILL	303
HATTIE HILL	307
OLIVER HILL	311
REBECCA BROWN HILL	315

TANNY HILL	321
ELIZABETH HINES	323
CHARLES HINTON	327
CHARLES HINTON	331
BEN HITE	335
BETTY HODGE	337
MINNIE HOLLOMON	341
H. B. HOLLOWAY	343
PINK HOLLY	363
DORA HOLMES	365
ELIJAH HENRY HOPKINS	367
NETTIE HOPSON	377
MOLLY HORN	379
CORA L. HORTON	383
LAURA HOUSE	389
AUNT PINKEY HOWARD	391
PINKIE HOWARD	407
JOSEPHINE HOWELL	409
AULINE HOWELL PEARL	413
MOLLY HUDGENS	417
CHARLIE HUFF	419
LOUVENIA HUFF	421
MRS. ANNA HUGGINS	423
MARGRET HULM	429
JOHN HUNTER	431
WILLIAM HUNTER	439
IDA BLACKSHEAR HUTCHINSON	441

CORNELIA ISHMON 453
JACK ISLAND 455
MARY ISLAND 465
HENRIETTA ISOM 467

— — 1937
Interviewer: Miss Irene Robertson
Person interviewed: Charlie Gadson
Brinkley, Arkansas
Age: 67

CHARLIE GADSON

"I was born in Barnwell County, South Carolina. My parents' name was Jane Gadson, Aaron Gadson. My mother master was Mr. Owens. That is all I ever knowed bout him. My father's master was Rivers and Harley Gadson.

"They said they was to get something but they moved on. At the ending of that war the President of the United States got killed. They wouldn't knowed they was free if they hadn't made some change. I don't know what made them think they would get something at freedom less somebody told them they would.

"I work at the oil mill and at sawmilling. I been farmin' mostly since I been here. I got kidney trouble and rheumatism till I ain't no count. I own a house and lot in Brinkley."

United States. Work Projects Administration

Interviewer: Samuel S. Taylor
Person interviewed: Dr. D. B. Gaines
1720 Izard Street, Little Rock, Arkansas
Age: 75

DR. D. B. GAINES

"I was born in 1863 and am now seventy-five years old. You see, therefore, that I know nothing experimentally and practically about slavery.

"I was born in South Carolina in Lawrence County, and my father moved away from the old place before I had any recollection. I remember nothing about it. My father said his master's name was Matthew Hunter.

"I was named for my father's master's brother, Dr. Bluford Gaines. My name is Doctor Bluford Gaines. Of course, I am a doctor but my name is Doctor.

"My father's family moved to Arkansas, in 1882. Settled near Morrilton, Arkansas. I myself come to Little Rock, Arkansas, in 1885, October eighth. Worked in the homes of white families for my board and entered Philander Smith College October 8, 1885. Continued to work with Judge Smith of the Arkansas Supreme Court until I graduated from Philander Smith College. After graduating I taught school and was elected Assistant Principal of the Little Rock Negro High School in 1891. Served three years. Accumulated sufficient money and went to Meharry Medical College, Nashville, Tennessee. Graduated there in 1896. Practiced for five years in the city of Little Rock. Entered permanently upon the ministry in 1900. Was called to the Mount Pleasant Baptist Church where I have been pastoring for thirty-nine years the first Sunday in next May.

"The first real thing that made me switch from the medicine to the ministry was the deep call of the ministry gave me more interest in the Gospel than the profession of medicine furnished to me. In other words, I discovered that I was a real preacher and not a real doctor.

"Touching slavery, the white people to whom my parents belonged were tolerant and did not allow their slaves to be abused by patrollers and outsiders.

"My mother's people, however, were sold from her in very early life and sent to Alabama. My mother's maiden name was Harriet Smith. She came from South Carolina too. Her old master was a Smith. My mother and father lived on adjoining plantations and by permission of both overseers, my father was permitted to visit her and to marry her even before freedom. Out of regard for my father, his master bought my mother from her master. I think my father told me that the old master called them all together and announced that they were free at the close of the War. Right after freedom, the first year, he remained on the farm with the old master. After that he moved away to Greenville County, South Carolina, and settled on a farm, with the brother-in-law of his old master, a man named Squire Bennett. He didn't go to war.

"There was an exodus of colored people from South Carolina beginning about 1880, largely due to the Ku Klux or Red Shirts. They created a reign of terror for colored people in that state. He joined the exodus in 1882 and came to Arkansas where from reports, the outlook seemed better for him and his family. He had no trouble with the Ku Klux in Arkansas. He maintained himself here by farming."

Opinions

"It is my opinion that from a racial standpoint, the lines are being drawn tighter due to the advancement of the Negro people and to the increased prejudice of the dominant race. These lines will continue to tighten until they somehow under God are broken. We believe that the Christian church is slowly but surely creating a helpful sentiment that will in time prevail among all men.

"It appears from a governmental standpoint that the nation is doomed sooner or later to crash. Possibly a changed form of government is not far ahead. This is due to two reasons: (1) greed, avarice, and dishonesty on the part of public people; (2) race prejudice. We believe that the heads of the national government have a far vision. The policies had they been carried out in keeping with the mind of the President, would have worked wonders in behalf of humanity generally. But dishonesty and greed of those who had the carrying out of these policies has destroyed their good effect and the fine intentions of the President who created them. It looks clear that neither the Democratic nor the Republican party will ever become sufficiently morally righteous to establish and maintain a first-class humanitarian and unselfish government.

"It is my opinion that the younger generation is headed in the wrong direction both morally and spiritually. This applies to all races. And this fact must work to the undoing of the government that must soon fall into their hands, for no government can well exist founded upon graft, greed, and dishonesty. It seems that the younger group are more demoralized than the younger group were two generations ago. Thus the danger both to church and state. Unless the church can catch a firmer grip upon the younger group than it has, the outlook is indeed gloomy.

"We are so far away from the situation of trouble in Germany, that it is difficult to know what it is or should be. But one thing must be observed—that any wholesale persecution of a whole group of people must react upon the persecutors. There could no cause arise which would justify a governmental power to make a wholesale sweep of any great group of people that were weak and had no alternative. That government which settles its affairs by force and abuse shows more weakness than the weak people which it abuses.

"We need not think that we are through with the job when we kill the weaker man. No cause is sufficient for the destruction of seven hundred thousand people, and no persecutor is safe from the effects of his own persecution."

Interviewer's Comment

The house at 1720 Izard is the last house in what would otherwise be termed a "white" block. There appears to be no friction over the matter.

Note that if you were calling Dr. Gaines by his professional title and his first name at the same time, you would say Dr. Doctor Bluford Gaines. He has attained proficiency in three professions—teaching, medicine, and the ministry.

Dr. Gaines is poised in his bearing and has cultured tastes and surroundings—neat cottage, and simple but attractive furnishings.

He selects his ideas and words carefully, but dictates fluently. He knows what he wants to say, and what he omits is as significant as what he states.

He is the leader type—big of body, alert of mind, and dominant. It is said that he with two other men dominated Negro affairs in Arkansas for a considerable period of time in the past. He does not give the impression of weakness now.

Despite his education, contacts, and comparative affluence, however, his interview resembles the type in a number of respects—the type as I have found it.

United States. Work Projects Administration

Interviewer: Miss Irene Robertson
Person interviewed: Mary Gaines
Brinkley, Arkansas
Age: Born 1872

MARY GAINES

"I was born in Courtland, Alabama. Mother was twelve years old at the first of the surrender.

"Grandfather was a South Carolinian. Master Harris bought him, two more, his brothers and two sisters and his mother at one time. He was real African. Grandma on mother's side was dark Indian. She had white hair nearly straight. I have some of it now. Mother was lighter. That is where I gets my light color.

"Master Harris sold mother and grandma. Mother said she was fat, tall strong looking girl. Master Harris let a Negro trader have grandma, mother and her three brothers. They left grandpa. Master Harris told the nigger traders not divide grandma from her children. He didn't believe in that. He was letting them go from their father. That was enough sorrow for them to bear. That was in Alabama they was auctioned off. Master Harris lived in Georgia. The auctioneer held mother's arms up, turned her all around, made her kick, run, jump about to see how nimble and quick she was. He said this old woman can cook. She has been a good worker in the field. She's a good cook. They sold her off cheap. Mother brought a big price. They caught on to that. The man nor woman wasn't good to them. I forgot their names what bought them. The nigger traders run her three brothers on to Mississippi. The youngest one died in Mississippi. They never seen the other two or heard of them till after freedom. They went back to Georgia. All of them went back to their old home place.

"In Alabama at this new master's home mother was nursing. Grandma and another old woman was the cooks. Mother went to their little house and told them real low she had the baby and a strange man in the house said, 'Is that the one you goiner let me have?' The man said, 'Yes, he's goiner leave in the morning b'fore times.'

"The new master come stand around to see when they went to sleep. That night he stood in the chimney corner. There was a little window; the moon throwed his shadow in the room. They said, 'I sure do like my new master.' Another said, 'I sure do.' The other one said, 'This is the best place I ever been they so good to us.' Then they sung a verse and prayed and got quiet. They heard him leave, seen his shadow go way. Heard his house door squeak when he shut his door. Then they got up easy and dressed, took all the clothes they had and slipped out. They walked nearly in a run all night and two more days. They couldn't carry much but they had some meat and meal they took along. Their grub nearly give out when they come to some camps. Somebody told them, 'This is Yankee camps.' They give them something to eat. They worked there a while. One day they took a notion to look about and they hadn't gone far 'fore Grandpa Harris grabbed grandma, then mama. They got to stay a while but the Yankees took them to town and Master Harris come got them and took them back. Their new master come too but he said his wife said bring the girl back but let that old woman go. Master Harris took them both back till freedom.

"When freedom come folks shout and knock down things so glad they was free. Grandpa come back. Master Harris said, 'You can have land if you can get anything to work.' Grandpa took his bounty he got when he left the army and bought a pair of mules. He had to pay rent the third year but till then he got what they called giving all that stayed a start.

"Grandma was Mariah and grandpa was Ned Harris. The two boys come back said the baby boy died at Selma, Alabama.

"Grandpa talked about the War when I was a child. He said he was in the Battle of Corinth, Mississippi. He said blood run shoe mouth deep in places. He didn't see how he ever got out alive. Grandma and mama said they was glad to get away from the camps. They looked to be shot several times. Colored folks is peace loving by nature. They don't love war. Grandpa said war was awful. My mother was named Lottie.

"One reason mother said she wanted to get away from their new master, he have a hole dug out with a hoe and put pregnant women on their stomach. The overseers beat their back with cowhide and them strapped down. She said 'cause they didn't keep up work in the field or they didn't want to work. She didn't know why. They didn't stay there very long. She didn't want to go back there.

"My life has never been a hard one. I have always worked. Me and my husband run a cafe till he got drowned. Since then I have to work harder. I wash and iron, cook wherever some one comes for me. When I was a girl I was so much like mother—a fast, strong hand in the field, I always had work.

"Mother said, 'Eat the beans and greens, pot-liquor and sweet milk, make you fat and lazy.' That was what they put in the children's wooden trays in slavery. They give the men and women meat and the children the broth and dumplings, plenty molasses. Sunday mother could cook at home in slavery if she'd 'tend to the baby too. All the hands on Harrises place et dinner with their family on Sunday. He was fair with his slaves.

"For the life of me I can't see nothing wrong with the times. Only thing I see, you can't get credit to run crops and folks all trying to shun farming. When I was on a farm I dearly loved it. It the place to raise young black and white both. Town and cars ruined the country."

Interviewer's Comment

Owns two houses in among white people.

Interviewer: Miss Irene Robertson
Person interviewed: William Gant
Forrest City, Arkansas
Age: 101

WILLIAM GANT

"I was one hundred and one years old last Saturday (1938). I was born in Bedford County, middle Tennessee. My parents' names was Judy and Abraham Gant. They had the same master. They had three boys and two girls. Our owners was Jim Gant and Elizabeth Gant. Ma had seven children, four gals and three boys. We called her Miss Betsy. Jim Gant owned seven hundred acres of good land in one body and some more land summers else. My young masters and mistresses was: Malindy, Jennie, Betsy, Mary, Jim, John, Andy. They had twenty-five or thirty slaves I knowed. He was pretty good to his slaves. He didn't whoop much. Give 'em three or four licks. He fed 'em all well. We had warm clothes in winter.

"I never seen nobody sold. My brothers and sisters was divided out. Miss Betsy was my young mistress. I could go to see all my folks. I never seen no hard times in my life. I had to work or be called lazy. I loved to work. I been in the field when the sun come up and got part my ploughing done. Go back to the house and eat and feed my mule, rest around in the shade. Folks didn't used to dread work so bad like they do now. I lay down and rest in the heat of the day. They had big shade trees for us niggers to rest under, eat under, spring water to drink. I'd plough till smack dark I couldn't see to get to the barn. We had lighted knots to feed by. The feed be in the troughs and water in the big trough in the lot ready. My supper would be hot too. It would be all I could eat too. Yes, I'd be tired but I could sleep till next morning.

"We had big todoos along over the country. White and black could go sometimes. Picnics and preachings mostly what I went to. Sometimes it was to a house covering, a corn shucking, a corn shelling, or log rolling. We went on hunts at night some.

"Sassy (saucy) Negroes got the most licks. I never was sassy. I never got but a mighty few licks from nobody. We was slaves and that is about all to say.

"I learned to fiddle after the fiddler on the place. Uncle Jim was the fiddler. Andy Jackson, a white boy, raised him. He learned him to read and write in slavery. After slavery I went to learn from a Negro man at night. I learned a little bit. My master wouldn't cared if we had learned to read and write but the white folks had tuition school. Some had a teacher hired to teach a few of them about. I could learned if I'd had or been 'round somebody knowed something. He read to us some. He read places in his Bible. Anything we have and ask him. We didn't have books and papers. I loved to play my fiddle, call figures, and tell every one what to do. I didn't take stock in reading and writing after the War.

"My parents had the name of being a good set of Negroes. She was raised by folks named Morrow and pa by folks named Strahorn. When ma was a little gal the Morrows brought her to Tennessee. My parents both raised in South Carolina by the Morrows and Strahorns. I was twenty years old in the War.

"They had a big battle seven or eight miles from our homes. It started at daylight Sunday morning and lasted till Monday evening. I think it was Bragg and Buel. The North whooped. It was a roar and shake and we could hear the big guns plain. It was in Hardin County close to Savannah, Tennessee. It was times to be scared. We was all distressed.

"My master died, left her a widow.

"We farmed, made thirty or forty acres of wheat, seventy-five acres of oats, some rye. I pulled fodder all day and take it down at night while the dew would keep it in the bundle. Haul it up. We was divided out when the War was on.

"Somebody killed Master Jim Gant. He was murdered in his own house. They never did know who done it. They had two boys at home. One went visiting. They knocked her and the boy senseless. It was at night. They was all knocked in the head.

"Will Strahorn owned my wife. He was tolerable good to his Negroes. Edmond Gant was a black preacher in slavery. He married us. He married us in white folks' yard. They come out and looked at us marry. I had to ask my master and had to go ask for her then. Our children was to be Strahorn by name. Will would own them 'cause my wife belong to him. My first wife had five girls and three boys. My wife died. I left both my two last wives. I never had no more children but them eight.

"Freedom—my young master come riding up behind us. We was going in dragging our ploughs. He told us it was freedom. The Yankees took everything. We went to Murray County to get my horse. I went off the next day. The Yankees stayed in Lawrence County. The Yankees burnt Tom Greenfield out. Tom and Jim had joining farms. They took everything he had. Took his darkies all but two girls. He left. Jim was good and they never went 'bout him. Jim stayed at home. I went over there. He put me on his brother's place.

"I come to Arkansas by train. I come to Jackson, Tennessee, then to Forrest City, brought my famlee. My baby child is grown and married.

"The Ku Klux never bothered me. It was a mighty little I ever seen of them.

"I never have had a hard time. I have worked hard. I been ploughing, hoeing, cradling grain, picking cotton all my life. I love to plough and cradle grain. I love to work.

"There is a big difference now and the way I was raised up. They used to be whooped and made mind. They learned how to work. Now the times run away from the people. They used to buy what they couldn't raise in barrels. Now they buy it in little dabs. I ain't used to it. White folks do as they pleases and the darkies do as they can. Everybody greedy as he can be it seem like to me. Laziness coming on more and more every year as they grow up. I ain't got a lazy bone in me. I'm serving and praising my Lord every day, getting ready to go over in the next world."

JAN 14 1938
Interviewer: Miss Irene Robertson
Person interviewed: Mike Genes
Holly Grove, Ark.
Age: 72

MIKE GENES

"I heard folks talk is all I know bout slavery. I was born in Arkansas. My mother was Sara Jane Whitley. My father was _____ Genes. My mother came here from Tennessee wid Henderson Sanders. I was raised on the Duncan place. My mother raised us a heap like old times. I got fire tongs now she had. She made ash cakes and we had plenty milk. I got her old pot hooks too. She cooked cracklin' bread in the winter and black walnut bread the same way. We made palings and boards for the houses and barns. Jes gradually we gittin' away from all that. Times is changing so fast.

"I heard 'em say in slavery they got 'em up fore day and they worked all day. Some didn't have much clothes. I can remember three men twisting plow lines. They made plow lines.

"I vote if I have a chance, but I really don't care bout it. I don't know how to keep up to vote like it ought to be.

"This young generation may change but if they don't they air a knock out. They do jes anyway and everyway. They don't save and cain't save it look like, way we got things now. Folks don't raise nothin' and have to buy so much livin' is hard. Folks all doin fine long as the cotton is to pick. This is two reconstructions I been through. Folks got used to work after that other one and I guess they have to get used to work this time till it get better. I don't know what causes this spell of hard times after the wars."

Interviewer: Miss Irene Robertson
Person interviewed: Jennie Wormly Gibson
Biscoe, Arkansas
Age: 49

JENNIE WORMLY GIBSON

"Gran'ma was Phoebe West. Mama was Jennie West. Mama was a little girl when the Civil War come on. She told how scared her uncle was. He didn't want to go to war. When they would be coming if he know it or get glimpse of the Yankee soldiers, he'd pick up my mama. She was a baby. He'd run for a quarter of a mile to a great big tree down in the field way back of the place off the road. He never had to go to war. Ma said she was little but she was scared at the sight of them clothes they wore. Mama's and grandma's owners lived at Vicksburg a lot of the time but where that was at Washington County, Mississippi. They had lots of slaves.

"Grandma was a midwife and doctored all the babies on the place. She said they had a big room where they was and a old woman kept them. They et milk for breakfast and buttermilk and clabber for supper. They always had bread. For dinner they had meat boiled and one other thing like cabbage, and the children got the pot-liquor. It was brought in a cart and poured in wooden troughs. They had gourds to dip it out with. They had gourds to drink their cool spring water with.

"Daylight would find the hands in the field at work. Grandma said they had meat and bread and coffee till the war come on. They had to have a regular meal to work on in the morning.

"Grandma said their something to eat got mighty slim in war times and kept getting slimmer and slimmer. They had plenty sorghum all the time. Them troughs was hewed out of a log and was washed and hung in the sun till next mealtime. They cooked in iron pots and skillets on the fire. Grandma worked where they put her but her main trade was seeing after the sick on that place.

"They had a fiddler on the place and had big dances now and then.

"This young generation won't be advised no way you can fix it. I don't know what in the world the folks is looking about. The folks ain't good as they used to be. They shoots craps and drinks and does low-down things all the time. I ain't got no time with the young generation. Times gone to pieces pretty bad if you axing me."

Interviewer: Watt McKinney
Person interviewed: James Gill
R.F.D. Marvell, Arkansas
Age: 86
Occupation: Farmer

JAMES GILL

"Uncle Jim" Gill, an ex-slave eighty-six years of age, owns a nice two hundred acre farm five miles north of Marvell where he has lived for the past thirty-five years. "Uncle Jim" is an excellent citizen, prosperous and conservative and highly respected by both white and colored. This is molasses making time in the South and I found "Uncle Jim" busily engaged in superintending the process of cooking the extracted juice from a large quantity of sorghum cane. The familiar type of horse-power mill in which the cane is crushed was in full operation, a roaring fire was blazing in the crudely constructed furnace beneath the long pan that contained the furiously foaming, boiling juice and that "Uncle Jim" informed me was "nigh 'bout done" and ready to drain off into the huge black pot that stood by the side of the furnace. The purpose of my visit was explained and "Uncle Jim" leaving the molasses making to some younger Negro accompanied me to the shade of a large oak tree that stood near-by and told me the following story:

"My ole mars, he was name Tom White and my young mars what claimed me, he was name Jeff. Young mars an' me was just 'bout same age. Us played together from time I fust riccolect till us left de ole home place back in Alabama and lit out for over here in Arkansas.

"Ole mars, he owned a heap of niggers back dere where us all lived on de big place but de lan', it was gittin' poor an' red and mought near wore out; so ole mars, he 'quired a big lot of lan' here in Arkansas in Phillips County, but you know it was all in de woods den 'bout fifteen miles down de ribber from Helena and just thick wid canebrakes. So he sont 'bout twenty famblies ober here end dats how us happened to come 'cause my pappy, he was a extra blacksmith and carpenter and ole mars knowed he gwine to haf to hab him to 'sist in buildin' de houses and sich like.

"Though I was just 'bout seben year ole den, howsomeever, I 'member it well an' I sure did hate to leave de ole home where I was borned and I didn' want leave Mars Jeff either and when Mars Jeff foun' it out 'bout 'em gwine take me he cut up awful and just went on, sayin' I his nigger and wasn't gwine 'way off to Arkansas.

"Ole mars, he knowed my mammy and pappy, dey wasn't gwine be satisfied widout all dere chillun wid 'em, so en course I was brung on too. You see, ole mars and he fambly, dey didn' come and we was sont under de oberseer what was name Jim Lynch and us come on de train to Memphis and dat was when I got so skeered 'cause I hadn' nebber seen no train 'fore den an' I just hollered an' cried an' went on so dat my mammy say if I didn' hush up she gwine give me to de paddy rollers.

"Dey put us on de steamboat at Memphis and de nex' I 'member was us gittin' off at de landin'. It was in de winter time 'bout las' of January us git here and de han's was put right to work clearin' lan' and buildin' cabins. It was sure rich lan' den, boss, and dey jus' slashed de cane and deaden de timber and when cotton plantin' time come de cane was layin' dere on de groun' crisp dry and day sot fire to it and burned it off clean and den planted de crops.

"Ole mars, he would come from Alabama to see 'bout de bizness two an' three times every year and on some of dem 'casions he would bring Mars Jeff wid him and Mars Jeff, he allus nebber failed to hab somethin' for me, candy and sich like, and dem times when Mars Jeff come was when we had de fun. Us just run wild playin' and iffen it was in de summer time we was in de bayou swimmin' or fishin' continual but all dem good times ceasted atter a while when de War come and de Yankees started all dere debbilment. Us was Confedrits all de while, leastwise I means my mammy an' my pappy and me an' all de res' of de chillun 'cause ole mars was and Mars Jeff would er fit 'em too and me wid him iffen we had been ole enough.

"But de Yankees, dey didn' know dat we was Confedrits, dey jus' reckon we like most all de res' of de niggers. Us was skeered of dem Yankees though 'cause us chillun cose didn' know what dey was and de oberseer, Jim Lynch, dey done tole us little uns dat a Yankee was somepin what had one great big horn on he haid and just one eye and dat right in de middle of he breast and, boss, I sure was s'prized when I seen a sure 'nough Yankee and see he was a man just like any er de res' of de folks.

"De war tore up things right sharp yit an' still it wasn't so bad here in Arkansas as I hear folks tell it was back in de yolder states like Tennessee, Alabama, and Georgia. De bes' I riccolect de Yankees come in here 'bout

July of de year and dey had a big scrap in Helena wid 'em and us could hear de cannons fifteen miles off and den dey would make dere trips out foragin' for stuff, corn and sich, and dey would take all de cotton dey could fin', but our mens, dey would hide de cotton in de thickets an' canebrakes iffen dey had time or either dey would burn it up 'fore de Yankees come if dey could. I 'member one day we had on han' 'bout hundred bales at de gin and a white man come wid orders to de oberseer to git rid of it, so dey started to haulin' it off to de woods and dey hauled off 'bout fifty bales and den dey see dey wasn't goin' to hab time to git de res' to de woods and den dey commenced cuttin' de ties on de bales so dey could set fire to dem dat dey hadn' hid yit and 'bout dat time here come one of Mr. Tom Casteel's niggers just a flyin' on a mule wid a letter to de white man. Mr. Tom Casteel, he had he place just up de ribber from us, on de island, and when he gived de letter to de man an de man read it, he said de Yankees is comin' and he lit out for de ribber where de boat was waitin' for him and got 'way and dere was all dat loose cotton on de groun' and us was skeered to sit fire to de cotton den and 'bout dat time de Yankees arive and say don' you burn dat cotton and dey looked all ober de place and find de bales dat was hid in de woods and de nex' day dey come and haul it off and dey say us niggers can hab dat what de ties been cut on and my mammy, she set to work and likewise de odder women what de Yankees say can had de loose cotton and tie up all dey can in bags and atter dat us sold it to de Yankees in Helena for a dollar a poun' and dat was all de money us had for a long time.

"How-some-ever us all lived good 'cause dere was heap of wild hogs an' 'possums and sich and we had hid a heap of corn and us did fine. Sometimes de war boats, dey would pass on de ribber—dat is de Yankee boats—and us would hide 'hind de trees and bushes and see dem pass. We wouldn't let dem see us though 'cause we thought dey would shoot. Heap en heap er times sojers would come by us place. When de Yankees ud come dey would ax my mammy, 'Aunt Mary, is you seen any Se-cesh today?' and mammy, she ud say 'Naw suh' eben iffen she had seen some of us mens, but when our sojers ud come and say, 'Aunt Mary, is you seen ary Yankee 'round here recent?' she ud allus tell dem de truf. Dey was a bunch of us sojers, dat is de Confedrits, what used to stay 'round in de community constant, dat we knowed, but dey allus had to be on de dodge 'cause dere was so many more Yankees dan dem.

"Some of dese men I 'member good 'cause dey was us closest neighbors and some of dem libed on 'j'ining places. Dere was Mr. Lum Shell, Mr. Tom Stoneham, Mr. Bob Yabee, Mr. Henry Rabb and Mr. Tom Casteel. Dem I 'member well 'cause dey come to us cabin right of'en and mammy, she ud cook for 'em and den atter de niggers git dey freedom dey could leave de place any time dey choose and every so of'en mammy ud go to Helena and gin'rally she took me wid her to help tote de things she get dere. Ole Mr. Cooledge, he had de biggest and 'bout de onliest store dat dere was in Helena at dat time. Mr. Cooledge, he was a ole like gentleman and had everything most in he store—boots, shoes, tobacco, medicine en so on. Cose couldn't no pusson go in an' outen Helena at dat time— dat is durin' war days—outen dey had a pass and de Yankee sojer dat writ de passes was named Buford en he is de one what us allus git our passes from for to git in en out and 'twasn't so long 'fore Mr. Buford, he git to know my mammy right well and call her by her name. He, just like all de white mens, knowed her as 'Aunt Mary', but him nor none of de Yankees knowed dat mammy was a Confedrit and dats somepin I will tell you, boss.

"Dese sojers dat I is just named and dat was us neighbors, dey ud come to our cabin sometimes en say, 'Aunt Mary, we want you to go to Helena for us and git some tobacco, and mebbe some medicine, and so on, and we gwine write ole man Cooledge er note for you to take wid you'; and mammy, she ud git off for town walking and ud git de note to ole man Cooledge. Ole man Cooledge, you see, boss, he sided wid de Confedrites too but he didn' let on dat he did but all de Confedrit sojers 'round dar in de county, dey knowed dey could 'pend on him and when my mammy ud take de note in ole man Cooledge, he ud fix mammy up in some of dem big, wide hoop skirts and hide de things 'neath de skirts dat de men sont for. Den she and sometimes me wid her, us would light out for home and cose we allus had our pass and dey knowed us and we easy git by de pickets and git home wid de goods for those sojer men what sont us.

"Speakin' from my own pussonal 'sperience, boss, de niggers was treated good in slavery times, dat is dat was de case wid my mars' peoples. Our mars wouldn't hab no mistreatment of his niggers but I'ze heered tell dat some of de mars was pretty mean to dere niggers, but twasn't so wid us 'cause us had good houses and plenty somepin to eat outen de same pot what de white folks' victuals cooked in and de same victuals dat dey had. You see dat ole kittle settin' ober dar by de lasses pan right now? Well, I is et many a meal outen dat kittle in slavery times 'cause dat is de very same kittle dat dey used to cook us victuals in when us belonged to ole mars, Tom White, and lived on he place down on de ribber. It was den, boss, just same wid white men as 'tis in dis day and time. Dere is heap of good white folks now and dere is a heap of dem what ain't so good. You know dat's so, boss, don't you?

"When de niggers been made free, de oberseer, he called all de peoples up and he says, 'You all is free now and you can do like you please. You can stay on here and make de crops ur you can leave which-some-ever you want to do.' And wid dat de niggers, dat is most of dem, lef' like when you leave de lot gate open where is a big litter of shotes and dey just hit de road and commenced to ramble. Most of 'em, dey go on to Helena and gits dey grub from de Yankees and stay dar till de Yankees lef'.

"But us, we stay on de place and some more, dey stay too and you know, boss, some of dem niggers what belonged to old mars and what he was so good to, dey stole mighty nigh all de mules and rode dem off and mars, he never git he mules back. Naw suh, dat he didn'. De war, it broke ole mars up and atter de surrender he jus' let he Arkansas farm go an' never come back no more. Some of de older peoples, dey went back to Alabama time er two and seen ole mars but I nebber did git to see him since us was sot free. But Mars Jeff, he comed here all de way from de home in Alabama way atter he was growed. It's been 'bout fifty year now since de time he was here and I sure was proud to see him, dat I was, boss, 'cause I sure did love Mars Jeff and I loves him yit to dis day iffen he still lives and iffen he daid which I ain't never heered er not, den I loves and 'spects he memory.

"Yas suh, boss, times is changed sure 'nough but like I 'splained 'bout white folks and it's de same wid niggers, some is good and trys to lib right en some don' keer and jus' turns loose en don' restrain demselves.

"You know, boss, dere is heaps of niggers wid white blood in 'em and dat mess was started way back yonder I reckon 'fore I was ever borned. Shucks, I knowed it was long afore den but it wasn't my kine er white folks what 'sponsible for dat, it was de low class like some of de oberseers and den some of de yother folks like for instance de furriners what used to come in de country and work at jobs de mars ud give 'em to do on the places like carpentrying an' sich. I knowed one bad case, boss, dat happened right dere by us place and dat was de oberseer who 'sponsible for dat and he was de oberseer for a widow oman what lived in Helena and dis white man runned de place an' he hab he nigger oman and she de mama of 'bout six chillun by dis man I tellin' you 'bout, three gals and three boys, and dem chillun nigh 'bout white and look just like him and den he move off to some yother part of de county and he git married dere to a white oman but he take he nigger fambly wid him just de same and he built dem a house in de middle of de place he done bought and he keep 'em dere eben though he done got him a white wife who he lib wid also and, boss, since I done told you he name don't tell I said so 'cause de chillun, dey is livin' dere yet and some of dem is gettin' old deyselves now but, boss, I don't 'spect I is tellin' you much you don't already know 'bout dat bunch."

Interviewer: Beulah Sherwood Hagg
Person interviewed: Mrs. Cora Gillam
1023 Arch Street, Little Rock, Arkansas
Age: 86
[Scratching Pacified Master.]

MRS. CORA GILLAM

"I have never been entirely sure of my age. I have kept it since I was married and they called me fifteen. That was in '66 or '67. Anyhow, I'm about 86, and what difference does one year make, one way or another. I lived with master and mistress in Greenville, Mississippi. They didn't have children and kept me in the house with them all the time. Master was always having a bad spell and take to his bed. It always made him sick to hear that freedom was coming closer. He just couldn't stand to hear about that. I always remember the day he died. It was the fall of Vicksburg. When he took a spell, I had to stand by the bed and scratch his head for him, and fan him with the other hand. He said that scratching pacified him.

"No ma'am, oh no indeedy, my father was not a slave. Can't you tell by me that he was white? My brother and one sister were free folks because their white father claimed them. Brother was in college in Cincinnati and sister was in Oberlin college. My father was Mr. McCarroll from Ohio. He came to Mississippi to be overseer on the plantation of the Warren family where my mother lived. My grandmother—on mother's side, was full blood

Cherokee. She came from North Carolina. In early days my mother and her brothers and sisters were stolen from their home in North Carolina and taken to Mississippi and sold for slaves. You know the Indians could follow trails better than other kind of folks, and she tracked her children down and stayed in the south. My mother was only part Negro; so was her brother, my uncle Tom. He seemed all Indian. You know, the Cherokees were peaceable Indians, until you got them mad. Then they was the fiercest fighters of any tribes.

"Wait a minute, lady. I want to tell you first why I didn't get educated up north like my white brother and sister. Just about time for me to be born my papa went to see how they was getting along in school. He left my education money with mama. He sure did want all his children educated. I never saw my father. He died that trip. After awhile mama married a colored man name Lee. He took my school money and put me in the cotton patch. It was still during the war time when my white folks moved to Arkansas; it was Desha county where they settle. Now I want to tell you about my uncle Tom. Like I said, he was half Indian. But the Negro part didn't show hardly any. There was something about uncle Tom that made both white and black be afraid of him. His master was young, like him. He was name Tom Johnson, too.

"You see, the Warrens, what own my mother, and the Johnsons, were all sort of one family. Mistress Warren and Mistress Johnson were sisters, and owned everything together. The Johnsons lived in Kentucky, but came to Arkansas to farm. Master Tom taught his slaves to read. They say uncle Tom was the best reader, white or black, for miles. That was what got him in trouble.

Slaves was not allowed to read. They didn't want them to know that freedom was coming. No ma'am! Any time a crowd of slaves gathered, overseers and bushwhackers come and chased them; broke up the crowd. That Indian in uncle Tom made him not scared of anybody. He had a newspaper with latest war news and gathered a crowd of slaves to read them when peace was coming. White men say it done to get uprising among slaves. A crowd of white gather and take uncle Tom to jail. Twenty of them say they would beat him, each man, till they so tired they can't lay on one more lick. If he still alive, then they hang him. Wasn't that awful? Hang a man just because he could read? They had him in jail overnight. His young master got wind of it, and went to save his man. The Indian in uncle Tom rose. Strength—big extra strength seemed to come to him. First man what opened that door, he leaped on him and laid him out. No white men could stand against him in that Indian fighting spirit. They was scared of him. He almost tore that jailhouse down, lady. Yes he did. His young master took him that night, but next day the white mob was after him and had him in jail. Then listen what happened. The Yankees took Helena, and opened up the jails. Everybody so scared they forgot all about hangings and things like that. Then uncle Tom join the Union army; was in the 54th Regiment, U. S. volunteers (colored) and went to Little Rock. My mama come up here. You see, so many white folks loaned their slaves to the cessioners (Cecessionists) to help build forts all over the state. Mama was needed to help cook. They was building forts to protect Little Rock. Steele was coming. The mistress was kind; she took care of me and my sister while mama was gone.

"It was while she was in Little Rock that mama married Lee. After peace they went back to Helena and stayed two years with old mistress. She let them have the use of the farm tools and mules; she put up the cotton and seed corn and food for us. She told us we could work on shares, half and half. You see, ma'am, when slaves got free, they didn't have nothing but their two hands to start out with. I never heard of any master giving a slave money or land. Most went back to farming on shares. For many years all they got was their food. Some white folks was so mean. I know what they told us every time when crops would be put by. They said 'Why didn't you work harder? Look. When the seed is paid for, and all your food and everything, what food you had just squares the account.' Then they take all the cotton we raise, all the hogs, corn, everything. We was just about where we was in slave days.

"When we see we never going to make anything share cropping, mother and I went picking. Yes ma'am, they paid pretty good; got $1.50 a hundred. So we saved enough to take us to Little Rock. Went on a boat, I remember, and it took a whole week to make the trip. Just think of that. A whole week between here and Helena. I was married by then. Gillam was a blacksmith by trade and had a good business. But in a little while he got into politics in Little Rock. Yes, lady. If you would look over the old records you would see where he was made the keeper of the jail. I don't know how many times he was elected to city council. He was the only colored coronor Pulaski county ever had. He was in the legislature, too. I used to dress up and go out to hear him make speeches. Wait a minute and I will get my scrap book and show you all the things I cut from the papers printed about him in those days....

"Even after the colored folks got put out of public office, they still kept my husband for a policeman. It was during those days he bought this home. Sixty-seven years we been living right in this place—I guess—when did you say the war had its wind up? It was the only house in a big forest. All my nine children was born right in this house. No ma'am, I never have worked since I came here. My husband always made a good living. I had all I could do caring for those nine children. When the Democrats came in power, of course all colored men were let out of office. Then my husband went back to his blacksmith trade. He was always interested in breeding fine horses. Kept two fine stallions; one was named 'Judge Hill', the other 'Pinchback'. White folks from Kentucky, even, used to come here to buy his colts. Race people in Texas took our colts as fast as they got born. Only recently we heard that stock from our stable was among the best in Texas.

"The Ku Kluxers never bothered us in the least. I think they worked mostly out in the country. We used to hear terrible tales of how they whipped and killed both white and black, for no reason at all. Everybody was afraid of them and scared to go out after dark. They were a strong organization, and secret. I'll tell you, lady, if the rough element from the north had stayed out of the south the trouble of reconstruction would not happened. Yes ma'am, that's right. You see, after great disasters like fires and earthquakes and such, always reckless criminal class people come in its wake to rob and pillage. It was like that in the war days. It was that bad element of the north what made the trouble. They tried to excite (incite) the colored against their white friends. The white folks was still kind to them what had been their slaves. They would have helped them get started. I know that. I always say that if the south could of been left to adjust itself, both white and colored would been better off.

"Now about this voting business. I guess you don't find any colored folks what think they get a fair deal. I don't, either. I don't think it is right that any tax payer should be deprived of the right to vote. Why, lady, even my children that pay poll tax can't vote. One of my daughters is a teacher in the public school. She tells me they send out notices that if teachers don't pay a poll tax they may lose their place. But still they can't use it and vote in the primary. My husband always believed in using your voting privilege. He has been dead over 30 years. He had been appointed on the Grand Jury; had bought a new suit of clothes for that. He died on the day he was to go, so we used his new suit to bury him in. I have been getting his soldier's pension ever since. Yes ma'am, I have not had it hard like lots of ex-slaves.

"Before you go I'd like you to look at the bedspread I knit last year. My daughters was trying to learn to knit. This craze for knitting has got everybody, it looks like. I heard them fussing about they could not cast on the stitches. 'For land's sakes,' I said, 'hand me them needles.' So I fussed around a little, and it all came back. What's funny about it is, I had not knitted a stitch since I was about ten. Old mistress used to make me knit socks for the soldiers. I remember I knit ten pair out of coarse yarn, while she was doing a couple for the officer out of fine wool and silk mixed. I used to knit pulse warmers, and 'half-handers',—I bet you don't know what they was. Yes, that's right; gloves without any fingers, 'cepting a thumb and it didn't have any end. I could even knit on four needles when I was little. We used to make our needles out of bones, wire, smooth, straight sticks,—anything that would slip the yarn. Well, let me get back to this spread. In a few minutes it all came back. I began knitting washrags. Got faster and faster. Didn't need to look at the stitches. The girls are so scared something will happen to me, they won't let me do any work. Now I had found something I could do. When they saw how fast I work, they say: 'Mother, why don't you make something worth while? Why make so many washrags?' So I started the bedspread. I guess it took me six months, at odd times. I got it done in time to take to Ft. Worth to the big exhibit of the National Federation of Colored Women's Clubs. My daughter was the national president that year. If you'll believe it, this spread took first prize. Look, here's the blue ribbon pinned on yet. What they thought was so wonderful was that I knit every stitch of it without glasses. But that is not so funny, because I have never worn glasses in my life. I guess that is some more of my Indian blood telling.

"Sometimes I have to laugh at some of these young people. I call them young because I knew them when they were babies. But they are already all broken down old men and women. I still feel young inside. I feel that I have had a good life."

— 11 1938
Interviewer: Samuel S. Taylor
Person interviewed: J. N. Gillespie
1112 Park Street, Little Rock, Arkansas
Age: 75

J. N. GILLESPIE

"I was born near Galveston, in Texas, January 19, 1863, so they tell me. I been in this town and been living right here at 1112 Park Street for fifty-three years and ain't never had no trouble with anybody.

"My grandparents were Gillespie's. My grandma was an Indian woman. She was stolen off the reservation—her and her daughter. The daughter was about twelve years old and big enough to wait table. Both of them were full blooded Cherokee Indians. My grandma married a slave, and when she growed up, my mother married a slave; but my mother's parents were both Indians, and one of my father's parents was white, so you see about three-fourths of me is something else. My grandmother's name before her first marriage was Courtney and my mother's first name was Parthenia.

"When they were stolen, they were made slaves. Nick Toliver bought 'em. He was their first master, far as I heard 'em say. After old man Nick Toliver died, Tom Brewer bought my mother. Toliver and Brewer were the only two masters she had.

"After freedom came, my grandma took back her own name, Gillespie. Grandma's second husband was named Berry Green. She was free and in the Indian reservation when she married Gillespie, but she was a slave when she married Berry Green.

"After my mother came to be of age, she married a man named Willis. He was a slave. That is why I am like I am now. If my grandma had stayed in the nation, I never would have been a slave, and I wouldn't need to be beatin' around here trying to get just bread and meat.

"After freedom, she taken her mother's name by her free husband, Gillespie, and she made her husband take it too. That how I got the name of Gillespie."

Occupation of Forefathers

"After they were made slaves, my grandmother cooked and my mother waited table and worked as a house girl. My grandma used to make clothes too, and she could work on one of these big looms."

Patrollers

"My mother told me that when the boys would go out to a dance, they would tie a rope across the road to make the horses of the patrollers stumble and give the dancers time to get away. Sometimes the horses' legs would be broken."

Subject's Occupation

"I wants to work and can't get work; so they ain't no use to worry. I used to cook. That is all I did for a living. I cooked as long as I could get something for it. I can't get a pension."

Slave Houses

"I didn't see no log houses when I growed up. Everything was frame."

Right After the War

"Right after the War, my mother stayed around the house and continued to work for her master. I don't know what they paid her. I can't remember just how they got free but I think the soldiers gave 'em the notification. They stayed on the place till I was big enough to work. I didn't do no work in slave time because I wasn't old enough."

Choked on Watermelon Seeds

"One day I was stealing watermelons with some big boys and I got choked on some seeds. The melon seeds got in my throat. I yelled for help and the boys ran away. Old Tom Brewer made me get on my hands and jump up and down to get the seeds out."

Leaving Galveston

"I was a small boy, might have been seven or eight years old, when I left Galveston. We came to Bradley County, here in Arkansas. From Bradley my mother took me to Pine Bluff. After I got big I went back to Texas. Then I came from Texas here fifty-three years ago, and have been living here ever since, cooking for hotels and private families.

"I never was arrested in my life. I never been in trouble. I never had a fight. Been living in the same place ever since I first came here—right here at 1112 Park Street. I belong to the Christian Church at Thirteenth and Cross Streets. I quit working around the yard and the building because they wouldn't pay me anything. They promised to pay me, but they wouldn't do it."

Interviewer's Comment

Gillespie has an excellent reputation, as indeed have most of the ex-slaves in this city. He is clear and unfaltering in his memory. He is deliberate and selects what he means to tell. He is never discourteous. He is a little nervous and cannot be held long at a time. Indian characteristics in him are not especially prominent, but you note them readily after learning of his ancestry. He is brown but slightly copper in color, and his profile has the typical Indian appearance. He is a little taciturn, and sometimes acts on his decisions before he announces them. I cultivated him about three weeks.

Interviewer: Samuel S. Taylor
Person interviewed: Will Glass
715 W. Eighth Street, Little Rock, Arkansas
Age: 50
Occupation: All phases of paving work
[Bit Dog's Foot Off]

WILL GLASS

"My grandfather was named Joe Glass. His master was named Glass. I forget the first name. My grandfather on my mother's side was named Smith. His old master was named Smith. The grandfather Joe was born in Alabama. Grandfather Smith was born in North Carolina."

Whippings

"There were good masters and mean masters. Both of my old grandfathers had good masters. I had an uncle, Anderson Fields, who had a tough master. He was so tough that Uncle Anderson had to run away. They'd whip him and do around, and he would run away. Then they would get the dogs after him and they would run him until he would climb a tree to get away from them. They would come and surround the tree and make him come down and they would whip him till the blood ran, and sometimes they would make the dogs bite him and he couldn't do nothing about it. One time he bit a dog's foot off. They asked him why he did that and he said the dog bit him and he bit him back. They whipped him again. They would take him home at night and put what they called the ball and chain on him and some of the others they called unruly to keep them from running away.

"They didn't whip my grandfathers. Just one time they whipped Grandfather Joe. That was because he wouldn't give his consent for them to whip his wife. He wouldn't stand for it and they strapped him. He told them to strap him and leave her be. He was a good worker and they didn't want to kill him, so they strapped him and let her be like he said."

Picnics

"Both of my grandfathers said their masters used to give picnics. They would have a certain day and they would give them all a good time and let them enjoy themselves. They would kill a cow or some kids and hogs and have a barbecue. They kept that up after freedom. Every nineteenth of June, they would throw a big picnic until I got big enough to see and know for myself. But their masters gave them theirs in slavery times. They gave it to them once a year and it was on the nineteenth of June then.

"Grandfather Joe said when he wanted to marry Jennie, she was under her old master, the man that Anderson worked under. Old man Glass found that Grandfather Joe was slipping off to old man Field's to see Grandma Jennie, who was on Field's place, and old man Fields went over and told Glass that he would either have to sell Glass to him or buy Jennie from him. Old man Glass bought Jennie and Grandfather Joe got her.

"After old man Glass bought Jennie, he held up a broom and they would have to jump over it backwards and then old man Glass pronounced them man and wife.

"Grandfather Joe died when I was a boy ten years old. Grandfather Smith died in 1921. He was eighty years old when he died. Grandfather Joe was seventy-two years old when he died. He died somewhere along in 1898."

Whitecaps

"I heard them speak of the Ku Klux often. But they didn't call them Ku Klux; they called them whitecaps. The whitecaps used to go around at night and get hold of colored people that had been living disorderly and carry them out and whip them. I never heard them say that they whipped anybody for voting. If they did, it wasn't done in our neighborhood."

Worship

"Uncle Anderson said that old man Fields didn't allow them to sing and pray and hold meetings, and they had to slip off and slip aside and hide around to pray. They knew what to do. People used to stick their heads under washpots to sing and pray. Some of them went out into the brush arbors where they could pray and shout without being disturbed.

"Grandfather Joe and Grandfather Smith both said that they had seen slaves have that trouble. Of course, it never happened on the plantations where they were brought up. Uncle Anderson said that they would sometimes go off and get under the washpot and sing and pray the best they could. When they prayed under the pot, they would make a little hole and set the pot over it. Then they would stick their heads under the pot and say and sing what they wanted."

Slave Sales

"Grandfather Joe and Grandfather Smith used to say that when a child was born if it was a child that was fine blooded they would put it on the block and sell it away from its parents while it was little. Both of my grandfathers were sold away from their parents when they were small kids. They never knew who their parents were.

"When my oldest auntie was born, my mother said she was sold about two years before freedom. Aunt Emma was only two years old then when she was sold. Mother never met her until she was married and had a family. They would sell the children slaves of that sort at auction, and let them go to the highest bidder."

Opinions

"My grandfather brought me up strictly. I don't know what they thought about the young people of their day, but I know what I think. I will tell you. At first I searched myself. Kids in the time I came along had to go by a certain rule. They had to go by it.

"We don't see to our children doing right as our parents saw to our doing. It would be good if we could get ourselves together and bring these young people back where they belong. What ruined the young folks is our lack of discipline. We send them to school but that is all, and that is not enough. We ought to take it on ourselves to see that they are learning as they ought to learn and what they ought to learn.

"I belong to Bethel A. M. E. Church. I married about 1919, November 16. I have just one kid and two grand kids."

United States. Work Projects Administration

— 13 1937
Interviewer: Miss Irene Robertson
Person interviewed: Frank William Glenn
Des Arc, Arkansas
Age: 73

FRANK WILLIAM GLENN

"I was born June 1864 in Des Arc. My parents named Richard Lewis Glenn and Pleasant Glynn. My mama died when I was small. I recollect hearing em say the southern women oughtn't marry the Yankee men, there was so much difference in their lives. A few widows and girls did marry Yankee men, very few. Southern folks jes' hated em.

"Master Wash Glenn had a son named Boliver. He may had more. I don't know much about em. We stayed there after the war for a long time then went to work for Mr. Bedford Bethels father. We worked there a long time then went to work for Mr. Jim Erwin. My papa always farmed. I heard my mama say she washed and sewed during slavery. There was three boys and one girl in our famlee. I heard bout the bushwhackers and Ku Klux. I was too young to tell bout what they did do. I never did see none dressed up.

"I don't fool wid votin' much. I have voted. I don't understand votin' much and how they run the govermint. My time of usefulness is nearly gone.

"The present time serves me hard. I got my leg caught in a wagon wheel and so sprained I been cripple ever since. The rheumatiz settles in it till I can't sleep at night. My wife quit me. I got two boys in Chicago, the girl and her ma in Brinkley. They sho don't help me. I have to rent my house. I don't own nuthin'. I work all I'm able.

"The present generation is selfish and restless. I don't know what goner become of em. Times is changing too fast for me. I jess look on and wonder what going to come on next."

Interviewer: Miss Irene Robertson
Person interviewed: Ella Glespie
Brassfield, Arkansas
Age: 71

ELLA GLESPIE

"I was born the third year after the surrender. I was born in Okolona, Mississippi. My parents was Jane Bowen and Henry Harrison. Ma had seven children. They lived on the Gates place at freedom. I'm the onliest one of my kin living anywheres 'bout now. Ma never was sold but pa was.

"Parson Caruthers brought pa from Alabama. He was a good runner and when he was little he throwd his hip outer j'int running races. Then Parson Caruthers learnt him a trade—a shoemaker. When he was still nothing but a lad he was sold for quite a sum of money. When emancipation come on he could read and write and make change.

"So den he was out in the world cripple. He started teaching school. He had been a preacher, too, durin' slavery. He preached and taught school. He was justice of the peace and representative for two terms from Chickasaw County in the state legislature. I heard them talk about that and when I started to school Mr. Suggs was the white man principal. Pa was one teacher and there was some more teachers. He was a teacher a long time.

He was eighty odd and ma was sixty odd when she died. Both died in Mississippi.

"My folks said Master Gates was good. I knowd my pa's young Master Gates. Pa said he never got a whooping. They made a right smart of money outen his work. He said some of the boots he made brung high as twenty dollars. Pa had a good deal of Confederate bills as I recollects. Ma said some of them on Gates' place got whoopings.

"When they would be at picnics and big corn shellings or shuckings either, all Gates' black folks was called 'Heavy Gates'; they was fed and treated so well. I visited back at home in Mississippi. Went to the quarters and all nineteen years ago. I heard them still talking about the 'Heavy Gates'. I was one the offspring.

"Ma cooked for her old mistress years and years. Mrs. Rogers in South Carolina give ma to Miss Rebecca, her daughter, and said, 'Take good care of her, you might need her.' They come in ox wagons to Mississippi. Ma was a little girl then when Miss Rebecca married Dr. Bowen. Ma hated to leave Miss Rebecca Bowen 'cause in the first place she was her half-sister. She said Master Rogers was her own pa. Her ma was a cook and house girl ahead of her. Ma was a fine cook. Heap better than I ever was 'cause she never lacked the stuff to fix and I come short there.

"I heard ma tell this. Wherever she lived and worked, at Dr. Bowen's, I reckon. The soldiers come one day and took their sharp swords from out their belts and cut off heads of turkeys, chickens, geese, ducks, guineas, and took a load off and left some on the ground. They picked up the heads and what was left and made a big washpot full of dumplings. She said the soldiers wasted so much.

"When I was young I seen a 'style block' at Holly Springs, Mississippi. I was going to Tucker Lou School, ten miles from Jackson. That was way back in the seventies. A platform was up in the air under a tree and two stumps stood on ends for the steps. It was higher than three steps but that is the way they got up on the platform they tole me.

"I think times are a little better. I gits a little ironing and six dollars and commodities. The young generation is taking on funny ways. I think they do very well morally 'cepting their liquor drinking habits. That is worse, I think. They are advancing in learning. I think times a little better.

"My husband had been out here. We married and I come here. I didn't like here a bit but now my kin is all dead and I know folks here better. I like it now very well. He was a farmer and mill man."

United States. Work Projects Administration

Interviewer: Mary D. Hudgins
Person Interviewed: Joe Golden
Age: 86
Home: 722 Gulpha Street, Hot Springs, Ark.

JOE GOLDEN

"Yes, ma'am to be sure I remembers you. I knew your father and all his brothers. I knew your mother's father and your grandmother, and all the Denglers. Your grandpappy was mighty good to me. Your grandmother was too. Many's the day your uncle Fred followed me about while I was hunting. I was the only one what your grandpappy would let hunt in his garden. Yes, ma'am! If your grandmother would hear a shot across the hill in the garden, she'd say, 'Go over and see who it is.' And your grandfather would come. He'd chase them away. But if it was me, he'd go back home and he'd tell her, 'It's just Joe. He's not going to carry away more than he can eat. Joe'll be all right.'

"Yes, ma'am. I was born down at Magnet Cove. I belonged to Mr. Andy Mitchell. He was a great old man, he was. Did he have a big farm and lots of black folks? Law, miss, he didn't have nothing but children, just lots of little children. He rented me and my pappy and my mother to the Sumpters right here in Hot Springs.

"I can remember Hot Springs when there wasn't more than three houses here. Folks used to come thru and lots of folks used to stay. But there wasn't more than three families lived here part of the time.

"Yes, ma'am we worked. But we had lots of fun too. Them was exciting times. I can remember when folks got to shooting at each, other right in the street. I run off and taken to the woods when that happened.

"No, miss, we didn't live in Hot Springs all thru the war. When the Federals taken Little Rock they taken us to Texas. We stayed there until '68. Then we come back to Hot Springs.

"Yes, miss, Hot Springs was a good place to make money. Lots of rich folks was coming to the hotels. Yes, ma'am, I made money. How'd I make it? Well lots of ways. I used to run. I was the fastest runner what was. Folks would bet on us, and I'd always win. Then I used to shine shoes. Made money at it too. Lots of days I made as much as $4 or $5. Sometimes I didn't even stop to eat. But I was making money, and I didn't care.

"Then there was a feller, a doctor he was. He give me a gun. I used to like to hunt. Hunted all over these mountains[1], hunted quail and hunted squirrel and a few times I killed deers. The man what gave me the gun he promised me twenty five cents apiece for all the quail I could bring him. Lots of times I came in with them by the dozen.

"I tried to save my money. Didn't spend much. I'd bring it home to my mother. She'd put it away for me. But if my pappy knowed I got money he'd take it away from me and buy whiskey. You might know why, miss. He was part Creek—yes ma'am, part Creek Indian.

"Does you remember chinquapins? They used to be all over the hill up yonder.[1] I used to get lots of them. Sell them too. One time I chased a deer up there[1]. Got him with a knife, didn't have a gun. The dogs cornered him for me. Best dog I ever had, his name was Abraham Lincoln. He was extra good for a possom dog. Once I got a white possom in the same place I got a deer. It was way out yonder—that place there ain't nothing but rocks. Yes, ma'am, Hell's Half Acre.[2]

"Yes, miss, I has made lots of money in my time. Can't work none now. Wish you had got to me three years ago. That was before I had my stroke. Can't think of what I want to say, and can't make my mouth say it. You being patient with me. I got to take time to think.

"Me and my wife we gets along pretty well. We have our home, and then I got other property.[3] We was real well off. I had $1200 in the bank—Webb's Bank when it failed.[4] Never got but part of my money back.

"When I sold out my bootblack stand I bought a butcher shop. I made a lot of money there. I had good meat and folks, black folks and white folks came to buy from me. So you remembers my barbecue, do you? Yes, miss, I always tried to make it good. Yes, I remembers your pappy used to always buy from me.

"Your grandmother was a good woman. I remember when your Uncle Freddy had been following me around all day while I was hunting—it was in your grandpappy's garden—his vineyard too—it was mighty big. I told Freddy he could have a squirrel or a quail. He took the squirrel and I gave him a couple of quail too. Went home with him and showed your grandmother how they ought to be fixed.

"I can remember before your father lived in Hot Springs. He and his brothers used to come thru from Polk County. They'd bring a lot of cotton to sell. Yes, ma'am lots of folks came thru. They'd either sell them here or go on to Little Rock. Lots of Indians—along with cotton and skins they'd bring loadstone. Then when your pappy and his brothers had a hardware store I bought lots of things from them. Used to be some pretty bad men in Hot Springs—folks was mean in them days. I remember when your father kept two men from killing each other. Wish, I wish I could remember better. This stroke has about got me.

"Yes, miss, that was the garden. I used to sell garden truck too. Had a bush fence around it long before a wire one. Folks used to pass up other folks to buy truck from me. Your mother did.

"Life's been pretty good to me. I've lived a long time. And I've done a lot. Made a lot of money, and didn't get beyond the third grade.[5] Can't cultivate the garden now. My wife does well enough to take care of the yard. She's a good woman, my wife is.

"So you're going to Fayetteville to see Miss Adeline? I remember Miss Adeline.[6] She worked for your pappy's brother didn't she. Yes, I knowed her well. I liked her.

"Yes miss, I'm sort of tired. It's hard to think. And I can't move about much. But I got my home and I got my wife and we're comfortable. Thank you."

Interviewer's note:

I left him sitting and rocking gently in a home-made hickory stationary swing eyes half closed looking out across his yard and basking in the warm sunshine of late afternoon.

FOOTNOTES:

[1] Units of Hot Springs National Park.

[2] Spot without soil or vegetation—broken talus rock.

[3] Home clean, well painted and cared for, two story, large lot. Rental cottage, good condition, negro neighborhood.

[4] Bank owned and operated for and by negroes—affiliated with headquarters of large national negro lodge.

[5] No public schools in Hot Springs until the late 70s.

[6] The Adeline Blakely of another Arkansas interview with slaves.

United States. Work Projects Administration

Interviewer: Miss Irene Robertson
Person interviewed: Jake Goodridge
Clarendon, Arkansas
Age: 97? 87 is about correct
Born August 4, 1857

JAKE GOODRIDGE

"I was born close to Jackson, Tennessee in Madison County. My master was Hatford Weathers. His wife's name was Susan Weathers. They had a big family—John, Lidy, Mattie, Polly, Betty, and Jimmy, that I recollect and there might er been some more.

"My parents' names was Narcissus and Jacob Goodridge. I had one brother that was a Yankee soldier, and five sisters. One sister did live in Texas. They all dead fur as I know. We got scattered. Some of us got inherited fore freedom. Jake Goodridge took me along when he went to the army to wait on him. Right there it was me an' my brother fightin' agin one 'nother.

"When we come to St. Charles we come to Memphis on freight boxes—no tops—flat cars like. There a heap more soldiers was waiting. We got on a boat—a great big boat. There was one regiment—Indiana Cavalry, one Kansas, one Missouri, one Illinois. All on deck was the horses. There was 1,200 men in a regiment and four regiments, 4,800 horses and four cannons. There was not settin' down room on the boat. They captured my master and sent him to prison. First they put him in a callaboose and then they sent him on to prison and they took me to help them. They made a waitin' boy of me. I didn't lack none of 'em. They cussed all the time. I heard they paroled my master long time after the war.

"They would shoot a cannon, had a sponge on a long rod. They wipe it out and put in another big ball, get way back and pull a rope. The cannon fire agin. Course I was scared. I was scared to death bout two years, that 'bout how long I was in the war. I was twelve or fourteen years old. I recollect it as well as if it was yesterday. They never had a battle at St. Charles while I was there. They loaded up the boat and took us to Little Rock. They mustered out there. The Yankee soldiers give out news of freedom. They was shouting 'round. I jes' stood around to see whut they goiner do next. Didn't nobody give me nuthin'. I didn't know what to do. Everything going. Tents all gone, no place to go stay and nothin' to eat. That was the big freedom to us colored folks. That the way white folks fightin' do the colored folks. I got hungry and naked and cold many a time. I had a good master and I thought he always treated me heap better than that. I wanted to go back but I had no way. I made it down to St. Charles in 'bout a year after the surrender. I started farmin'. I been farmin' ever since. In Little Rock I found a job in a tin pin alley, pickin' up balls. The man paid me $12 a month, next to starvation. I think his name was Warren Rogers.

"I went to Indian Bay 'bout 1868 and farmed for Mr. Hathway, then Mr. Duncan. Then I come up to Clarendon and been here ever since.

"One time I owned 40 acres at Holly Grove, sold it, spent the money.

"I too old, I don't fool wid no votin'. I never did take a big stock in sich foolishness.

"I live wid my daughter and white folks. The Welfare give me $8 a month. We got a garden. No cow. No hog. No chickens.

"The present conditions seem pretty bad. Some do work and some don't work. Nobody savin' that I sees. Takes it all to live on. I haben't give the present generation a thought."

United States. Work Projects Administration

Interviewer: Miss Irene Robertson
Person interviewed: John Goodson (Goodrum)
Des Arc, Arkansas
Age: Born in 1865

JOHN GOODSON (GOODRUM)

"My master was Bill Goodrum. I was born at Des Arc out in the country close by here. My mother was a house woman and my father was overseer. I was so little I don't remember the war. I do remember Doc Rayburn. I seed him and remember him all right. He was a bushwacker and a Ku Klux they said. I don't remember the Ku Klux. Never seed them.

"I heard my parents say they expected the government to divide up the land and give them a start—a home and some land. They got just turned out like you turn a hog out the pen and say go on I'm through wid you.

"I heard them set till midnight talking 'bout whut all took place during the Civil War. The country was wild and it was a long ways between the houses. There wasn't many colored folks in this country till closin' of the war. They started bringing 'em here. Men whut needed help on the farms.

"All my life I been cooking. I cooked at hotels and on boats. I cooked some in restaurants. They say it was the heat caused me to go blind. I cooked up till 1927. The last folks I cooked for was on a boat for Heckles and Wade Sales up at Augusta, Arkansas. I done carpentry work some when I was off of a cooking job. I never liked farmin' much. I have done a little of that along between times too. My main job is cooking.

"I voted along when I could see. I ain't voted lately. I sho lacks this President.

"I had a house and lot—this one, but I couldn't pay taxes. We still living in it. We got a garden. No hog, no cow. We made our home when I cooked and my wife washed and ironed.

"I think this new generation of colored folks is awful. They can get work if they would do it. Times is gettin' worse. They work some if the price suit 'em, if it don't, they steal. They spend 'bout all they make for shows, whiskey and I don't know whut all.

"The Social Welfare gives me $8 a month. My wife does all the washing and ironin' she can get. We are doing very well.

"I don't understand much 'bout votin' and picking out canidates. It don't hurt if the women want to vote.

"Only songs I ever heard was corn songs. I don't remember none. They make 'em up out in the fields. Some folks good at making up songs. One I used to hear a whole heap was 'It goiner be a hot time in the old time tonite.' Another one 'If you liker me liker I liker you. We both liker the same.' I don't remember no more them songs. I used to hear 'em a whole lots. Yes out in the fields."

Interviewer: Thomas Elmore Lucy
Person interviewed: George Govan
Russellville, Arkansas
Age: 52

GEORGE GOVAN

"George Govan is my name, and I was born in Conway County somewheres in December 1886—I guess it was about de seventeenth of December. We lived there till 1911, when I come to Pope County. Both my parents was slaves on de plantation of a Mr. Govan near Charleston, South Carolina. Dat's where we got our name. Folks come to Arkansas after dey was freed. No sir, I ain't edicated—never had de chance. Parents been dead a good many years.

"Yas suh, my folks used to talk a heap and tell me lots of tales of slavery days, and how de patrollers used to whip em when dey wanted to go some place and didn't have de demit to go. Yas suh, dey had to have a demit to go any place outside work hours. Dey whipped my mother and father both sometimes, and dey sure was afraid of dem patrollers. Used to say, 'If you don't watch out de patrollers'll git you.' Dey'd catch de slaves and tie em up to a tree or a pos' and whip em wid buggy whips and rawhides.

"Some of de slaves was promised land and other things when dey was freed, and some wasn't promised nothin'. Some got land and a span of mules, and some didn't get nothin'. No suh, my daddy didn't farm none at first after he was freed because he didn't have no money to buy land, but he done odd jobs here and there till he come to Arkansas seven or eight years after the War.

"Yes, I owns my own home; been livin' in it for ten years, since I've been workin' as janitor at dis Central Presbyterian Church. I belongs to de Missionary Baptis' Church, but my parents were both Methodists.

"Sure did have lots of good songs in de old days, like 'Old Ship of Zion' and 'On Jordan's Stormy Banks.' Used to have one that begins 'Those that 'fuse to sing never knew my God.' It was a purty piece; and then there was another one about a 'Rough, rocky road.'

"De young people today has much better opportunities than when I was a child, and much better than dey had in slavery days, because dar ain't no patrollers to whip em. Most of em dese days has purty good behavior, and I think dey're better than in de old days.

"I has always voted regularly since I come of age— votes de Republican ticket. Can't read but a little, but I never had any trouble about votin'."

NOTE: George Govan is an intelligent Negro, fairly neat in his dress, very tall and erect in stature. Brogue quite noticeable, and occasional idioms that make his interview interesting and personal.

Interviewer: Mrs. Bernice Bowden
Person interviewed: Julia Grace
819 N. Spruce Street, Pine Bluff, Arkansas
Age: 75

JULIA GRACE

"I was seventy-four this last past fourth of July. I was born in Texas. My mother was sent to Texas to keep from bein' freed.

"Ad March and Spruce McCrary is the onliest white folks I remember bein' with. I don't know whether they was our owners or not.

"My father was sent to North Carolina and I never did see him no more.

"After freedom they brought us back here from Texas and we worked on the McCrary plantation.

"In slavery days mama said she and my father stayed in the woods most of the time. That's when they was whippin' 'em.

"My mother come from Richmond, Virginia. Petersburg was her town. She belonged to the Wellses over there.

"After her master got his leg broke, the rest was so mean to her she run off a couple times, so they sold her. Put her up on the tradin' block—like goin' to make a speech. Stripped 'em naked. The man bid 'em off like you'd bid off oxen.

"Mama told me her missis, after her husband died, got so mean to her she run off till her old missis sold her. They weighed 'em and stripped 'em naked to see if they was anything wrong with 'em and how they was built and then bid 'em off.

"Mama said she never would a been in Arkansas if they hadn't been so mean to her. They were too compulsive on 'em—you know, hard taskmasters.

"After freedom Ad March went back to North Carolina and Spruce McCrary come here to Pine Bluff.

"Fust time I moved here in town was in 1888. I stayed ten months, then I went back to the country. I aimed to go to Fort Smith but I got to talkin' with my playmates and I didn't have too much money, and I stayed till I didn't have enough money left to keep me till I could get a job. So I stayed here and worked for Mrs. Freemayer till I got so I couldn't work. She's the one got me on this relief.

"I went to school one session in 1886. Sam Caeser, he was a well-known teacher. He got killed here in Pine Bluff.

"I can't sweep and I can't iron. I got a misery in my back. I washes my clothes and spreads 'em out till they dry. Then I puts 'em on and switches into church and ev-er'body thinks they has been ironed.

"They ain't but one sign I believes in and that's peckerwoods. Just as sure as he pecks three times, somebody goin' to move or somebody goin' to die. Just as sure as you live somebody goin' out.

"One time one of my grandchildren and a friend of mine was walkin' through the woods and we missed the main road we aimed to ketch, and we got into a den of wild hogs. I said, 'Lord, make 'em stand still till we get out of here.' One of 'em was that tall and big long ears hung down over his eyes. That was the male, you know. I reckon they couldn't see us and we walked as easy as we could and we got away and struck the main road. I reckon if they could a seen us we would a been 'tacked but we got away. I had heard how they made people take to trees, and I was scared.

"Have you ever seen a three-legged cow? Well, I have. I looked at her good. She was grown and had a calf."

United States. Work Projects Administration

— 11 1938
Interviewer: Samuel S. Taylor
Person interviewed: Charles Graham
616 W. 27th Street, North Little Rock, Arkansas
Age: 79
[Freed in '63]

CHARLES GRAHAM

"I was born September 27, 1859, Clarksville, Tennessee. I don't remember the county. There are several Clarksvilles throughout the South. But Clarksville, Tennessee is the first and the oldest.

"I got a chance to see troops after the Civil War was over. The soldiers were playing, boxing, and the like. Then I remember hearing the cannons roar—long toms they used to call 'em. My uncle said, 'That is General Grant opening fire on the Rebels.'

"The first clear thing I remember was when everybody was rejoicing because they were free. The soldiers were playing and boxing and chucking watermelons at one another. They had great long guns called muskets. I heard 'em say that Abraham Lincoln had turned 'em loose. Where I was at, they turned 'em loose in '63. Lincoln was assassinated in '65. I heard that the morning after it was done. We was turned loose long before then.

"I was too young to pay much attention, but they were cutting up and clapping their hands and carrying on something terrible, and shouting, 'Free, free, old Abraham done turned us loose.'

"I was here in them days! Heard those long toms roar! General Grant shelling the Rebels!"

Patrollers

"I don't remember much about the patrollers except that when they been having dances, and some of them didn't have passes, they'd get chased and run. If they would get catched, them that didn't have passes would get whipped. Them that had them, they were all right."

Amusements

"They had barbecues. That's where the barbecues started from, I reckon, from the barbecues among the slaves.

"They would have corn shuckings. They would have a whole lot of corn to shuck, and they would give the corn shucking and the barbecue together. They would shuck as many as three or four hundred bushels of corn in a night. Sometimes, they would race one another. So you know that they must have been some shucking done.

"I don't believe that I know of anything else. People were ignorant in those days and didn't have many amusements."

Occupations

"I used to be a regular miller until they laid the men off. Now I don't have no kind of job at all."

Right after the War

"Some of the slaves went right up North. We stayed in Clarksville and worked there for a year or two. In 1864, we went to Warren County, Illinois. They put me in school. My people were just common laborers. They bought themselves a nice little home.

"My mother's name was Anna Bailis and my father's name was Charles Morrill. I don't remember the names of their masters.

"I was raised by my uncle, Simon Blair. His master used to be a Bailis. My father, so I was told, went off and left my mother. She was weak and ailing, so my uncle took me. He took me away from her and carried me up North with them. My father ran away before the slaves were freed. I never found out what became of him.

"I stayed in Illinois from the time I was five or six years old up until I was twenty-one. I left there in 1880. That is about the time when Garfield ran for President. I was in Ohio, seen him before he was assassinated in 1882. Garfield and Arthur ran against Hancock and English. They beat 'em too."

Little Rock

"I used to go from place to place working first one place and then another—going down the Mississippi on boats. Monmouth, Illinois, where I was raised—they ain't nothing to that place. Just a dry little town!"

Opinions

"The young people nowadays are all right. There is not so much ignorance now as there was in those days. There was ignorance all over then. The Peckerwoods wasn't much wise either. They know nowadays though. Our race has done well in refinement.

"I find that the Negro is more appreciated in politics in the North and West than in the South. I don't know whether it will grow better or not.

"I'll tell you something else. The best of these white people down here don't feel so friendly toward the North."

Interviewer: Samuel S. Taylor
Person interviewed: James Graham
408 Maple Street, Little Rock, Arkansas
Age: 75
["Free Negroes"]

JAMES GRAHAM

"I was born in South Carolina, Lancaster County, about nine miles from Lancaster town. My father's name was Tillman Graham and my mother's name was Eliza.

"I have seen my grandfathers, but I forget their names now. My father was a farmer. My father and mother belonged to this people, that is, to the Tillmans.

"On my father's side, they called my people free Negroes because they treated them so good. On my mother's side they had to get their education privately. When the white children would come from school, my mother's people would get instruction from them. My mother was a maid in the house and it was easy for her to get training that way."

United States. Work Projects Administration

Interviewer: Mrs. Bernice Bowden
Person interviewed: Marthala Grant
2203 E. Barraque, Pine Bluff, Arkansas
Age: 77

MARTHALA GRANT

"All I can remember is some men throwin' us up in the air and ketchin' us, me and my baby brother. Like to scared me to death. They had on funny clothes. Me and my brother was out in the yard playin'. They just grabbed us up and threw us up and ketched us.

"My mother would tell us bout the war. She had on some old shoes—wooden shoes. Her white folks name was Hines. That was in North Carolina. I emigrated here when they was emigratin' folks here. I was grown then.

"Durin' the war I heered the shootin' and the people clappin' their hands.

"My mother said they was fightin' to free the people but I didn't know what freedom was. I member hearin' em whoopin' and hollerin' when peace was 'clared and talkin' bout it.

"Yes'm I went to school some—not much. I learned a right smart to read but not much writin'.

"We'd go up to the white folks house every Sunday evenin' and old mistress would learn us our catechism. We'd have to comb our heads and clean up and go up every Sunday evenin'. She'd line us up and learn us our catechism.

"We stayed right on there after the war. They paid my mother. I picked cotton and nussed babies and washed dishes.

"I was married when I was twenty. Never been married but once and my husband been dead nigh bout twenty years."

"When I come here this town wasn't much—sure wasn't much. Used to have old car pulled by mules and a colored man had that—old Wiley Jones. He's dead now.

"I had eleven childen. All dead but five. My boy what's up North went to that Spanish War. He stayed till peace was declared.

"After we come to Arkansas my husband voted every year and worked the county roads. I guess he voted Republican.

"I can't tell you bout the younger generation. They so fast you can't keep up with them. I really can't tell you."

Interviewer: Samuel S. Taylor
Person interviewed: Wesley Graves
817 Hickory Street, North Little Rock, Arkansas
Age: 70
[Father Taught Night School]

WESLEY GRAVES

"My father's white folks were named Tal Graves. My mother was a McAdoo. Her white folks were McAdoos. Some of them are over the river now. He's a great jewelryman now.

"I was born in Trenton, Tennessee. My father was born 'round in Humboldt, Tennessee. My mother was born in Paris, Tennessee and moved out in the country near Humboldt. He met my mother out there and married her just a little bit before the War. He was a slave and she was too.

"He didn't go to the War; he went to the woods. He got to chasing 'round. His young mistress married. She married a Graves. That was the name we was freed under. She was a Shane.

"She educated my father. When she come from school, she would teach him and just carry him right on through the course that way. That was a good while before the War. Her father gave him to her when she married Graves. He was a little boy and she kept him and educated him. Graves ran a farm. I don't know just what my father did when he was little. He was raised up as a house boy. Very little he ever done in the field. I don't know what he did after he grew up and before freedom came. After peace was declared, he taught in night school. He preached too. His first farming was done a little after he come out here. I was about seven years old then. That was in the year 1873.

"My mother's full name was Adeline McAdoo. Before freedom she did housework. She was a kind a pet with the white folks. She didn't do much farming. My mother and father had six children—five boys and one girl. All born after freedom. There were three ahead of me. The oldest was born before the War, not afterward.

"In my country where I was raised the Negroes weren't freed until 1865. My uncle, Jim Shane—that is the only name I ever knew him by—, he ran away and come to this country and made money enough to come back and buy his freedom. Just about time he got himself paid for, the War closed and he would have been freed anyway. The money wouldn't have done him no good anyhow because it was all Confederate money, and when the War closed, that wasn't no good.

"My father ran away when the War broke out. His master wanted to carry him to the army with him and he run off and stayed in the woods three years. He stayed until his little mistress wrote him a letter and told him she would set him free if he would come home. He stayed out till the War closed. He wouldn't take no chances on it.

"The pateroles made my father do everything but quit. They got him about teaching night school. That was after slavery, but the pateroles still got after you. They didn't want him teaching the Negroes right after the War. He had opened a night school, and he was doing well. They just kept him in the woods then."

Ku Klux

"There was a bunch of Ku Klux that a colored man led. He was a fellow by the name of Fount Howard. They would come to his house and he would call himself showing them how to catch old people he didn't like. He told them how to catch my old man. I have heard my mother tell about it time and time again. The funny part of it was there was a cornfield right back of the kitchen. Just about dusk dark, he got up and taken a big old horse pistol and shot out of it, and when he fired the last shot out of it, a white man said, 'Bring that gun here.' Believe me he cut a road through that field right now.

"They stayed 'round for a little while and tried to bully his people. But the old lady stood up to them, so they finally carried her and her children in the house and told her to tell him to come on back they wouldn't hurt him. And they didn't bother him no more.

"My mother's master told my mother that she was free. He called all the slaves in and told them they were free as he was. I don't think he give them anything when they were freed. He was a kind a poor fellow. Didn't have but six or seven slaves. He offered to let them stay and make crops. My father had a better job than that. Did you ever know Bishop Lane out in Tennessee? My father and he were ordained at the same time in the some C. M. E. Church. Then he moved to Kentucky and joined the A. M. E. Church. My father died in 1875 and my mother in 1906.

"I have been married forty-seven years. I married on the twenty-sixth day of December in 1889. I heard my mother and father say that they married in slavery time and they just jumped over a broom. I don't belong to no church. I am off on a pension. I got a good job doin' nothing. My pension is paid by the Railroad.

"I put up forty-four years as a brakeman and five years on ditching trains before I went to braking. My old road master put me on the braking. A fellow got his fingers cut off and they turned his keys over to me and put me to braking and I went there and stayed.

"I have two children. Both of them are living—a girl and a boy. I have had a big bunch of young people 'round me ever since I married. Raised a couple of nephews. Then my two. All of them married. That is my daughter's oldest child right there. (He pointed to a pretty brownskin girl—ed.)

"My father died when I was eight, and I was away from home railroading most of the time and didn't hear much about old times from my mother. So that's all I know.

"I have lived right here on this spot for forty-three years. About 1893 I bought this place and have lived here ever since. This was just a big woods and weed patch then. There weren't more than about six houses out here this side of the Rock Island Railroad.

"I commenced voting in 1889. Cast my first ballot then. I never had any trouble about it."

Interviewer: Miss Irene Robertson
Person interviewed: Ambus Gray
R.F.D. #1. Biscoe, Arkansas
Age: 80

AMBUS GRAY

"I was ten year old when the Civil War come on. I was born Tallapoosy County, Alabama. I belong to Jim Gray. I recollect the paddyrollers. I don't recollect the Ku Klux Klan. There was twelve boys and two girls in our family in time. I was among the older set.

"Bout all I remembers bout slavery was how hard the hands had to work. We sho did haf to work! When we wasn't clerin new ground and rollin pine logs an burnin brush we was er buildin fences and shuckin an shellin corn. Woman you don't know nufin bout work! We cler new groun all day den burn brush and pile logs at nite. We build fences all day and kill hogs and shuck corn dat night. No use to say word bout bein tired. Never heard nobody complainin. They went right on singin or whislin'. Started out plowin and drappin corn then plantin' cotton. Choppin' time come on then pullin' fodder and layin' by time be on. Be bout big meetin time and bout fo that or was over everybody was dun in the cotton field till dun cold weather. I remembers how they sho did work.

"Both my parents was field hands. They stayed on two years after the war was over. Jim Gray raised red hogs and red corn, whooper-will peas. He kept a whole heap of goats and a flock of sheep.

"We didn't see no real hard times after the war. We went to Georgia to work on Armstrongs farm. We didn't stay there long. We went to Atlanta and met a fellar huntin' hands down at Sardis, Mississippi. We come on there. Rob Richardson brought the family out here. I been here round Biscoe 58 years when it was sho nuf swamps and woods.

"I don't think the Ku Klux ever got after any us but I seen em, I recken. I don't know but mighty little. The paddyrollers is what I dreaded. Sometime the overseer was a paddyroller. My folks didn't go to war. We didn't know what the war was for till it had been going on a year or so. The news got circulated round the North was fighting to give the black man freedom. Some of em thought they said that so they'd follow and get in the lines, help out. Some did go long, some didn't want to go get killed. Nobody never got nuthin, didn't know much when it was freedom. I didn't see much difference for a year or more. We gradually quit gettin' provisions up at the house and had to take a wagon and team and go buy what we had. We didn't have near as much. Money then like it is now, it don't buy much. It made one difference. You could change places and work for different men. They had overseers just the same as they did in slavery.

"The Reconstruction time was like this. You go up to a man and tell him you and your family want to hire fer next year on his place. He say I'm broke, the war broke me. Move down there in the best empty house you find. You can get your provisions furnished at certain little store in the closest town about. You say yesser. When the crop made bout all you got was a little money to take to give the man what run you and you have to stay on or starve or go get somebody else let you share crop wid them. As the time come on the black man gets to handle a little mo silver and greenbacks than he used to. Slaves didn't hardly ever handle any money long as he live. He never buy nothin, he have no use for money. White folks burried money durin the war. Some of them had a heap of money.

"I have voted but I don't keep up wid it no mo. It been a long time since I voted. This is the white folks country an they goiner run it theirselves. No usen me vote. No use the women votin as I see it. Jes makes mo votes to count. The rich white man is goiner run the country anyhow.

"I farmed all my life. I been here in Biscoe fifty-eight years. I worked for Richardson, Biscoe, Peeples, Nail. I owned a home, paid $150 for it. I made it in three years when we had good crops.

"Times are harder now than I ever seen em here. If you have a hog you have to pen it up and buy feed. If you have a cow, when the grass die, she is to feed. If you have chickens there ain't no use talkin, they starve if you don't feed em. No money to buy em wid an no money to buy feed for em. Times is hard. Durin the cotton boom times do fine (cotton picking time). The young folks is happy. They ain't got no thought of the future. Mighty hard to make young folks think they ever get old. Theys lookin at right now. Havin em a good time while they young."

United States. Work Projects Administration

Interviewer: Miss Irene Robertson
Person interviewed: Green Gray
R.F.D. #1 Biscoe, Arkansas
Age: 70—73?

GREEN GRAY

"I was born after de war in Alabama. Then we went to Atlanta, Georgia. Bout the first I recollect much bout was in Atlanta. I was seventeen years old. They was building the town back up where it had been burnt. If you was a carpenter you could get rough work to do. My father was a farmer and had a family; soon as he could he come with a man he met up wid to Sardis, Mississippi. He had twelve children. Some of em born down in Mississippi. The reason we all went to Atlanta was dis—we was workin fer a man, white man, named Armstrom. White woman told me go do somethin, bring in a load er wood I think it was, and my mother told me not to do it. He and my father had a fuss an he tied my father to some rails and whooped him. Soon as they done that we all left. They hunted us all night long. Crowd white folks said they goiner kill us. Some fellow come on to Atlanta and told us bout em huntin us. Thater way folks done. It muster been bout the very closin of the war cause I heard em say I was give to my young mistress, Sallie Gray. I don't remember who they say she married. I never did live wid em long fore my papa took me.

"The first free school was in Pinola County, Mississippi. I went to it. The teacher was a white man named George Holliday.

"I votes a Republican ticket. Miss, I don't know nothin much bout votin, cassionly I vote to help my side out a little. We used to elect our town officers here in Biscoe but the white folks run it now. Professor Hardy and Professor Walker was the postmasters (both Negroes) for a long while. John Clay was constable and Oscar Clark magistrate (both Negroes). One of the school board was Dr. Odom (Negro). They made pretty fair officers.

"I was a cow herder, and a fire boy, and a farmer. When I come to Biscoe I was a farmer. I married and had two children. My wife lef me and went wid another fellar then she jumped in the river right down yonder and drowned. I started workin at the sawmill and workin in the lumber. I owns a little home and a spot of ground it on 25' × 90'. I made it workin fer Mr. Betzner (white farmer). I'm farmin now.

"Times is hard. You can't get no credit. Between times that you work in the crop it is hard to live. Used to by workin hard and long hours could make a good livin. Wages better now, $1 to $1.75 a day. Long time ago 60¢ a day was the price. Then you could buy meat five and six cents a pound. Now it 20¢. Flour used to be 40¢ a sack. Now it way outer sight. The young folks don't work hard as I used to work but they has a heap better chance at edgercation. Some few saves a little but everything jes so high they can't get ahead very much. It when you get old you needs a little laid by."

Interviewer: Mrs. Bernice Bowden
Person interviewed: Neely Gray
818 E. Fifteenth, Pine Bluff, Arkansas
Age: 87

NEELY GRAY

"I was born in Virginia. Dr. Jenkins bought my mother from a man named Norman. Brought us here on the boat. I know I was walkin' and talkin'. I don't remember about the trip, but I remember they said they had to keep me out from fallin' in the river. I was too playified to remember anything about it.

"Durin' the War I was a girl six or seven years old. Big enough to nuss my mother's next chile, and she was walkin' and talkin' 'fore surrender.

"My mother was pushin' a hundred when she died. I was her oldest chile. Sold with her.

"Dr. Jenkins had three women and all of 'em had girls. Raised up in the house. Dr. Jenkins said, 'Doggone it, I want my darkies right back of my chair.' He never did 'buse his colored folks. He was a 'cepted (exceptional) man—so different. I never saw the inside of the quarters.

"Dr. Jenkins' house wasn't far from the river. You could hear the boats goin' up and down all night.

"I was scared of the Yankees 'cause they always p'inted a gun at me to see me run. They'd come in the yard and take anything they wanted, too.

"After surrender mama went and cooked for a man named Hardin.

"Hardest time I ever had was when I got grown and had to take care of my mother and sister. Worked in the field.

"I was married out from behind a plow. Never farmed no more.

"My fust husband was a railroad man. I tried to keep up with him but he went too fast; I couldn't keep up. He got so bad they finally black-balled him from the road.

"I tell you nobody knows what it is till you go through with it. I've had my bitters with the sweet.

"Been married four times and I've buried two husbands. I just raised one chile and now she's dead. But I got great-grandchillun—third generation—in Houston, Texas, but I never hear from 'em.

"I get along all right. The Welfare helps me and I try to live right."

Interviewer: Mrs. Bernice Bowden
Person interviewed: Nely Gray
821 E. 18th Avenue, Pine Bluff, Arkansas
Age: 84
Occupation: Does a little quilting

NELY GRAY

"Yes ma'm, I was sold from Richmond, Virginia. Dr. Jenkins bought my mother when I was a little girl walkin' and talkin'. Put me up on the block and sold me too. I was bout three years old.

"Dr. Jenkins was mighty good to his hands. Say he was goin' to raise his little darkies up back of his chair. He thought lots of his colored folks.

"I member seein' the Rebels ridin' horses, three double, down the road time of the war. I used to run off from mama to the county band—right where the roundhouse is now. Mama used to have to come after me. You know I wasn't no baby when I shed all my teeth durin' slavery days.

"Yankee soldiers? Oh Lord—seed em by fifties and hundreds. Used to pint the gun at me jest to hear me holler and cry. I was scared of em. They come in and went in Dr. Jenkins' dairy and got what they wanted. And every morning they'd blow that bugle, bugle as long as a broom handle. Heard em blow 'Glory, Glory Hallelujah'. I liked to hear em blow it.

"Yankees marched all up and down the river road. They'd eat them navy beans. I used to see where they throwed em in the fence corner. Saw so many I don't like em now. They called em navy beans and I called em soldier beans.

"I member it well. I'm a person can remember. Heap a folks tell what other folks see but I tell what I see. Don't tell what nobody told me and what I heard.

"I member when they had the battle in Pine Bluff. We was bout three miles from here when they fit-up here. I member all of it.

"They started to send us to Texas and we got as far as the ravine when they heard the Yankees wasn't comin' so we went back home.

"I stayed round the house with the white folks and didn't know what nothin' was till after surrender. We stayed with Dr. Jenkins for a week or two after surrender, then a man come and took my mother down in the country. I don't know what she was paid—she never did tell us her business.

"I was mama's onliest girl and she worked me day and night. Hoed and picked cotton and sewed at night. Mama learned me to knit and I used to crochet a lot. She sure learned me to work and I ain't sorry.

"I worked in the field till I come out to marry a railroad man. I never went to school but two or three months in my life directly after freedom. My husband was a good scholar and he learned me how to read and write. I learned my daughter how to read and write so when she started to school they didn't have to put her in the chart class.

When she was six years old she could put down a figger as quick as you can.

"Been married four times and they's all dead now. Ain't got nobody but myself. If it wasn't for the white folks don't know what I'd do.

"I used to cook for Dr. Higginbotham when she had company. She couldn't do without old Nely. One time she sent for me to cook some hens. I soaked em in soda water bout an hour and fried em and you couldn't tell em from friers.

"I'm weak in my limbs now but I believe in stirrin'. Welfare helps me but I quilts for people. Yes'm, I stirs—if I didn't I just couldn't stand it.

"This here younger generation is gone. They ain't goin'—they's gone. Books ain't done no good. I used to teach the Bible lesson once a week, but I don't fool with em now. Ain't got no manners—chews gum and whispers.

"I got great grand children lives in Houston and they don't give me a penny. I don't know what I'd do if twasn't for the Welfare.

"Used to wash and iron. I've ironed twenty shirts in one-half a day."

United States. Work Projects Administration

MAY 11 1938
Interviewer: Miss Irene Robertson
Person interviewed: "Happy Day" Green
Near Barton and Helena, Arkansas
Age: Grown during the Civil War

GREEN NEAR BARTON AND HELENA

"I don't know how old I is, young mistress. I was here 'fore the Civil War, young mistress. I was born in South, Alabama, young mistress. Well, it was nigh Montgomery, Alabama, young mistress. My mama name Emily Green. She had three children to my knowing. I don't know no father. My owner was Boss William Green, young mistress. His wife was Miss Lizabuth, young mistress. They did have a big family, young mistress. To my knowing it was: Billy, Charlie, Bunkum, Ida, Mary, Sally, Jimmy, Buddy. I never went to school a day in my life, young mistress. When I come on big 'nuff to work I had to help keer for mama and two girl sisters, young mistress.

"When I come to this state, Van Vicks and Bill Bowman immigrated one hundred head of us. They landed some of us at Helena. Our family was landed at Phillips Bayou, young mistress.

"I was a cowboy, me and George. He was another black boy, young mistress. We kept flies offen Boss William Green and Miss Lizabuth, young mistress. They took naps purt nigh every day when it be the long days (in summer), young mistress. Mama was milk woman. Boss William Green had goats and 'bout a dozen heads of milch cows, young mistress. I was willed to Mars Billy. He went off to war and died 'fore the War begun, young mistress.

"Nobody run 'way from Boss William Green. He told 'em if they run off he would whoop 'em. He didn't have no dogs, young mistress. They be a white man near by owned nigger hounds, young mistress. He take his hounds, go hunt a runaway, young mistress. You would pay him, I reckon, young mistress.

"I did get some whoopings, young mistress. They used a cow hide strap on me, young mistress. They blistered me a right smart, young mistress.

"We didn't have so much to eat. They give us one peck meal, four pounds meat a week. Mama done our cooking, young mistress. We had good clothes, warm clothes, woolen clothes, young mistress. We had a few sheep about the place. We had a few geese 'mong the turkeys, guineas, ducks, and chickens. They kept the peafowls for good luck, young mistress.

"Fur a fact they had a big garden, young mistress. Boss William Green worked the garden. He made us pull the plow—four of us boys. He said the stock would tromp down more'n they'd make, young mistress. Two of his boys and me and George pulled his plough. We had a big garden.

"I chopped in the field, picked up chips on the clearings. I chopped cook wood right smart, young mistress.

"When freedom come on, grandpa come after mama. Boss William Green told her, 'You free.' He give her ten bushels corn, good deal of meat—back bone and spareribs. He come one Saturday evening, young mistress. She took 'long whatever she had at our house in the way of clothing and such lack, young mistress. Well, grandpa was share crapping, young mistress.

"The Ku Kluckses come one night. They kept us getting 'em water to run through something under their sheets. The water was running out on the ground. We did see it for a fact, young mistress. We was scared not to do that. They was getting submission over the country, young mistress They would make you be quiet 'long the roadside, young mistress. They would make you be quiet where you have meeting. They would turn the pots down on the floor at the doors, young mistress. The Ku Kluckses whooped some, tied some out to trees and left 'em. They was rough, young mistress.

"I worked in the field all my life.

"Times is good fer me, young mistress. I live with my niece. I get twelve dollars assistance 'cause I been sick, young mistress. I owns a pony. All I owns, young mistress.

"I hab voted, young mistress. I'm too old to vote now, young mistress. I reckon I voted both ways some, young mistress.

"Young folks is so strong and happy they is different from old folks, young mistress."

United States. Work Projects Administration

Interviewer: Watt McKinney
Person interviewed: Henry Green
Barton, Arkansas
Age: 90

HENRY GREEN

Uncle Henry Green, an ex-slave ninety years of age, is affectionately known throughout a large part of Phillips County as "Happy Day". This nickname, acquired in years long past, was given him no doubt partly on account of his remarkably happy disposition, but mainly on account of his love for the old religious song, "Happy Day", that Uncle Henry has enjoyed so long to sing and the verses of which his voice still carries out daily over the countryside each morning promptly at daybreak and again at sundown.

Uncle Henry and his old wife, Louisa, live with Uncle Henry's sister, Mattie Harris, herself seventy-five years of age, on a poor forty acre farm that Mattie owns in the Hyde Park community just off the main highway between Walnut Corner and West Helena. Henry acts as janitor at the Lutherian Church at Barton and the three do such farming as they are able on the thin acres and with the few dollars that they receive each month from the Welfare Board together with the supplies furnished them at the Relief Office these three old folks are provided with the bare necessities sufficient to sustain them.

Uncle Henry, his wife and sister Mattie are the most interesting of the several ex-slave Negroes in this county whom it has been my pleasure and good fortune to interview. As I sat with them on the porch of their old, rambling log house the following incidents and account of their lives were given with Uncle Henry talking and Mattie and Louisa offering occasional explanations and corrections:

"Yes sir, Boss Man, my right name is Henry Green but eberybody, dey all calls me 'Happy Day'. Dat is de name whut mos' all calls me fer so long now dat heap of de folks, dey don't eben know dat my name is sho nuf Henry Green. I sho ain't no baby, Boss Man, kase I is been here er long time, dat I is, and near as I kin cum at hit I is ninety years old er mo, kase Mattie sey dat de lady in de cotehouse tell her dat I is ninety-fo, en dat wuz three years er go. I is er old nigger, Boss Man, en er bout de onliest old pusson whut is lef er round here in dis part of de county. I means whut is sho nuf old, en what wuz born way bak in de slabery times, way fo de peace wuz 'clared.

"Us wuz borned, dat is me en sister Mattie, er way bak dere in Souf Alabama, down below Montgomery, in de hills, en on de big place whut our ole marster, William Green, had, en whar de tanyard wuz. Yo see, old marster, he runned er big tanyard wid all de res of he bizness, whar dey tan de hides en mek de shoes en leather harness en sich lak, en den too, marster, he raise eberything on de place. All whut he need fer de niggers en he own fambly, lak cotton, wheat, barley, rice en plenty hogs en cows. Iffen peace hadn't er been 'clared en Marse Billy hadn't er died I wuz gwine ter be Marse Billy's property, kase I wuz already willed ter Marse Billy. Marse Billy wuz old Marster William Green's oldest son chile, en Marse Billy claimed me all de while. Marse Billy, he went off to de War whar he tukkin sik en died in de camp, 'fore he cud eben git in de fitin.

"Atter de War wuz ober en peace cum, my grandmammy en my grandpappy, dey cum en got my mammy en all us chillun en tuk us wid dem ter Montgomery, en dat wuz whar us wuz when dem two Yankee mens immigrated us here ter Arkansas. Dey immigrated er bout er hundred head er niggers at de same time dat us cum. My grandpappy en my grandmammy, dey didn't belong ter old Marster William Green. I jist don't know whut white folks dey did belong ter, but I knows dat dey sho cum en got my mammy en us chillun. Old marster, he neber mine dem er leavin' en tole 'em dat dey free, en kin go if us want ter go, en when us left old marster gib mammy ten bushels er corn en some hog heads en spareribs en tole her ter bring de chillun bak er gin 'fore long kase he gwine ter gib all de chillun some shoes at de tanyard, but us neber did go bak ter git dem shoes kase we wuz immigrated soon atter den.

"No sir, Boss Man, we don't know nuthin' 'bout who our pappy wuz. Dar wuzn't no niggers much in slabery times whut knowed nuthin' 'bout dey pappys. Dey jes knowed who dey mammys is. Dats all dey knowed 'bout dat. Us neber hab no pappy, jes er mammy whut wuz name Emily Green.

"Boss Man, yo see how black I is en kinky dat my hair is en yo can see dat me en sister Mattie is sho pure niggers wid no brown in us. Well, yo know one thing, Boss Man, en dis is sho whut my mammy done tole us er heap er times, en dat is dat when I wuz born dat de granny woman runned ter old mis en tell her ter cum en look at dat baby whut Emily done gibed birth ter, and dat I wuz nigh 'bout white en hed straight hair en blue eyes, en when old mis seed me dat she so mad dat she gib mammy er good stroppin kase I born lak dat but hit warn't long atter I born 'fore I gits black, en old mis see den dat I er pure nigger, en den she tell mammy dat she sorry dat she stropped her 'bout me being white en er habin blue eyes en straight hair. No sir, Boss Man, I jes don't know how cum I change but dat sho is whut mammy did tell us. Sister Mattie, she know dat.

"Yes sir, Boss Man, I kin tell you all er bout de old slabery times, en cordin ter whut I'se thinkin', en fer as me myself is, wid de times so tight lak dey is now days wid me, and all de time be er stud'in' 'bout how ter git er long, hit wud be er heap better fer hit to be lak hit wuz den, kase us neber hed nuthin ter worry 'bout den cept ter do dat whut we wuz tole ter do, en all de eatin' en de cloes wuz gib ter us. Our marster trained us up right, fer ter do our wuk good en ter obey whut de white folks sey en ter sho be polite to de white folks, en atter us lef old marster den our mammy she trained us de same way, en we is always polite, kase manners is cheap.

"All de nigger chillun in slabery time wore slips, bofe de gals en de boys. Dere wuzn't no breeches fer de little ones eben atter dey git old enuf ter wuk en go ter de fiel's, dey still wear dem slips, en dey used ter feed us outen dem big wooden bowls whut dey mix de bread up in, wid sometimes de pot-likker, en sometimes mostly wid de milk, en de chillun, dey go atter dat grub en git hit all ober dey faces en dey hands en dey slips en er bout de time dey git through eatin' de old mis she cum out en when dey through old mis, she hab 'em ter wash dey hands en faces nice en clean.

"On dem Sundays dat de marster want all de niggers ter go ter church fer de preachin', he send dem all de order ter wash up good en clean en put on dey clean cloes en git ready fer de preachin', en fust ter cum up dar whar he waitin' ter see dat dey look good en nice en clean, en when us git up dar ter de house lookin' fresh en good, de marster's folks, dey talk lak dis ter one er nudder; dey sey: 'Look er here at my nigger, Henry, dat boy is lookin' fine. He is gwine ter be er big healthy man en er good wukker,' en atter dey all done looked all de niggers ober dey tell 'em ter be gwine on ter de church en dey go on en sit in de bak behine all de white folks en hear de white man preach. Dar wuzn't no nigger preachers in dem days dat I ever seed.

"Now I know dat yo has heard of dem paddyrollers. Well, I tell yo, Boss Man, dem paddyrollers, dey wuz bilious. Dey wuz de mens whut rid out on de roads at night ter see dat all dem niggers whut wuz out en off dey marster's places hed er pass from dey marsters. Dem paddyrollers, dey wud stop er nigger whut dey find out at night en sey, 'Boy, whar yo gwine? En is yo got yo pass?' En de Lawd help dem niggers whut dey cotch widout dat pass. Iffen er nigger be cotch out et night widout de pass writ down on de paper frum he marster, en dem paddyrollers cotch him, dat nigger sho haf ter do sum good prayin' en pretty talkin' er else dey tek him ter whar dey got four stobs drove down in de groun en dey tie he hans en feet ter dem stobs en den ware him out wid er big heaby strop. De mostest reason dat sometimes de niggers out at night is on account dey courtin' some gal whut libes on some udder place. When yo see de paddyrollers er comin' en yo ain't got no pass writ down on de paper en yo don't want ter git er stroppin, den de onliest thing fer yo ter do is ter run en try ter git on yer marster's place 'fore dey git yo, er try ter dodge 'em er somepin lak dat. Iffen de paddyrollers got dem nigger hounds wid 'em when de nigger break en run, den de onliest thing dat de nigger kin do den is ter wuk de conjure. He kin wuk dat conjure on dem hounds in seberal different ways. Fust, he kin put er liddle tuppentine on he feet er in he shoe, en er lot er times dat will frow de hounds off de track, er else, iffen he kin git er hold er some fresh dirt whar er grabe ain't been long dug, en rub dat on he feet, den dat is er good conjure, en mo dan dat iffen he kin git ter catch er yearlin calf by der tail en step in de drappins whar dat calf done runned er long wid him er holdin' on ter de tail, den dat is a sho conjure ter mak dem hounds lose de track, en dat nigger kin dodge de paddyrollers.

"Lak I sey, Boss Man, 'bout de onliest thing dat de niggers in slabery time wud lebe de place at night fer, wud be dey courtin', en mostly den on er Wednesday er Saturday night, so I gwine ter tell yo how dey sometimes dodge de paddyrollers whilst dey courtin' dere wimmens at night. Yo see, mos' all de wimmens, dey be er wukkin at night on dey tasks dat dere old mis gib 'em ter do, er weavin' er de cloth. Dese wimmens wud be er settin' 'roun de fire weavin' de cloth en de nigger be dar too er courtin' de gal, en all ter once here cum dem paddyrollers, some at de front door en some at de back door, en when de wimmens er hear 'em er comin', dey raise er loose plank in de flo whut dey done made loose fer dis bery puppus, en de nigger he den drap right quick down 'neath de flo twix de jists, en de wimmens den slap de plank right bak in place on top er de man ter hide him, so iffen de paddyrollers does come in dat dey see dat dere ain't no man in dar. Dat wuz de way dat de niggers used ter fool 'em heap er times.

"I 'members dem days well when de War gwine on yit I neber did see no Yankee mens er tall, en de closest dat us eber cumbed ter see de Yankees wuz dat time when old marster hed de horn blowed ter signal de niggers ter git de kerrige hosses en de milk cows off ter de woods kase he had done heard dat de Yankees wuz er cumin, but dey missed us en dem Yankees, dey neber find old marster's place. I seed some of our sojer mens do, once, atter us lef old marster en go ter Montgomery wid our grandpappy. Dese sojer mens, dey come in ter town on de train bak frum de War whar dey been fitin fer so long, en dey happy en singin', dey so glad dat peace done 'clared. Hit wuz er whole train full er dem Fedrit sojers, en dey wimmens en chilluns all dere er huggin' en er kissin' 'em ginst dey git off de train en gibin 'em cakes en sich good things ter eat.

"Yes sir, Boss Man, de niggers wuz treated good in slabery times en wuz trained up right, ter wuk, en obey, en ter hab good manners. Our old marster, he neber wud sell er nigger en he feed 'em good, en dey lub en 'spected him. Yo sho hed better 'spect him, en iffen yo didn't dat strop wud be er flyin'. All er old marster's niggers wuz good multiplyin' peoples. Dey sho wuz, en dey raise big famblies. Dats one thing whut er woman hed ter be in dem days er she sho be sold quick. Iffen she ain't er good multiplier dey gwine ter git shut er her rail soon. Day tuk extra pains wid dem good multiplyin' wimmins too en neber gib dem no heaby wuk ter do no mo dan weavin' de cloth er sich roun de place.

"Whilst our old marster, he neber sell no niggers, de speculators, dey hab 'em fer sale er plenty, en I has seed 'em er passin' in de road en er long string er gwine ter de place whar de sale gwine ter be. 'Fore dey git ter de sale place dey roach dem niggers up good jes lak dey roach er mule, en when dey put 'em on de block fer de white mens ter bid de price on 'em den dey hab 'em ter cut de shines en de pidgeon wing fer ter show off how supple dey is, so dey bring de bes' price.

"Dey neber hed no farm bells in slabery times fer ter ring en call de hans in en outen de fiel's. Dey hed horns whut dey blowed early en late. De wuk wud go on till hit so dark dat dey can't see. Den de horn wud blow en de niggers all cum in en git dey supper, en cook dey ash cakes in de fire whut dey build in dey own cabins. Boss Man, is yo eber et er ash cake? I don't 'spects dat yo know how ter mek one er dem ash cakes. I gwine ter tell yo how dat is done. Fust yo git yo some good home groun meal en mix hit well wid milk er water en a liddle salt an bakin' powder whut yo mek outen red corn cobs, den yo pat dem cakes up right good en let 'em settle, den put 'em in de hot ashes in de fireplace en kiver 'em up good wid some mo hot ashes en wait till dey done, en Boss Man, yo sho is got er ash cake dat is fitten ter eat. Dats de way dat us made 'em in slabery times en de way dat us yit meks 'em. Us didn't know whut white bread wuz in de old days, hardly, 'ceptin sometimes 'roun de marster's kitchen er nigger wud git er hold of er biscuit. All de bread dat de slabe niggers git wud be made outen cornmeal er dem brown shorts whut de marsters gib 'em in de rashions.

"Us wuz all well fed do in slabery times en kept in good fat condition. Ebery once in er while de marster wud hab er cow kilt en de meat 'stributed out mongst de folks en dey cud always draw all de rashions dat dey need.

"Dey used ter hab dem big corn shuckin's too in de old days. De corn wud be piled up in er pile es big es er house en all de han's wud be scattered out roun' dat pile er corn shuckin' fas' as dey cud, en atter dey done shucked dat pile er corn, ole marster wud hab two big hogs kilt en cooked up in de big pots en kittles, en den dem niggers wud eat en frolic fer de longes', mekin music wid er hand saw en er tin pan, en er dancin', en laffin, en cuttin' up, till dey tired out. Dem wuz good days, Boss Man. I sho wish dat I cud call dem times bak ergin. De marsters whut hed de big places en de slabe niggers, dey hardly do no wuk er tall, kase dey rich wid niggers en lan', en dem en dey famblies don't hab no wuk ter do, so de old marsters en de young marsters, dey jes knock erbout ober de country on dey hosses, en de young misses en de old misses, dey ride er bout in de fine kerrige wid de coachman er doin' de drivin'. Dey hab de oberseers ter look atter de mekin er de crops, so de bosses, dey jes sort er manage, en see dat de bizness go on de right way.

"De marsters en de misses, dey look atter dere niggers good do en see dat dey keep demselves clean en 'spectible, en try ter keep de disease outen 'em. Ebery Monday mornin' dey gib 'em all er little square, brown bottle er bitters fer dem ter take dat week. Dat wuz dere medicine, but iffen er nigger do git sick, den dey sent fer de doctor right er way en hab de doctor ter 'zamine de sick one en sey, 'Doctor, kin you do dat nigger eny good?' er 'Do whut yo kin fer dat nigger, Doctor, kase he is er valuable han' en wuth muney.'

"I neber wuz sick none do in my life, but I jes nathally been kilt, near 'bout, one time in de gin when my head git cotched twixt de lever en de band wheel en Uncle Dick hed ter prize de wheel up offen my head ter git me loose, en dat jes nigh 'bout peeled all de skin offen my head. Old marster, he gib me er good stroppin fer dat too. Dat wuz fer not obeyin', kase he hed done tole all us young niggers fer ter stay 'way frum de gin house.

"I wuzn't gwine ter be trained up ter wuk in de fiel's, I wuz trained ter be er pussonal servant ter de marster, en sister Mattie, she wuz gwine ter be trained up ter be er house woman, en so wuz my old woman, Louisa, kase her mammy wuz er house woman herself fer her white folks in South Carolina, so I rekkin dats de reason us always thought we so much en better 'en de ginral run er niggers.

"Yes sir, Boss Man, de niggers is easy fooled. Dey always is been dat way, en we wuz fooled er way frum Alabama ter Arkansas by dem two Yankee mens, Mr. Van Vleet en Mr. Bill Bowman, whut I tole yo er bout, dat brung dat hundred head er folks de time us cum. Dey tole us dat in Arkansas dat de hogs jes layin' er roun already baked wid de knives en de forks stickin' in 'em ready fer ter be et, en dat dere wuz fritter ponds eberywhars wid de fritters er fryin' in dem ponds er grease, en dat dar wuz money trees whar all yo hed ter do wuz ter pik de money offen 'em lak pickin' cotton offen de stalk, en us wuz sho put out when us git here en fine dat de onliest meat ter be hed wuz dat whut wuz in de sto, en dem fritters hed ter be fried in de pans, en dat dar warn't no money trees er tall. Hit warn't long 'fore my grandpappy en my grandmammy, dey lef 'en went bak ter Alabama, but my mammy en us chillun, we jes stayed on right here in Phillips County whar us been eber since, en right en dat room right dar wuz whar us old mammy died long years er go.

"Well, Boss Man, yo done ax me en I sho gwine ter tell yo de truf. Yes sir, I sho is voted, en I 'members de time well dat de niggers in de cotehouse en de Red Shirts hab ter git 'em out. Dat wuz de bes' thing dat dey eber do when dey git de niggers outen de cotehouse en quit 'em frum holdin' de offices, kase er nigger not fit ter be no leader. I neber cud wuk under no nigger. I jes nathally neber wud wuk under no nigger. I jist voted sich er length er time, en when de Red Shirts, dey say dat er nigger not good enuf ter vote, en dey stopped me frum votin', en I don't mess wid hit no mo.

"Yes sir, Boss Man, I blebe dat de Lawd lef' me here so long fer some good puppose, en I sho hopes dat I kin stay here fer er heap er mo years. I jes nathally lubes de white folks en knows dat dey is sho gwine ter tek care of old 'Happy Day', en ain't gwine ter let me git hurt.

"De young niggers in dis day sho ain't lak de old uns. Dese here young niggers is jes nathally de cause of all de trubble. Dey jes ain't been raised right en ter be polite lak de old ones, lak me, I don't hold it er gin yo, kase, mebbe yo pappy en yo mammy owned my pappy en my mammy in slabery times en whupped 'em, kase I 'spects dat dey needed all de punishment whut dey got. All de education whut I got, Boss Man, is jes ter wuk, en obey, en ter lib right.

"I knows dat I ain't here far many mo years, Boss Man, en I sho hopes dat I kin git ter see some of my marsters, de Greens, ergin, 'fore I goes. I ain't neber been back since I lef, en I ain't neber heard frum none of 'em since I been in Arkansas, en I know en cose dat all de old uns is gone by now, but I 'spects dat some of de young uns is lef yit. I wud sho lak ter go back dar ter de old place whar de tanyard wuz, but I neber wud hab dat much money ter pay my way on de train, en den, I don't rekkin dat I cud fine de way nohow. I wud git some of de white folks ter write er letter back dar fer me iffen I know whar ter send hit, er de name of some of my young marsters whut mebbe is dar still. Yes sir, Boss Man, I sho hopes dat I kin see some of dem white folks ergin, en dat some of dese days dey will fine me. Yo know I is de janitor at de church at Walnut Corner whar de two hard roads cross, en whar all de cars cum by. De cars, dey cum by dar frum eberywhars, en so ebery Sunday morning atter I gits through er cleanin' up de church, I sets down on de bench dar close ter Mr. Gibson's sto, whar dey sell de gasolene en de cold drinks, en whar de cars cum by frum eberywhar, en I sets dar er lookin' at all dem white folks er passin' in dey cars, en sometimes dey stop fer ter git 'em some gasolene er sumpin, en I says ter myself dat mebbe one er my young marsters sometimes gwine ter be in one of dem cars, en gwine ter drive up dar er lookin' fer me. Er heap er times when de cars stop dar will be er white gentman in de cars whut git out en see me a settin' dar on de bench, en he sey, 'Uncle, yo is rail old, ain't yo?' An den he ax me my name en whar I borned at, en er heap er times dey buy me er cigar. Well, Boss Man, dats how cum I sets on dat bench dar at de road crossin' at Walnut Corner ebery Sunday, mos' all day, atter I gits through er cleanin' up de church, jes settin' dar watchin' dem cars cum by en 'spectin one of dese days fer one of my young marsters ter drive up en ter fine me er settin' dar waitin' fer him, en when he cum, iffen he do, I know dat he sho gwine ter tek me back home wid him."

United States. Work Projects Administration

Interviewer: Mrs. Bernice Bowden
Person interviewed: Frank Greene
2313 Saracen Street, Pine Bluff, Arkansas
Age: 78

FRANK GREENE

"Yes'm, I can remember the Civil War and the Yankees, too. I can really remember the Yankees and my old boss. I can't remember everything but I can remember certain things just as good.

"Dr. Ben Lawton was my old boss. That was in South Carolina. That was what they called Buford County at that time.

"Had a place they called the Honey Hill Fight. I used to go up there and pick up balls.

"I can remember the Yankees had little old mules and blue caps and the folks was runnin' from 'em.

"I remember old boss run off and hid from 'em—first one place and then another.

"I remember the Yankees would grab up us little folks and put us on the mules—just for fun you know. I can remember that just as well as if 'twas yesterday—seems like.

"They burned old boss's place down. He had five or six plantations and I know he come back and rebuilt after peace declared, but he didn't live long.

"He wasn't a mean man. He was good to his folks. We stayed there two years after surrender and when I come to this country, I left some of my uncles on that same place.

"I remember a white gentlemen in South Carolina would just jump his horse over the fence and run over the folks, white and black, cotton and all. He was a rich man and he'd just pay 'em off and go on. He wouldn't put up the fence neither. He was a hunter—a sporting man.

"Me? Yes ma'am, I used to vote—the Republican ticket. We ain't nothin' now, we can't vote. I never had any trouble 'bout votin' here but in the old country we had some trouble. The Democrats tried to keep us from votin'. Had to have the United States soldiers to open the way. That was when Hays and Wheeler was runnin'.

"Here in the South the colored folks is free and they're not free. The white folks gets it all anyway—in some places.

"But they ain't nobody bothered me in all my life— here or there.

"I went to school some after the war. Didn't have very much, but I learned to read and write and 'tend to my own affairs.

"I have done farm work all my life and some public work. I got the same ambition to work as I used to have but I can't hold it. I start out but I just can't hold it.

"Just to pass my opinion of the younger generation, some of 'em level-headed, but seems to me like they is a little rougher than they was in my day.

"I think every one should live as an example for those coming behind."

United States. Work Projects Administration

MAY 11 1938
Interviewer: Samuel S. Taylor
Person interviewed: George Greene
Temporary—1700 Pulaski St., Little Rock, Ark.
Permanent—Wrightsville, Ark.
Age: 85?

GEORGE GREENE

Birth and Age

"I don't know when I was born. I don't know exactly, but I was born in slavery time before the War began. I was big enough to wait on the table when they was fighting. I remember when they was setting the Negroes free. I was born in Aberdeen, Mississippi, in Monroe County. Seven miles from the town of Aberdeen, out on the prairies, that is where I was born.

"I figure out my age by the white woman that raised me. She sent me my age. When they was working the roads, my road boss, I told him I was forty-five years old and he didn't believe it. So I sent to the white woman that raised me from a month-old child. When I left her, I'd done got grown. Her name was Narcissus Stephenson; she had all our ages and she sent mine to me.

"She may be dead now. I could've stayed right there if she isn't dead, because she never did want me to come away. Right out in Arkansas, I come,—to my sorrow. Well, I done right well till I got crippled. Got hit by an automobile. That's what I'm doin' here now."

Parents and Relatives

"My father's name was Nathan Greene. I reckon he went by that name, I can't swear to it. I wasn't with him when he died. I was up in Mississippi on the Mississippi River and didn't get the news in time to get there till after he was dead. He was an old soldier. When the Yankees got down in Mississippi, they grabbed up every nigger that was able to fight. If I'd get his furlough papers, I'd a been drawin' pension before I did. But his brother was with him when he died and he let the dismiss papers get lost, and nobody got nothin'. Don't draw nothin' from it at all. Couldn't find the papers when I was down there.

"I don't know whether my father used his master's name or his father's name. His father's name was Jerry Greene, and his master's name was Henry Bibb. I don't know which name he went by, but I call myself Greene because his father's name was Jerry Greene. No Bibb owned him at first. Jerry Greene was born in North, Alabama in Morgan County. That's where he was born. Bibb bought him and brought him down to Mississippi where I was born. Lord! Old Man Bibb owned a lot of 'em, too. My father and grandfather were both colored but my grandfather was an old yellow man. You know, he had to take his color after his papa. I don't know my great-grandfather's name. They can't tell nothin' 'bout that in them days. His papa, my grandfather's papa, I can't tell for sure whether he was white or black.

"My mother's name was Adeline Greene. Grandpa's wife's name was Louisa. She was one of these kinder mixed with Indian. She lived to see a many a year before she died. She lived to be a hundred and fifteen years of age before she died. I knowed Grandma Louisa. Up until I was a man grown. She was about my color with long straight hair and black (hair). Old Lady Bibb was her mistress. She died way after freedom.

"I don't know mama's age. I was here in Arkansas when she died. Didn't know she was dead until a month after she was buried. She died in Mississippi. Grandma, mama, and all of them died in Mississippi.

"My grandma on my mother's side was named—I can't remember her name, but I knowed her. I can't remember what the old man's name was neither. It's been so long it just went from my memory. They never told me much neither. Folks didn't talk much to children in those days. I wouldn't hardly have thought of it now anyway."

House and Furniture

"A old log house was what I was born in,—when I come out from Mississippi that old house was still standing. Aw, they put up houses them days. It had one room. Didn't have but one room,—one window, one door,— didn't have but one door to go in and out. I remember that well. Didn't have no whole parcel of doors to go in and out. Plank floors. I wasn't born on the dirt! I was born on planks. Our house was up off the ground. We had a board roof. We used four foot boards. Timber was plentiful then where they could make boards easy. Boards was cheap. There wasn't no such things as shingles. Didn't have no shingle factories.

"We didn't have nothing but on old wooden bed. It wasn't bought. It was made. Made it at home. Carpenter made it. Making wooden beds was perfect then. They'd break down every two or three years. They lasted. There was boards holding then. Wasn't no slats nor nothing. Nail them boards to the post and to the sides of the house, and that was the end of it with some people. We had a corded bed. Put them ropes through the sides and corded them up there as tight as Dick's hatband—and they stayed. They made their own boards, and made their own ropes, and corded them together, and they stayed. Chairs! Shucks! They just took boxes. They made chairs too—took shucks and put bottoms in them. Them chairs lasted. Them shucks go way, they'd put more there. Wish I had one of them chairs now. We made a box and put our rations in it. Them days they made what they called cupboards. They made anything they wanted to. When they got free, they'd buy dishes. When they got free, boxes and cupboards went out of style. They bought safes. There wasn't no other furniture. We used tin pans for dishes in slavery time. When we got free, we bought plates.

"When them pans fell they didn't break. They even as much as made their own trays to make bread in. They would take a cypress tree and dig it out and them scoundrels lasted too. Don't see nothin' like that now. Tin pan is big enough to make up bread in now. In them days they made anything. Water buckets,—they did buy them. Old master would give 'em a pass to go get 'em. Anything they wanted, he would give 'em if he thought it necessary. Old master would get 'em all the buckets. He was good and he would buy what you would ask him for. They made milk buckets. They made 'em just like they make 'em now."

Work of Family in Slave Time

"My people were all field hands. My master had a great big farm—three or four hundred acres. I waited table when I was a little chap and I learned to plow before the War was over."

Good Master

"Old Man Bibb was as good and clever a man as ever you knowed. That overseer down there, if he whipped a man Old Man Bibbs would say, 'Here's your money. Don't want you beating up my niggers so they can't work. I don't need you.' He'd tell 'im quick he don't need him and he can git. That's the kind of man he was. Wouldn't let you be mobbed up. He was a good christian man. I'll give that to him. In the time of the War when they was freeing slaves and I was a little old eight-year-old kid, there was a little old Dutchman, a Tennessee man, he came out in the country to get feed. Out there in Alabama.

"I was in Alabama then. The white woman that raised me had taken me there. She had done married again and left me with mama awhile. While I was little, that was. When I was about seven, she came and got me again and carried me down in Alabama and raised me with her children. That white woman never called me nothin' but baby as long as she lived. You know she cared for me just like I was one of her's. When a person raise a child from a month old she can't help from loving it.

"This Dutchman come and asked me where my parents was and I told him they was in Mississippi. He slipped me away from my folks and carried me to Decatur and they got cut off there. He was a Yankee soldier, and old Forrest's army caught 'em and captured me and then carried me first nearly to Nashville. They got in three miles of the town and couldn't get no closer. They ran us so we never got no res' till we got to Booneville, Mississippi. Then I sent word to Bibb and my uncle came up and got me. Him and Billie Bibb, my young master. Billie Bibb was a soldier too. He was home on a furlough. I was glad to see him because I tell you in the army there was suffering. But I'll tell you I'll give them credit, those Tennessee men took care of me just as though I was their own. I was in a two mule wagon. I drove it. I was big enough to drive. The ambulance man stopped in Nashville to see his folks and got a furlough and went on home."

Work

"I learned how to work—work in the field. Wasn't nothing but field work. I learned how to hoe first. But in Alabama I learned how to plow. I didn't want to be no hoe man; I wanted to plow. When I went back to Mississippi, they put me on the plow. I was just eight years old when I learned to plow."

Share cropping

"Right after freedom, I just kept on plowing. We share cropped. My mama and I would take a crop. She'd work. We'd all work like the devil until I got a job and went to town. She was willing to let me go. That was when I married too."

How Freedom Came

"All I know about freedom was Old Man Henry Bibb come out and told us we was free. That is how I came to know it. He came out there on the farm and said, 'Well, you all free as I am. You can stay here if you want to or you can go somewhere else.' We stayed. Mama stayed there on the farm plumb till she come to town. I don't know how many years. I was there in town and so she come onto town later. Moved in with the people she was with. They gave up their place. I was nineteen years old when I left the country. My mother gave me her consent,—to marry then, too. She came to town a few years later.

"The slaves weren't given nothin' after they was freed. Nothing but what they worked for. They got to be share croppers."

Ku Klux Klan

"The Ku Klux never bothered me but they sure bothered others. Way yonder in Mississippi directly after the surrender, they'd hated it so bad they killed up many of them. They caught white men there and whipped them and killed them. They killed many a nigger. They caught a white man there and whipped him and he went on up to Washington, D. C. and came back with a train load of soldiers. They came right down there in the south end of our town and they carried them Ku Kluxers away by train loads full. They cleaned out the east side of the river. The Ku Klux had been stringing up niggers every which way. 'Twasn't nothin' to find a nigger swinging up in the woods. But those soldiers come from Washington City. If they didn't clean 'em up, I'll hush.

"I don't know what become of 'em. They never did come back to Aberdeen."

Occupations Followed and Life Since Freedom

"I ain't worked a lick in four or five years. If I lived to see August tenth, I will be eighty-six years old. I used to follow railroading or saw milling or farming. That is what I followed when I was able to work. The last work I did was farming, working by the day—a dollar and a half a day. And they cut it down and cut me down. Now they ain't giving nothing. If a man gets six bits a day he doing good. Harder times in Arkansas now than I have ever seen before. If a man is able to take care of his family now, he is doing well. They don't give niggers nothing now.

"The only way I live is I get a little pension. They give me eight dollars a month and commodities. That is all I live on now. That keeps me up, thank God. I have been getting the pension about ever since they started. I reckon it is about two years. I have been receiving it every month. It ain't failed yet. They been taking care of me pretty well ever since they started. First start it wasn't nothin' but rations. They give me groceries enough to las' me every month. I had a wife then.

"I have been a widow now four years. Four years I've been a widow. But there ain't nothin' like a man staying in his own house. I have made out now for four years. Right there cooking and washing for George! I didn't have nothing else to do. Fellow can't tell what day the Lord will say, 'Stop', but as long as I am this way, I'll keep at it.

"This soreness in my leg keeps me in bad shape. I came here to get my leg fixed. It gets so I can't walk without a stick. I don't like to stay with other folks. They're sinners and they use me sorta sinful—speak any sort of language. But they sure 'nough treats me nice.

"I got my leg hurt last December. Car ran into me at Wrightsville, and knocked me down and threw me far as from here to that thing (about fifteen feet). After they flung me down, I was flat on my back a long while. I couldn't move. When a fellow gets old and then gets crippled up, it's hard. But I'm gettin' 'long pretty well now, 'cept that this leg ain't strong."

DEC — 1937
Interviewer: Miss Irene Robertson
Person interviewed: Andrew Gregory
Brinkley, Arkansas
Age: 74

ANDREW GREGORY

"I was born in Carroll County, Tennessee. My mother was owned by Houston. She said when war was declared he was at a neighbor's house. He jumped up and said, 'I gonner be the first to kill a Yankee.' They said in a few minutes he fell back on the bed dead. My father owner was Tillman Gregory. After freedom he stayed on sharecroppin'. From what he said that wasn't much better than bein' owned. They had to work or starve. He said they didn't make nobody work but they didn't keep nobody from starvin' if they didn't go at it. They was proud to be free but that didn't ease up the working.

"My people stayed on in Tennessee a long time. When I was nineteen years old they was making up a crowd to come here to work. Said the land was new. I come wid them. It was a big time. We come on the Hardcash (steamboat). I farmed and cleared land all my life. I sold wood, hauled wood. I've done all kinds of form work. I get $12 from the Welfare Association.

"The young generation is a puzzle to me. That why I stand and watch what they do. The folks make the times. It's a puzzle to me too."

United States. Work Projects Administration

Interviewer: Miss Irene Robertson
Person interviewed: Annie Griegg
                    Madison, Arkansas
Age: 84

ANNIE GRIEGG

"I was born a slave, born in Nashville, Tennessee. I was sold twice. I don't recollect my mother; I was so small when I was parted from her. I had two sisters and I recollect them. One of my sisters was sold the same day I was sold and I recollect my other sister was named Rebecca. I never seen her no more after I was sold. I was the youngest.

"Mother belong to Captain Walker. That was before the Civil War so I know he wasn't an officer in it. His daughter married a man named Mr. Foster. Captain Walker had give me to his daughter when she married. They lived in Nashville, Tennessee too. Mr. Foster sold me and Captain Walker sold my sister Ann and Mr. Bill Steel Henderson at Columbia, Tennessee bought us both and give my sister to his widowed sister for a house girl and nurse and he kept me.

"They lived close to us and my sister stayed at our house nearly all the time. My sister and me was sold for the some price, $100 a piece. She could count and knew a dollar. She had some learning then. I never went to school a day in my life.

"The first block was a big tree and stumps sawed off for steps by the side of it. The big tree had been sawed off up high. The man cried me off standing on the next stump step. My sister told me our mother was a cook at Captain Walker's. She told me my father was a Foster. It was my understanding that he was a white man. My sister was darker than I was. Mr. Foster sold me for a nurse. Mr. Henderson's sister was name Mrs. McGaha (?). My sister nursed and cooked. I nursed three children at Mr. Henderson's. He was good to me. I loved the children and they was crazy about me. He sold me to Mr. Field Mathis. I nursed four children for them. I never did know why I was sold. Mr. Henderson was heap the best. Mr. Henderson never hit me a lick in his life.

"Mathis was cruel. He drank all the time. He got mad and stamped my hand. I nearly lost the use of my hand. It was swollen way up and hurt and stayed riz up till his cousin noticed it. He was a doctor. He lived in the other end of the house—the same house. He found some bones was broke loose in my hand (right hand). Dr. Mathis (Dr. Mathis or Dr. Mathews who died at Forrest City, Arkansas) set his brother out about treating little nurse thater way. Told him he oughter be ashamed of hisself. Dr. Mathis splintered my hand and doctored it till it got well.

"Mr. Field Mathis was a merchant. They moved to Colt, Arkansas at the beginning of the War, Dr. and Mr. Field Mathis both. We come on the train and steamboats. It was so new to me I had a fine time but that is all I can tell about it. Mr. Field was cross with his wife. She was fairly good to me. I had all the cooking, washing and ironing to do before I left there.

"After we come to Arkansas I never got to see my sister. My husband was a good scholar. He could write. He wrote and wrote back to find my sister and mother but they never answered my letters. I asked everybody that come from there about my sisters and mother but never have heard a word. I slept on a pallet on the floor nearly all my life. I had a little bed at Mr. Henderson's.

"I didn't know it was freedom till one day when I was about fourteen or fifteen years old—judging from my size and what I done. I went off to a spring to wash. I had one pot of clothes to boil and another just out of the pot to rub and rinse. A girl come to tell me Mrs. Field had company and wanted me to come cook dinner. I didn't go but I told her I would be on and cook dinner soon as I could turn loose the washing. There was two colored girls and a white girl could done the cooking but I was a good cook. The girl put on the water for me to scald the chickens soon as she went to the house. When I got there Mrs. Field Mathis had a handful of switches corded together to beat me. I picked up the pan of boiling water to scald the chickens in. She got scared of me, told me to put the pan down. I didn't do it. I didn't aim to hurt her. I wouldn't throwed that boiling water on nothing. She sent to the store for her husband. He come and I told him how it was about the clothes and three girls there could cook without me. He got mad at her and said: 'Mary Agnes, she is as free as you are or I am. I'm not going to ever hurt her again and you better not.' That is the first I ever heard about freedom. It had been freedom a long time. I don't know how long then.

"I stayed on, washed out the clothes and strung them up that evening. I ironed all the clothes and cooked the rest of the week. Mr. Field got me a good home with some colored folks. He told me if I would go there he never would let nobody bother me and he never would mistreat me no more. I worked some for them but they paid me. She ought to thought a heap of me the way I cooked and worked for her. That was my freedom. I was sold on a platform to Mr. Mathis.

"After freedom I done field work. I never seen a Ku Klux in my life. I cooked out some and I married. I still cooked out. I was married once and married in a church. I have seven children living and seven dead.

"I live with my daughter and her family and I get $6 and commodities. I'm mighty thankful for that. It helps me a whole lots.

"I recken young folks do the best they know to do. Seems like folks are kinder hearted than they used to be. Times have changed a heap every way. Times is harder for poor folks than the others. It is a true saying that poor folks have hard ways and rich folks have mean ways. They are more selfish. I always had to work hard. Both times I was sold for $100."

Interviewer: Miss Irene Robertson
Persons interviewed: William and Charlotte Guess
West Memphis, Arkansas
Ages: 68 and 66

WILLIAM AND CHARLOTTE GUESS

William Guess

"I was born in Monroe County, Arkansas. Father come from Dallas, Texas when a young man before he married. Him and two other men was shipped in a box to Indian Bay. I've heard him and Ike Jimmerson laugh how they got bumped and bruised, hungry and thirsty in the box. I forgot the name of the other man in the box. They was sent on a boat and changed boats where they got tumbled up so bad. It was in slavery or war times one. White folks nailed them up and opened them up too I think. Father was born in Dallas, Texas. Mother was a small woman and come from Tennessee. Billy Boyce in Monroe County owned her. That is the most I ever heard my folks tell about the Civil War."

Charlotte Guess

"Mother was born in Dallas, Texas. She was born into slavery. She was a field woman. She was sold there and brought to Mississippi at about the close of the Civil War. She was sold from her husband and two children. She never seen them. She farmed cotton and corn in Texas. Her husband whooped her, so she was glad to be sold. She married after the surrender to another man in Mississippi. No, he didn't beat her. They had disputes. She was the mother of ten children. She lived to be 82 years old. She went from Arkansas back to Mississippi to die."

Interviewer's Note

It would be interesting if I could find out more about why the Negroes were sent in the box. He seemed not to know all about it. This Negro man when young was a light mulatto. He is light for his age. He looks and acts white. Has a spot on one eye.

Interviewer: Miss Irene Robertson
Person interviewed: Lee Guidon
Clarendon, Arkansas
Age: 89

LEE GUIDON

"Yes maam I sho was in the Cibil War. I plowed all day and me and my sister helped take care of the baby at night. It would cry and me bumpin' it. [In a straight chair, rocking.] Time I git it to the bed where its mama was it wake up and start cryin' all over again. I be so sleepy. It was a puny sort o' baby. Its papa was off at war. His name was Jim Cowan an' his wife Miss Margaret Brown 'fore she married him. Miss Lucy Smith give me and my sister to them. Then she married Mr. Abe Moore. Jim Smith was Miss Lucy's boy. He lay outen the woods all time. He say no needen him gittin' shot up and killed. He say let the slaves be free. We lived, seemed lack, on 'bout the line of York an' Union Counties. He lay out in the woods over in York County. Mr. Jim say all they fightin' 'bout was jealousy. They caught him several times but ebry time he got away frum 'em. After they come home Mr. Jim say they never win no war. They stole and starved out the South.

"They didn't want the slaves talkin' 'bout things. One time I got ruffed up and I say I was goin' to freedom—the wood whar Mr. Jim be—and I recollect we was crossin' over a railin' fence. My ma put her hand over my mouth like dis, and say you don't know anything 'bout what you sain' boy.

"I neber will forgit Mr. Neel. He was all our overseer. He say 'Lee Good Boy' plows so good. He never spoke an unkind word in his life to me. When I haf to go to his house he call me in an' give me hot biscuits or maybe a potato. I sure love potato [sweet potatoes]. He was a good old Christian man. The church we all went to was made outer hand hewd logs—great big things. My pa lived in Union County on the other side the church.

"He lived to be 103 years old. Ma lost her mind. They both died right here with me—a piece outer town. He was named Pompey and ma Fannie. Her name 'foe freedom was Fannie Smith, then she took the name Guidon.

"After freedom a heap of people say they was going to name their selves over. They named their selves big names then went roaming 'round lack wild, huntin' cities. They changed up so it was hard to tell who or whar anybody was. Heap of 'em died an' you didn't know when you hear 'bout it if he was your folks hardly. Some of the names was Abraham an' some called their selves Lincum. Any big name 'ceptin' their master's name. It was the fashion. I herd 'em talking 'bout it one ebenin' an' my pa say fine folks raise us an' we goiner hold to our own names. That settled it wid all of us.

"Ma was a sickly woman all her life. They kept her 'round the house to help cook and sweep the yards. Not a speck of grass, not a weed growd on her yard. She swep it 'bout two times a week. It was prutty and white. The sand jes' shined in the sun. Had tall trees in the yard.

"I can't recollect 'bout my papa's master cause I was raised at my mama's master's place. He said many and many a time Joe Guidon never had to whoop him. After he growd up he never got no whoopins a tall. Joe Guidon learned him to plow an' he was boss of the plow hands. His wife was named Mariah Guidon. He say she was a mighty good easy woman too.

"Saturday was ration day and Sunday visitin' day. But you must have your pass if you leave the farm an' go over to somebody elses farm.

"When I was a boy one thing I love to do was go to stingy Tom's still house. His name was Tom Whiteside. He sure was stingy and the meanest white man I ever seed. I went to the still house to beat peaches to make brandy. It was four miles over there and I rode. We always made least one barrel of peach brandy and one of cider. That would be vinegar 'nough by spring. 'Simmon beer was good in the cole freezin' wether too. We make much as we have barrels if we could get the persimmons. He had a son name Bill Whitesides.

"Once an old slave woman lost her mind. Stingy Tom sent her to get a Bull tongue and she chased after one of the bulls down at the lot tryin' to catch it. She set his barn fire and burned thirteen head of horses and mules together. Stingy Tom had the sheriff try to get her tell what white folks put her up to do it. He knowed they all hated him cause he jes' so mean. The old woman never did tell but they hung her anyhow. There was a big crowd to see it. Miss Lucy jes' cried and cried. She say Satan got no use for Stingy Tom he so mean. That the first person I ever seed hung. They used to hang folks a heap. The biggest crowds turned out to see it.

"The old woman's son he went to the woods he so hurt cause they going to hang his ma.

"The Missouri soldiers were worse than the Yankees. They waste an' steal your corn and take your horses. They brought a little girl they stole and let Stingy Tom have her. He kept her and treated her so mean. They thrash out wheat and put it on big heavy sheets to dry. The little girl had to sit outen the sun an' keep the chickens offen it. I seed him find her 'sleep and hit hard as he could in the face wid big old brush. It was old dogwood brush wid no leaves on it. He wouldn't let that little girl have no biskit on Sunday mornin'. Everybody had all the hot biskit they could eat on Sunday mornin'. Well after freedom, long time, her aunt heard she was down there and come an' got her. She grow up to be a nice woman. Them same Missouri soldiers took Henry Guidon (younger brother of Lee Guidon) off. Stole him from the master—stole his mule. They was so mean. They found out when they shoot, the mule so scared it would throw Henry. They kept it up and laughed. Course it hurt Henry. Liable to kill him. They say they making a Yankee soldier outen him that way. One night before they got too fur gone he rode off home. They burn whole cribs corn. Could smell it a long ways off. They was mean to eberybody.

"I recken I do know 'bout the Ku Kluck. I knowed a man named Alfred Owens. He seemed all right but he was a Republican. He said he was not afraid. He run a tan yard and kept a heap of guns in a big room. They all loaded. He married a southern woman. Her husband either died or was killed. She had a son living wid them. The Ku Kluck was called Upper League. They get this boy to unload all the guns (16 shooters). Then the white men went there.

The white man give up and said, 'I ain't got no gun to defend myself wid. The guns all unloaded an' I ain't got no powder and shot.' But the Ku Kluck shot in the houses and shot him up like lace work. He sold fine harness, saddles, bridles—all sorts of leather things. The Ku Kluck shure run them outen their country. They say they not going to have them 'round and they shure run them out, back where they came from.

"Charles Good had a blacksmith. They [the Missouri soldiers] opened a fence gap when they came through. They took him, tied him to a tree and shot him in the face with little shot. He suffered there till Wednesday when he was still living. They tied him to the tree wid his own gallowses. They was doubled and strong. Then some of them went down there and finished up the job beating him over the head with the guns till he was dead. The Ku Kluck broke up every gun they could find. They sure better not ketch a gun at the quarters of colored folks. They whoop him and break up the gun. Ask him where he got that gun and start more bad trouble.

"They packed a two-story jail so full of men they had orders to turn 'em out. Then they built a high fence 'bout eight foot tall and put 'em in it. They had lights and guards all 'round it. They kept 'em right out in the hot sun in that pen. That's where the Yankees put the Ku Klucks. Then they had trials and some was sent to Albany for three years and eight years and the like. They made glass at Albany. Them Yankees wouldn't let 'em have no bonds. Then the white folks told them they needn't settle among them. They owned all the land and wouldn't sell them a foot for nuthing. A heap of lawyers and doctors got in it. That fence was iron and bob wire. The Ku Kluck killed good men, but Republicans.

"We stayed on like we were 'cause we done put in the crop and the Ku Kluck never did bother us. We made a prutty good crop. Then we took our freedom. Started workin' fer money and part of the crop.

"I married in 1871. Me and Emma went to bed. Somebody lam on the door. Emma say 'You run they won't hurt me.' I say 'They kill me sure.' We stayed and opened the door. They pull the cover offen her looking. They lifted up a cloth from over a barrel behind the bed in the corner. I say that are a hog. He say we right from hell we ain't seen no meat. Then they soon gone. The moon shining so bright that night. They were lookin' for my wife's brother I heard 'em say. They say he done something or another.

"Charleston was the nearest a army ever come to me but I seed a heap of soldiers on the roads. One road was the Rock Hill road.

"One man I heard 'em talk cheap about had the guns and powder. They shot holes in the walls. He climbed up in the fireplace chimney and stood up there close to the brick. It was dark and they couldn't see him. They looked up the chimney but didn't see him. It was a two-story chimney. Lady if you ain't never seen one I can't tell you just how it was. But they shot the house full of holes and never harmed him.

"For them what stayed on like they were Reconstruction times 'bout like times before dat 'ceptin' the Yankees stole out an' tore up a scanlus heap. They tell the black folks to do something and then come white folks you live wid and say Ku Kluck whoop you. They say leave and white folks say better not listen to them old Yankees. They'll git you too fur off to come back and you freeze. They done give you all the use they got fer you. How they do? All sorts of ways. Some stayed at their cabins glad to have one to live in an' farmed on. Some runnin' 'round beggin', some hunting work for money an' nobody had no money 'ceptin' the Yankees and they had no homes or land and mighty little work fer you to do. No work to live on. Some goin' every day to the city. That winter I heard 'bout them starving and freezing by the wagon loads.

"I never heard nuthing 'bout votin' till freedom. I don't think I ever voted till I come to Mississippi. I votes Republican. That's the party of my color and I stick to them long as they do right. I don't dabble in white folk's buzness an' that white folks votin' is their buzness. If I vote I go do it and go on home.

"I been plowin' all my life and in the hot days I cuts and saws wood. Then when I gets outer cotton pickin' I put each boy on a load of wood an' we sell wood. Then we clear land till next spring. I don't find no time to be loafing. I never missed a year farming till I got the Brights disease an' it hurt me to do hard work. The last years we got $3 a cord. Farmin' is the best life there is when you are able.

"I come to Holly Springs in 1850, stopped to visit. I had six children and $90 in money. We come on the train. My parents done come on from South Carolina to Arkansas. Man say this ain't no richer land than you come from. I tried it seven years. I drove from there, ferried the rivers. It took a long time. We made the best crop I ever seed in 1888. I had eight children, my wife. I cut and hauled wood all winter. I soon had three teams haulin' wood to Clarendon. Some old men, [white men] mean things! Learned one of my boys to play craps. They done it to git his money.

"When I owned most I had six head mules and five head horses. I rented 140 acres of land. I bought this house and some other land about. The anthrax killed nearly all my horses and mules. I got one big fine mule yet. Its mate died. I lost my house. My son give me one room and he paying the debt off now. It's hard for colored folks to keep anything. Somebody gets it frum 'em if they don't mind.

"The present times is hard. Timber is scarce. Game is about all gone. Prices higher. Old folks cannot work. Times is hard for younger folks too. They go to town too much and go to shows. They going to a tent show now. Circus coming they say. They spending too much money for foolishness. It's a fast time. Folks too restless. Some of the colored folks work hard as folks ever did. They spends too much. Some folks is lazy. Always been that way.

"I signed up to the Governmint but they ain't give me nuthin' 'ceptin' powdered milk and rice what wasn't fit to eat. It cracked up and had black somethin' in it. A lady said she would give me some shirts that was her husbands. I went to get them but she wasn't home. These heavy shirts give me heat. They won't give me the pension an' I don't know why. It would help me buy my salts and pills and the other medicines like Swamp Root. They won't give it to me."

Interviewer: Miss Irene Robertson
Person interviewed: Linley Hadley
Madison, Arkansas
Age: 77

LINLEY HADLEY

"I was born the very day the Civil War started, April 12, 1861. I was born in Monroe County close to Aberdeen, Mississippi. My papa was named Dave Collins. He was born far back as 1832. He was a carriage driver.

"Mama was born same year as papa. She was a field hand and a cook. She could plough good as any man. She was a guinea woman. She weighed ninety-five pounds. She had fourteen children. She did that. Had six or seven after freedom. She had one slave husband. Her owners was old Master Wylie Collins and Mistress Jane. We come 'way from their place in 1866.

"I can recollect old Master Collins calling up all the niggers to his house. He told them they was free. There was a crowd of them, all mixes. Why all this took place now I don't know. Most of the niggers took what all they have on their heads and walked off. He told mama to move up in the loom house, if she go off he would kill her. We moved to the loom house till in 1866.

"One night some of the niggers what had been Collins' slaves come and stole all mama's children, toted us off on their backs at night. Where we come to cross the river, Uncle George Tunnel was the ferryman. He had raised mama at his cabin at slavery. He took us to his white folks. We lived with them a year and then mama moved on Bill Cropton's place and we lived there forty years. All the Croptons dead now.

"We come to Arkansas in 1891 close to Cotton Plant. 1898, I come to Madison. Been here ever since.

"Grandma belong to Master Rogers where we knowed George Tunnel. Mama, named Harriett, and Aunt Miller was sold. A man in Texas bought Aunt Miller. We never could hear a word from her. After freedom we tried and tried. Master Collins was mean. You couldn't lay your hand on mama's back without laying it on marks where she had been beat. All his niggers was glad to leave him. They stripped mama's clothes down to her waist and whooped her, beat the blood out with cowhides. Master Collins 'lowed his niggers to steal, then his girls come take some of it to their house to eat. Master Collins didn't have no boys.

"Papa was a little chunky man. He'd steal flour and hogs. He could tote a hog on his back. My papa went on off when freedom come. They was so happy they had no sense. Mama never seen him no more. I didn't neither. Mama didn't care so much about him. He was her mate give to her. I didn't worry 'bout him nor nobody then.

"Master Collins did give us plenty to wear and eat too. When I left there we all worked. Mama married ag'in. We kept on farming. I farmed all my life.

"I got a boy what works. We own our house and all this place (one-half acre). I don't get no help from nowhere. Seem like them what works and tries ought to be the ones to get help and not them what don't never pay no taxes. Fast generation it is now. But they don't bother me. I got a good boy. Times is hard. Everything you have to buy is high."

United States. Work Projects Administration

Interviewer: Miss Irene Robertson
Person interviewed: Anna Hall (mulatto)
Brinkley, Arkansas
Age: 68

ANNA HALL

"I don't know nuthin' cept what I heard folks talk 'bout when I was a child. I was born good while after that war. My folks lived in Scott County near Jackson, Mississippi when I was little and in slavery times too. My mother's mistress was Miss Dolly Cruder. She was a widow and run her own farm. I don't remember her. She give her own children a cotton patch apiece and give the women hands a patch about and they had to work it at night. If the moon didn't give light somebody had to hold a literd (lantern) not fur from 'em so they could see to hoe and work it out. I think she had more land then hands, what they made was to be about a bale around for extra money. It took all the day time working in the big field for Miss Dolly. I heard 'em say how tired they would be and then go work out their own patches 'fore they go to bed. I don't remember how they said the white girls got their cotton patches worked. And that is about all I remembers good 'nough to tell you.

"They didn't expect nothing but freedom out the war. The first my mother heard she was working doing something and somebody say, 'What you working fur don't you know you done free?' That the first she knowed she was free. They just passed the word round; that's how they heard it and the soldiers started coming in to their families. Some of them come back by themselves and some come riding several of them together.

"I know they didn't give my mother nothing after the war. She washed and ironed 'bout all her life.

"The young generation is doing better than we old folks is. If there is any work to get they gets it in preference to us. Education is helping some of 'em here in Brinkley. Some of the young ones gets good money. They teaches and cooks. Times is hard for some.

"I live wid my son. Yes he own his house. I gets $8 from the relief. We has 'bout 'nough to live on and dat is all."

Interviewer: Miss Irene Robertson
Person interviewed: Ellie Hamilton (male)
Clarendon, Arkansas
Age:

ELLIE HAMILTON

"I was born about near Holly Springs, Mississippi. My parents' masters' name William and Mary Ellen Jefferies. I don't know much 'bout them. My parents' name Neely and Amos Hamilton. I judge that was pa's master's name. They had eight children. Three of us living yet.

"I been farmin' and workin' 'round Clarendon ever since I was a chap. I work 'round hotels and stores and farm too.

"I votes when we have a leader for our party. It don't do no good. I never seed no good come outen the colored race votin' yet.

"Some ways times is much better, much better! Some ways they is worser. The people is educated better'n I had a chance at.

"Work wages is a heap better. I has worked for $7 a month. Now some can get $18 to $20 a week. But the young generation throwin' it away. They ain't going to save a bit of it. The present condition is worse morally. They used to could depend on a man. You can't hardly depend on the younger generation. They is so tricky.

Folks going too much. I recollect when I was a child I went to town one or two times a year. I didn't want all I seen there then neither. Seems lack folks spends so much money foolishly.

"I own a home, no cow, no hog, no land. Get $10 a month from the PWA.

"I come to Arkansas to farm. It is a fine farmin' country, Miss. My father died and left my mother wid seven children to raise. She come on out here to make a livin'.

"I remember when Tilden and Hendrick lost and Hayes and Wheeler was elected. They sung songs 'bout 'em and said 'Carve that possum nigger to the heart.' It done been so long since we sung them rally songs I forgot every line of all of them. People used to sing more religious songs seems like than they do now. They done gone wild over dancin' 'stead of singin'.

"I farmed for J. P. Cherry at Holly Springs from time I was eight year old till I was twenty-one year old. That's a long time to stay by one man ain't it?"

Interviewer: Miss Irene Robertson
Person interviewed: Josephine Hamilton
Hazen, Arkansas
Age: 77

JOSEPHINE HAMILTON

"I was born near Houston, Mississippi, in 1860. We lived about three miles north when I can first recollect. My mistress was named Frankie Hill and my master was Littleton Hill. I had some sisters and brothers dead but I had four brothers and one sister that got up grown. The first house I remembers living in was a plank house. Then we lived in a log house wid a stick-and-dirt chimney. I was wid my old master when he died of heart trouble. She lack to died too. We setting by de fire one night and he held the lamp on one knee and reading out loud. It was a little brass lamp with a handle to hook your finger in. He was a Baptist. He had two fine horses, a big gray one and a bay horse. Joe drove him to preaching. Miss Frankie didn't go. He said his haid hurt when dey went to eat dinner and he slept all the evening. He et supper and was reading. I was looking at him. He laid his haid back and started snoring. He had long white hair. I say 'Miss Frankie, he is dieing.' Cause he turned so pale. He was setting in a high back straight chair. We got him on the bed. He could walk when we held him up. His brother was a curious old man. He et morphine a whole heap. He lived by himself. I run fast as my legs would take me. Soon as I told him he blowed a long horn. They said it was a trumpet. You never seen such a crowd as come toreckly. The hands come and the neighbors too. It being dot time er night they knowed something was wrong. He slept awhile but he died that night. I stayed up there wid Miss Frankie nearly all de time. It was a mile from our cabin across the field. Joe stayed there some. He fed and curried the horses. Nom I don't remember no slave uprisings. They had overseers on every farm and a paddyroll. I learned to sew looking at the white folks and my ma showed me about cutting. There wasn't much fit about them. They were all tollerably loose. We played hiding behind the trees a heap and played in the moonlight. We played tag. We picked up scaley barks, chestnuts, and walnuts. Miss Frankie parched big pans of goobers when it was cold or raining. Some of the white folks was mean. Once young mistress was sick. She had malaria fever. I was sitting down in the other room. Young master was lying on de bed in the same room. A woman what was waiting on her brought the baby in to put a cloth on him. He was bout two months old, little red-headed baby. He was kicking and I got tickled at him. Young master slapped me. The blood from my nose spouted out and I was jess def for a long time. He beat me around till Miss Polly come in there and said 'You quit beating that little colored girl. You oughter be ashamed. Your wife in there nearly dead.' 'Yes maam, she did die.' I never will forgit Miss Polly. I saved one of the young mistress little girl bout seven or eight years old. Miss Frankie raised a little deer up grown. It would run at anybody. Didn't belong at the house. It got so it would run me. It started at the little girl and I pulled her in on the porch backwards and in a long hall. Her mama show was proud. Said the deer would paw her to death.

"I remembers everybody shouting and so glad they was free. It was a joyful time. If they paid my folks for work I didn't know it. We stayed on with Miss Frankie till I was grown and her son Billy Hill took her to Houston, Texas to live. Miss Sallie and Miss Fannie had been married a long time. We always had a house to live in and something to eat.

"I show never did vote. I would not know nothing about it. I think the folks is getting wiser and weaker. Some of us don't have much as we need and them that do have wastes it. I always lived on the farm till eight years ago when my husband died. I wasn't able to farm by myself. I didn't have no children. I come to Hazen to live wid dese here girls I raised. (Two girls.) They show is good to me. No maam I ain't never got no old age pension. They won't give it to me. We come to Arkansas in 1918. We lived down around Holly Grove. We had kin folks wrote about out here and we wanted to change. Long as I was able I had a good living but since I been so feeble I have to make out wid what the children bring me. I don't know if de times is getting any better, don't seem lack the people training their children a tall. They say they kaint do nothing wid em. I allus could do something wid dem I raised. I used to look at them and they minded me. The trouble is they ain't learning to work and won't do nothing less they going to get big pay. Then they run spend it fast as they can go for fool-bait."

Interviewer: Irene Robertson
Person interviewed: Josephine Hamilton
 Hazen, Arkansas

JOSEPHINE HAMILTON

If you borrow salt it is bad luck to pay it back.

Parch okra seed grind up or beat it up and make coffee.

Parch meal or corn and make coffee.

In slavery times they took red corn cobs burned them and made white ashes, sifted it and used it instead of soda.

Beat up charcoal and take for gas on the stomach.

Sift meal add salt and make up with water, put on collard leaf, cover with another collard leaf put on hot ashes. Cover with hot ashes. The bread will be brown, the collard leaves parched up, "It is really good." Roast potatoes and eggs in the ashes.

In slavery times they made persimmon beer. Had regular beer barrels made a faucet. Put old field hay in the bottom, persimmons, baked corn bread and water. Let stand about a week, a fine drink with tea cakes. It won't make you drunk.

Comb hair after dark makes you forgetful.

Asafoetida and garlic on the bait makes the fish bite well.

Rub fishing worms on the ground makes them tougher so you can put them on the hook.

Name of Interviewer: Martin—Pettigrew
Person interviewed: Peter Hamilton
Age: 68

PETER HAMILTON

"My mother made three crops after she wuz freed, and I wuz born when she made her third crop, so I thinks I wuz born 'round 1868. I wuz born in Bolivar County, Mississippi. My mother and father were slaves and belonged to the Harris family. Only one I 'members is my sister, she died. My brothers went off and worked on ships, and I never saw them no mo'.

"After freedom, my mother kept working for her marster and misstis, and they paid them for their work. They stayed on the same plantation until I wuz almost grown.

"At Christmas time, we had heaps to eat, cakes, homemade molasses candy that you pulled, popcorn, horse apples which wuz good, mo' better'n any apples we get these days.

"The white folks give gifts in the big house and mammy went to the house and the white folks give her the things to put in we nigger chilluns' stockings.

"We hung up our stockings in our house and up at the white house too. 'Fore Christmas, the white folks would tell us if we stole chickens, eggs, ducks and things, or go in the apple orchard, and wuz bad, Santa Claus would not come to us. But if we were good, he would bring gifts to us. 'Fore Christmas, the white folks would make a Santa Claus out of clothes and stuff it, put a pack on his back, and stand him up in the road. Colored chillun feared to go near him.

"I have never been arrested, never been in the jail house or calaboose. Went to school when I could.

"Traveled all over, worked on canal in South America.

"Name of boat I wuz on was the 'Clamshell, No. 4', with Captain Nelson, fum New York."

Interviewer: Miss Irene Robertson
Person interviewed: Lawrence Hampton
R.F.D., Forrest City, Arkansas
Age: 78

LAWRENCE HAMPTON

"I was born in Orangeburg, South Carolina. My parents' names was Drucilla and Peter Hampton. She was the mother of twelve children. They both b'long to John D. Kidd and Texas Kidd. To my knowing they had no children. They was old to me being a child but I don't reckon they be old folks. They had a plantation, some hilly and some bottom land. He had two or three hundred slaves. He was a good, good man. He was a good master. He had some white overseers and some black overseers. Grandpa Peter was one of his overseers. He was proud of his slaves. He was a proud man.

"We all had preaching clothes to wear. He had his slaves be somebody when they got out of the field. They went in washing at the fish pond, duck pond too. It was clear and sandy bottom. Wouldn't be muddy when a lot of them got through washing (bathing). They was black but they didn't stink sweaty. They wore starched clean ironed clothes. They cooked wheat flour and made clothes. When the War come on their clothes was ironed and clean but the wheat was scarce and the clothes got flimsy. John D. Kidd was loved by black and white. He was a good man. Grandpa George had a son sold over close to

Memphis. They had twelve children last letter mama had from them. I've never seen any one of them.

"Grandpa Peter was a overseer. After he was made overseer he was paid. That was a honor for being good all his life. When freedom come on he had ten thousand dollars. He was pure African, black as ace of spades. He give papa and the other four boys five hundred dollars a piece to start them farms. Papa died when he was sixty-five and grandma was about a hundred. Mama was seventy-five when she died. Grandpa was eighty-five when he died. They didn't know exactly but that was about their ages. It was a pretty big honor to be a carriage man. They had young men hostlers and blacksmiths.

"Freedom—The boys all stayed around and girls too. They bought places about. They never would charge John D. Kidd for work. They let the girls cook, milk, and set the fowls, long as the old couple lived. They never took no pay. They go in gangs and chop out his crop and big picnic dinners all they ever took from him. We all loved that old man.

"They done some whooping on the place but it was a shame. They got over it and went on dressed up soon as the task was done. Never heard much said about it. I never seen nobody whooped.

"My own folks whooped me. We was free then.

"I heard how easy to farm out in Arkansas. I come to Forrest City in 1884. I was 'bout twenty-five years old then. It was a mud hole is right. I farmed all my life. We made money.

"My color folks don't know how to take care of their money. They can make money but don't handle it long.

"I owns a home and twenty acres of land. I want to keep it. Me and my wife live out there. I had ten children and four of them still living. They all good children and I'm proud to own they mine.

"John D. Kidd had a lot of his wife's brothers that come visiting. I'd find out they be up there. Here I'd go. We'd swim, fish, ride, and I'd love to be around them and hear them talk. That was the kind of good times we had when I was a boy. I missed all that when I come here. It was sich fine farming land. I couldn't go back to stay. I been back numbers of times visiting.

"I heard of the Ku Klux but I never seen none of them. They was hot over there in South Carolina in some spots.

"I'm able by the grace of God to make my own humble living. Sometime I may like a little help but I ain't asked foe none yet.

"I heard this here about the Ku Klux in Forrest City. I heard different ones say. They was having a revival out here at Lane Chapel and the captain of the Ku Klux come in and they followed in their white clothes and he give the colored minister a letter. He opened it and it had some money for him. They went on off on their horses. I don't know when that was. I didn't see it, I heard about it."

Interviewer: Miss Irene Robertson
Person interviewed: Hannah Hancock
Biscoe, Arkansas?
Age: Past 80

HANNAH HANCOCK

"I was born in Chesterfield County, South Carolina. My mother's name was Chloa. We lived on Hardy Sellers plantation. She was the white folks cook. I et in the white folks kitchen sometimes and sometimes wid the other children at maw's house. Show my daddy was livin. But he lived on another man's farms. His master's name was Billy Hancock and his name was Dave. Der was a big family of us but dey all dead now but three of us. Ize got two sisters and a brother still livin, I reckon. I ain't seed them in a long time. Mrs. Sellers had several children but they were all married when I come along and she was a widow. Joe Pete was her son and he lived close, about a mile across the field, but it was farther around the road. Billy Hancock married Mrs. Sellers daughter. My mistress didn't do much. Miss Becky Hancock wove cloth for people. You could get the warp ready and then run in the woof. She made checked dresses and mingledy looking cloth. They colored the cloth brown and purple mostly. Mrs. Sellers get a bolt of cloth and have it all made up into dresses for the children. Sometimes all our family would have a dress alike. Yesm, we did like dot. Granny made de dresses on her fingers. She was too old to go to de field an she tote water from the big spring and sometimes she water de hands when dey be hoeing. She would cut and dry apples and peaches. Nobody knowed how to can. They dried de beef. It show was good. It was jess fine. No maam, Granny didn't have no patterns. She jess made our dresses lack come in her haid. We didn't get many dresses and we was proud of em and washed and ironed and took care of em.

"I recollects hearing de men talking about going off to war and em going. No jess de white men left from Mrs. Sellers place. De children didn't set around and hear all that was said. They sent us off to play in the play houses. We swept a clean place and marked it off and had our dolls down there. We put in anything we could get, mostly broken dishes. Yes maam, I had rag dolls and several of them. No wars real close but I could hear the guns sometimes.

"Mrs. Sellers had two large carriage horses. The colored boys took them down in the bottoms and took off a lot of the meat and groceries and hid them 'fo the Yankees come along. They didn't nebber fin them things. Mrs. Sellers was awful good and the men jess looked after her and took care of her. Me or maw stayed at the house with her all the time, day and night. When anybody got sick she sent somebody to wait on them and went to see what they needed and sometimes she had 'em brought up to the house and give 'em the medicine herself. She didn't have no foman. Uncle Sam and uncle John was the oldest and uncle Henry. They was the men on the farm and they went right on with the work. Folks had bigger families than they do now. They show did work, but de field work don't last all de time. They cleared land and fixed up the rail fences in the winter. A rail fence was on each side of a long lane that led down to the pasture.

The creek run through the pasture. It was show a pretty grove. Had corn shuckings when it was cold. We played base down there. We always had meat and plenty milk, collards and potatoes. Old missus would drip a barrel of ashes and make corn hominy in the wash pot nearly every week and we made all the soap we ever did see. If you banked the sweet potatoes they wouldn't rot and that's where the seed come from in the spring. In the garden there was an end left to go to seed. That is the way people had any seed. Times show have changed. I can't tell what to think. They ain't no more like than if they was another kind of folks. So much different. I jess look and live. I think they ought to listen to what you say. Say anything to them they say 'Kaint run my business.' I don't know if they spected anything from freedom. Seemed like they thought they wouldn't have to work if dey was free and dey wouldn't have no boss. Missus let a lot of her land grow up in pine trees. Said she had no money to pay people to work for her. Some of de families staid on. My maw and paw went on a farm on share not far from Mrs. Sellers. When she was going to have company or she got sick she sent for my maw. My maw washed and ironed for her till they moved plum off. They said somebody told them it was freedom. When dey picked up and moved off de missus show didn't give em nothing. They didn't vote. They didn't know how. I heard a lot about the Ku Klux Klan but I wasn't scared. I never did see none.

"De younger generation jess lives today and don't know what he'll do tomorrow or where he'll be. I ain't never voted and I don't know if my boys do or not.

"I never heard of uprisings. De paddyroll was to see after dot and Mrs. Sellers didn't have none. Uncle Sam and uncle John made em mind.

"Sing—I say dey did sing. Sing about the cooking and about the milking and sing in de field.

"I never did see nobody sold. But I heard them talk about selling em. They took em off to sell em. That was the worst part about slavery. The families was broke up. I never lived nowhere 'cept in South Carolina and Prairie County (Arkansas). My folks come here and they kept writing for me to come, and I come on the train. Mrs. Sellers son, Joe Sellers, killed himself, shot himself, one Sunday evening. Didn't know how come he done it. I was too little to know what they expected from the war. The colored folks didn't have nothing to do with it 'cept they expected to get freed. A heap of people went to the cities, some of them died. After freedom things got pretty scarce to eat and there was no money. I worked as a house girl, tended to the children, brushed the flies off the table and the baby when it slept and swept the house and the yard too. After I come here (to Arkansas) I married and I worked on the farms. We share cropped. I raised my children, had chickens, geese, a cow and hogs. When the cotton was sold we got some of it. Yes maam, I show had rether be out there if I could jess work. We lived on Mr. Dick Small's place till he sold out. We come to town a year and went back and made enough in one year to buy dis place. It cost $300. Jess my two sons and me. The others were married. My husband died on the farm. I come in town and done one or two washings a week. Yes maam I walked here and back. That kept me in a little money. It was about two miles. I washed for Mr. L. Hall and part of the time for Mrs. Kate Hazen. I guess they treated us right about the crop settlement. We thought they did. We knowed how much was made and how much we got. The cheatin come at the stores where the trading was done.

"I lives with my son and his wife. Sometimes I do my cooking and sometimes I eat in there. I get $8.00 from the RFC and prunes, rice, and a little dried milk. I buys my meal and sugar and lard and little groceries with the money. It don't buy what I used to have on the farm.

"I don't remember much about the war. I was so little. I heard them talk a lot about it and the way they killed folks. I thought it was awful. My hardest time is since I got old and can't work."

United States. Work Projects Administration

Name of Interviewer: Irene Robertson
Person interviewed: Hannah Hancock
Hazen, Arkansas
Age: 90

HANNAH HANCOCK

I asked her if she believed anyone could harm her and she said not not unless they could get her to eat or drink something. Then they might. She said a Gypsy was feeling her and slipped a dollar and a quarter tied up in her handkerchief from her and she never did know when or how she got it. Said she never believed their tales or had her fortune told. She didn't believe anyone could put anything under the door and because you walked over it you would get a "spell". She said some people did. She didn't know what they put under the doors. She never was conjured that she knew of and she doesn't believe in it. Said she had to work too hard to tell tales to her children but she used to sing. She can't remember the songs she sang. She can't read or write.

The old woman is blind and gray, wears a cap. Her Mistress was Mrs. Mary and her Master was Mr. Hardy Sellers in Chesterfield County, South Carolina. Her husband died and left her with six children. Her brother came with a lot of other fellows to Arkansas. "Everybody was coming either here or to Texas". Mr. David Gates at DeValls Bluff sent her a ticket to come to his farm. Her brother was working for Mr. Gates Wattensaw plantation and that is where she has been till a few years ago she moved to Hazen and lives with her son and his wife. She remembered when the Civil War soldiers took all their food, mules and hitched Mrs. Sellers driving horses to the surry and drove off. Her Mistress cried and cried. She said she had a hard time after she left Mr. and Mrs. Sellers, they was sure good to them and always had more than she had ever had since. She wanted to go back to South Carolina to see the ones she left but never did have the money. Said they lived on Mr. Dick Small's place and he was so good to her and her children but he is dead too now.

Interviewer: Samuel S. Taylor
Person interviewed: Julia E. Haney
1320 Pulaski Street, Little Rock, Arkansas
Age: 78

JULIA E. HANEY

"I was born in Gallatin, Tennessee, twenty-six miles north of Nashville, September 18, 1859. Willard Blue and Mary Blue were my master and my mistress.

"I wanted to put in for a pension and didn't want to tell a story about my age. In reading the Gazette, I found out that William Blue got shot by an insurance man in Dallas, Texas over a stenographer. I found out where my young master was and after allowing him time to get over his grief, I wrote to him about my age. He wrote me that Andrew was the oldest and he didn't know, so he sent my letter to Tacoma, Tennessee, to Henry Blue. Henry wrote to him and told him to look in the bottom of the wardrobe in the old family Bible. He looked there and found the Bible and sent my age to me. They wrote to me and sent me some money and were awful nice to me. They said that I was the only one of the slaves living."

Good Masters

"Our masters were awful good to us. They didn't treat us like we were slaves. My mother carried the keys to everything on the place. They lived in the city. They didn't live in the country. I came here in 1869."

Family

"My mother married a Thompson. Her married name was Margaret Thompson and her name before she married was Margaret Berth. Her master before she married was Berth. Her last master was Blue. Her mother's name was Cordelia Lowe. Her maiden name was Berth. When the old man Berth died, he made his will and Bullard Berth didn't want any slaves because he wanted to train his children to work. Willard, my mother's master, should have been a Berth because he was old man Berth's son, but he called himself Blue. It might have been that old man Berth was his stepfather. Anyway he went by the name of Willard Blue. He was an undertaker.

"My father's name was Oliver Thompson. I don't remember any of my father's people. His people were in Nashville, Tennessee, and my mother's people were in Gallatin, Tennessee. We were separated in slavery."

Separation of Parents

"I don't know how my mother and father happened to get together. They didn't belong to the same master. My father belonged to Thompson and lived in Nashville and my mother belonged to Blue in Gallatin. They were not together when freedom came and never did get together after freedom. They only had one child to my knowledge. I don't know how they happened to be separated. It was when I was too small. Nashville is twenty-six miles from Gallatin. Perhaps one family or the other moved away."

Patrollers

"I have heard my mother speak about the pateroles. I don't know whether they were pateroles or not. They had guards out to see if the slaves had passes and they would stop them when they would be going out for anything. They would stop my mother when she would be going out to get the cows to see if she had a pass."

Jayhawkers

"I never heard my mother speak of jayhawkers, but I have heard her say that they used to catch the slaves when they were out. I don't know whether it was jayhawkers or not. I don't know what they done with them after they caught them. I have heard other people speak of jayhawkers. My people were very good to us. They never bothered my mother. She could go and come when she pleased and they would give her a pass any time she told them she wanted one."

Really Scared to Death

"I know one thing my ma told me. When the soldiers came through, there was an old rebel eating breakfast at our place. He was a man that used to handcuff slaves and carry them off and sell them. He must have stolen them. When he heard that the Yankees were marching into town with all them bayonets shining, it scared him to death. He sat right there at the breakfast table and died. I don't know his name, but he lived in Tennessee."

Mother's Work

"My mother was a cook and she knitted. She molded candles and milked the cows, and washed and ironed. She and her children were the only slaves they owned. They never whipped my mother at all. I stayed in the house. They kept me there. I never had to do anything but keep the flies off the table when they were eating."

Schooling

"My grandfather gave me my schooling after I came here. I had come here in 1869. I went to school in Capitol Hill and Union Schools. Mrs. Hoover (white) was one of the teachers at Union School when I was there. She was a good teacher. Miss Lottie Andrews—she is a Stephens now—was another one of my teachers."

How Freedom Came

"My master came right on the back porch and called my mother out and told her she was free, that he wasn't going in no war. That was at the beginning when they were mustering in the soldiers to fight the War. And he didn't go neither. She stayed with him till after emancipation. She was as free as she could be and he treated her as nice as anybody could be treated. She had the keys to everything."

House, Furniture, and Food

"My mother had a little house back in the yard joined to the back porch and connected with the kitchen. It had one room. She did all cooking in his kitchen. Her room was just a bedroom.

"The furniture was a bed with high posters. It didn't have slats, it had ropes. It was a corded bed. They had boxes for everything else—for bureaus, chairs, and things."

Further Details about Schooling

"I went to school as far as the eighth grade. Professor Hale, Professor Mason, and Professor Kimball were some of the teachers that taught me. They all said I was one of the brightest scholars they had."

Later Life

"I married Cado Haney in 1882. He is dead now. He's been dead nearly forty years. We didn't live together but fifteen years before he died. We never had no children. After he died I laundried for a living until I got too old to work. Now I get old age assistance."

Interviewer's Comment

A mighty sweet old lady to talk to.

Interviewer: Pernella M. Anderson
Person interviewed: Rachel Hankins
El Dorado, Arkansas
Age: 88

RACHEL HANKINS

"I was born in Alabama. My old mistress and master told me that I was born in 1850. Get that good—1850! That makes me about 88 but I can't member the day and month. I was a girl about twelve or fourteen years old when the old darkies was set free. My old mistress and master did not call us niggers; they called us darkies. I can't recollect much about slavery and I can recollect lots too at times. My mind goes and comes. I tell you children you all is living a white life nowdays. When I was coming up I was sold to a family in Alabama by the name of Columbus. They was poor people and they did not own but a few slaves and it was a large family of them and that made us have to work hard. We lived down in the field in a long house. We ladies and girls lived in a log cabin together. Our cabin had a stove room made on the back and it was made of clay and grass with a hearth made in it and we cooked on the hearth. We got our food from old mistress's and master's house. We raised plenty of grub such as peas, greens, potatoes. But our potatoes wasn't like the potatoes is now. They was white and when you eat them they would choke you, especially if they was cold. And sorghum molasses was the only kind there was. I don't know where all these different kinds of molasses come from.

"They issued our grub out to us to cook. They had cows and we got milk sometimes but no butter. They had chickens and eggs but we did not. We raised cotton, sold part and kept enough to make our clothes out of. Raised corn. And there wasn't no grist mills then so we had a pounding rock to pound the corn on and we pound and pound until we got the corn fine enough to make meal, then we separated the husk from the meal and parched the husk real brown and we used it for coffee. We used brown sugar from sorghum molasses. We spun all our thread and wove it into cloth with a hand loom. The reason we called that cloth home-spun is because it was spun at home. Splitting rails and making rail fences was all the go. Wasn't no wire fences. Nothing but rail fences. Bushing and clearing was our winter jobs. You see how rough my hands is? Lord have mercy! child, I have worked in my life.

"Master Columbus would call us niggers up on Sunday evening and read the Bible to us and tell us how to do and he taught us one song to sing and it was this 'Keep Your Lamp Trimmed and Burning' and he'd have us to sing it every Sunday evening and he told us that that song meant to do good and let each other see our good. When it rained we did not have meeting but when it was dry we always had meeting.

"I never went to school a day in my life. I learned to count money after I was grown and married.

"My feet never saw a shoe until I was fourteen. I went barefooted in ice and snow. They was tough. I did not feel the cold. I never had a cold when I was young. If we had ep-p-zu-dit we used different things to make tea out of, such as shucks, cow chips, hog hoofs, cow hoofs. Ep-p-zu-dit then is what people call flu now.

"When war broke out I was a girl just so big. All I can recollect is seeing the soldiers march and I recollect them having on blue and gray jackets. Some would ride and some would walk and when they all got lined up that was a pretty sight. They would keep step with the music. The Southern soldiers' song was 'Look Away Down in Dixie' and the Northern soldiers' song was 'Yankee Doodle Dandy.' So one day after coming in from the field old master called his slaves and told us we was free and told us we could go or stay. If we stayed he would pay us to work. We did not have nothing to go on so we stayed and he paid us. Every 19th of June he would let us clean off a place and fix a platform and have dancing and eating out there in the field. The 19th of June 1865 is the day we thought we was freed but they tell me now that we was freed in January 1865 but we did not know it until June 19, 1865. Never got a beating the whole time I was a slave.

"I came to north Arkansas forty years ago and I been in Union County a short while. My name is Rachel Hankins."

Interviewer: Mrs. Bernice Bowden
Person interviewed: Mary Jane Hardridge
1501 West Barraque St., Pine Bluff, Ark.
Age: 85

MARY JANE HARDRIDGE

"Oh don't ask me that, honey. Yes, I was here in slavery days. I reckon I was here before the Civil War; I was born in '58. I'm right now in my birth county about four miles from this city.

"I can remember my young masters that went to war. One was named Ben and one Chris. Old master's name was James Scull. He was kinda mixed up—he wasn't the cruelest one in the world. I've heard of some that was worse than he was. I never suffered for nothin' to eat.

"I can tell you about myself as far back as I can remember. I know I was about thirteen or fourteen when the war ended.

"My father's birth home was in Virginia. His name was Flem Price and his father was a doctor and a white man. Mother's name was Mary Price and she was half Indian. You can tell that by looking at her picture. She was born in Arkansas.

"I can remember seeing the soldiers. I had to knit socks for them. Used to have to knit a pair a week. Yes ma'm I used to serve them. I had it to do or get a whippin'. I nursed and I sewed a little. My mother was a great seamstress. We did it by hand too. They didn't have no sewing machines in them times.

"When my white folks went on summer vacations—they was rich and traveled a great deal—mama always went along and she just left us children on the plantation just like a cow would leave a calf. She'd hate to do it though. I remember she went off one time and stayed three months and left me sick in the white folks house on a pallet. I know I just hollered and cried and mama cried too. There was another old colored lady there and she took me to her house. We lived right on the river where the boat landed and I remember the boat left at high noon and I cried all the rest of the afternoon.

"I remember the first Yankee I ever saw. They called him Captain Hogan. I had a white chile in my arms. He set there and asked the boss how many Negroes did he have and the boss said what was the news. He come out to let the Negroes know they was as free as he was and told Marse Jim to bring all of them back from Texas. I know I run and told mama and she said 'You better hush, you'll get a whippin'.'

"They sho didn't burn up nothin'—Just took the mules and horses. Now I remember that—they didn't burn up nothin' where I lived.

"I heard of the Ku Klux but I never seen any. We was expectin' 'em though at all times.

"My grandmother belonged to Creed Taylor and after freedom mama got her and she lived there with the Sculls two years. My mother and father was paid a salary and they paid me too—four dollars a month. And I remember mama never would let me have it—just give me what she wanted me to have. They treated us better than they did before the war. Cose they was a little rough, but they couldn't whip you like they did. They could threaten it though.

"I went to school just a little after freedom. Mama and papa wasn't able to send me. Wasn't no colored teachers competent to teach then and we had to pay the white teacher a dollar a month.

"I had very strict parents and was made to mind. When I went out I knew when I was comin' in. I had one daughter who died when she was eight years old and if I could bring her back now, I wouldn't do it cause I know she would worry me to death.

"I used to sew a lot for people in Pine Bluff but I am too old now. I own my home and I have some rooms rented to three young men students and I get a little help from the Welfare so I manage to get along.

"Well good-bye—I'm glad you come."

United States. Work Projects Administration

Interviewer: Mrs. Bernice Bowden
Person interviewed: Mary Jane Hardrige
1501 W. Barraque, Pine Bluff, Arkansas
Age: 79

MARY JANE HARDRIGE

"Well, I don't believe in signs much. My sister was sick about a year once. They said she had the T. B. (tuberculosis). One day I was there and she said, 'Sis, do you hear that peckerwood? He's drivin' a nail in my coffin.' And sure enough she died not long after.

"But let me tell you I had a peculiar dream yesterday morning just before day. There's a little child here. His mother died and left him, the baby child. I dreamt his mother brought him to me. She said, 'I brought my boy here and I want you to keep him.' I thought he come to me just as naked as he could be. He kept sayin', 'Come on, Mrs. Hardrige, and let's go home, I'm cold.' He didn't have a garment on. His mother was with him and she's dead you know.

"I mentioned it to one of my neighbors and she said it was a sign of some woman's death.

"I was very much devoted to the child. I love him, and that dream stayed with me all day. I don't know but I've always heard if you dream of the dead it's goin' to rain.

"I ain't four miles from where I was born. I was born across the river. We belonged to Jim Scull. I've lived all my life in Jefferson County."

Interviewer: Pernella Anderson
Person Interviewed: O. C. Hardy
El Dorado, Ark.
Age: 69

O. C. HARDY

"O. C. Hardy is my name and I is 69 years old. I like a lot of being a real old time slave, but I tell you I am a slave now, and ain't no 1800 slave. I was born way down in Louisiana. We lived on a plantation with some white people by the name of Chick Johnson. That is the first place I remember we ever stayin' on. My ma and pa slave for them folks. All of the children worked like slaves. What I mean by working like slaves—we didn't stop to get our breath until night. I was slavin' for just the white folks then and since I got grown and married I've been slavin' for my wife and children and the white folks. My mama and papa went in the name of their mistress and master's name and so did I, so we was all Hardys.

"Sixty-nine years ago the time wasn't like it is now. Everything was different. There was no cars, no airplanes, a few buggies, no trains. The go was ox teams and stage coaches. People used ox teams in place of mule and horse teams. Sometimes you would see ox teams with twelve and fourteen oxen. The ox wore yokes that sometime weigh a hundred or more pounds. The reason of that, they were so mean they had to wear them yokes to hold em down. One yoke would go across two oxen's heads. They could pull—oh my!—as much as some big trucks. We made much better crops back in the 1800s than we do now. The winters was much harder and you know the harder the winter the better the crop year you have. We always plowed and turned our ground over in the hard of winter—that was in order for the cold to kill all insect and germs in the ground. You see, worms eats up your seed and plant, and germs do your seed and plant just like they would do your body. So we got rid of them little hinderings. In January we was ready to get our corn ground ready for planting, and man! we raised some crops. I recollect one year way back yonder we had what they called a centennial snow—that was the biggest snow that's ever been and the best crop year I ever knowed. I started plowing when I was about eight. Before then all I can remember doin' was bushing. After gathering crops we split rails and built fences. We played on Sunday evening. Our sport was huntin', fishin', and bird thrashin' and trap settin'. To catch fish easy we baited snuff and tobacco on the hook. We used to be bad about stealin' watermelons, eggs, chickens and sweet potatoes and slippin' way down in the woods and cookin'.

"Wasn't no such things as screen windows and doors. That is some of this 1900 stuff to my knowing. Flies and mosquitos was plentiful. Our cooking was plain boiled or fried cause we cooked on fireplaces. Wasn't no stoves. We used all brown sugar from syrup that turned to sugar. White sugar is about forty years old to my knowings. My ma used to cook the best old syrup cake and syrup potatoes pudding. She knitted all our socks and sweaters for you couldn't buy things like that because stores was few and she spun and wove for the white folks and knitted too."

Interviewer: Miss Irene Robertson
Person interviewed: Rosa Hardy
Biscoe, Arkansas
Age: ?

ROSA HARDY

"I was born in Brownsville, Tennessee. My mother died when I was real young, and I had no father. Pike Sutton was mother's master. He was my old grandfather. He owned a big farm. Tove Sutton was his son and my father. Mother was light but not as light as I am. I had a sister older than I am I lived with. I never lived among white folks except in a town with them. I don't know a thing about my people to tell. I don't know my age. I give myself a birthday. I don't know the day nor month I was born. But I'm old. I can count back enough to tell that.

"I work in the sewing room. I'm the oldest woman in there at De Valls Bluff. I get twenty-one dollars and this month I am to get twenty-seven.

"If you don't have work times are not good. I know that. I don't hardly know the young generation. Of course I see them but that is all. They hurrying their way and I'm going my way."

United States. Work Projects Administration

Interviewer: Mrs. Bernice Bowden
Person interviewed: Ida Harper
819 West Pullen Street; Pine Bluff, Arkansas
Age: 93

IDA HARPER

"Now what you want with me? I was born in Mississippi. I come here tollable young. I'se ninety-three now.

"My old master mean to us. We used to watch for him to come in the big gate, then we run and hide. He used to come to the quarters and make us chillun sing. He make us sing Dixie. Sometimes he make us sing half a day. Seems like Dixie his main song. I tell you I don't like it now. But have mercy! He make us sing it. Seems like all the white folks like Dixie. I'se glad when he went away to war.

"But they used to feed you. Heap better meat than you get now. I tell you they had things to eat in them days.

"I 'member when the soldiers was comin' through and runnin' the white folks both ways. Law chile—you don't know nothin'! We used to hide in the cistern. One time when the Yankees come in a rush my brother and me hide in the feather bed.

"When the war ended, white man come to the field and tell my mother-in-law she free as he is. She dropped her hoe and danced up to the turn road and danced right up into old master's parlor. She went so fast a bird could a sot on her dress tail. That was in June. That night she sent and got all the neighbors and they danced all night long.

"I never went to school a day in my life. I wish I could read but they ain't no use wishin' for spilt milk.

"How long I been in Arkansas? Let me see how many chillun I had since I been to Arkansas. Let me see—I fotch four chillun with me and I'se the mother of ten.

"Yes'm I sho' has worked hard. I worked in the field and cooked and washed and ironed. But oh Lord I likes my freedom.

"I couldn't tell you what I think of this present generation. They is just like a hoss on the battle field—white and black. They say 'Grandma, you just an old fogy.'

"I think they is another slave-time gal down in the next block. You want me to show you?"

"In slavery times you used to carry a rabbit foot in your pocket to keep old massa from whippin' you."

"We used to play a game called 'Once Over.' Throw a ball over the house and if they caught it on the other side, they'd run around and try to catch you.

"Then we used to play 'Hide the Switch.' And if you found it, the others all run to keep from bein' hit. Oh Lawd, that's been a long time."

Interviewer: Watt McKinney
Person Interviewed: Abram Harris
Marvell, Arkansas, (6 miles west)
Age: 93

ABRAM HARRIS

Abram Harris, an ex-slave, just past ninety-three years of age lives with his daughter, Hannah, 70 years old, on the farm of Mrs. Alice Davison a few miles west of Marvell, Arkansas. The two of them have just completed, within the last few days, the harvesting of a small crop of cotton and corn, and Abram was found in a small thicket not far from their cabin where he was busily engaged in cutting some firewood for their winter use. A small tree had been felled and the old man was swinging his axe with the strength and enthusiasm of one far younger than he as the wood was being cut to the proper length for his heater. Interrupted at my approach, Abram laid aside the axe and greeted me with that courtesy so characteristic of an ex-slave. After stating the purpose of my visit, the old negro apparently pleased at this opportunity afforded him to rest and talk, sat on the body of the newly cut tree and told me the following story:

"Yes sir, Cap'n, my name is Abram Harris and I is jist past ninety-three year old. En cose I knows dat I don't look dat old en all de folks sey dat I acts er heap younger dan my age iffen I really is old as I claims, en I kin still wuk bettern heap dese young uns, kase I is always knowed how ter wuk. My old Boss Man teach me de tricks. He war er wukker he-self, en eberybody hed ter roll roun Old Marster. He neber low no lazy pussen ter stay wid him. Yes sir, Cap'n, I sho has kept up wid my age eber since dat time when Old Marster tole me how ole I is. Yo kin see dat I is er old nigger, kase dese here whiskers so white en de hair on my haid so white too. When ye see dat on er nigger yo kin know dat he er old pussen right off. I gwine ter tell yo, how cum dat I sho knows how old I is. Er heap er niggers, dey tell yo dat dey is so en so year old when dey aint no sich er thing en dey don't know dey age, but I does, en hit wus jes dis er way.

"I wus borned en raised in South Carolina not fur from Greenville en my Old Marster whut I belonged ter, wus Marse Hodges Brown, en my young Marster he wus Marse Hampton, en me en Marse Hampton wus sho born in de same mont en de same year, en de mont, hit wus October, en dats zackly whut Old Marster tole me, en Marse Hampton sed dat same thing. Us wus boys togedder, me en Marse Hampton, en wus jist er bout de same size, en Marse Hampton, he claimed me, en I gwine ter be his property when bofe us grown. Dat is iffen de war not cum on en Marse Hampton hadn't er got kilt in de battle. When de war fust brake out, Marse Hampton he too young den ter jine de troops, how-sum-eber he went ter jine up den when he older brudder, Marse Thad, jine up, but Old Mis she wud'nt hear ter Marse Hampton gwine off den, kase he not old enuf, en den, he Old Mis' baby chile. Marse Thad, he bout two er three year older dan Marse Hampton en he jine de troops at de fust muster en went off ter de war en fit de Yankees night bout two years when de ball shot him in de shoulder, en he wounded den en hab ter cum bak home fer ter git well ergin. Atter Marse Thad cum home en stay fer er mont er sich time fer he wound ter heal up, den he ready ter go bak ter de company, en Marse Hampton gwine ter be eighteen year old pretty soon den, so dey swade Old Mis ter let Marse Hampton go wid Marse Thad bak ter de war, so Old Mis en Old Marster, dey gib in en Marse Hampton lef wid Marse Thad ter jine up wid him in de same company whut he in when de ball hit him. Now dat wuz in de spring when Marse Hampton jine up wid de troops, en him en me gwine ter be eighteen dat fall in October, but hit twarnt as awful long fore Marse Hampton got kilt in de big battle, en Marse Thad too. Dey wuz bofe kilt in de charge, right dar on de bres-wuks, wid dey guns in dey hans, dem two young Marsters er mine, right dar in dat Gettysburg battle, dats whut Old Marster en Old Mis bofe tole me er meny er time, en I wus eighteen in dat October atter dat big fight whut Mars Thad en Marse Hampton git kilt in, en Marse Hodges writ hit down fer me on er paper, en ebery October since den I gits sumbody whut kin figger ter tell me how old I is so's I kin know en tell folks when dey ax me, en jes last mont, my gal Hannah figgered hit out er gin en she sey dat I is now ninety-three past, so dat is de way dat I gits at hit Cap'n. Now is dat right?

"My white folks wus sho good ter all dey niggers. Dere wus nigh bout no whippin er tall, least Old Marster neber did whip his slaves ter do no good, en he mos ginerally tole us mammies er pappies ter do de whippin er de chillun en de older boys en gals. He hab whip me do en he whip Marse Hampton too when us wus boys. Old Marster start in wid dat hickry en mek out lak he gwine ter frail us out, but atter he done landed er few licks on us, en den us commence hollerin lak he hirtin bad, den he quit whippin, dat de way Old Marster wus. He neber want ter hurt nobody.

"My pa wus name, Jake, en my Mammy wus named, Fanny, Old Marster bought dem from sum-whar, but I wus borned right dar, me en Delia en all de res er de chillun.

"Cap'n, wud ye lak fer me ter tell ye bout dat time dat me en Delia wuz stole? Well, we sho wux stole. De Speckle-ladies (speculators or traders) stole us er way frum Old Marster when us wus chillun, bout twelve er thirteen year old. Hit happened in de night, when dar warnt nobody dar in de quarters but de wimmin. Old Marster en all de men wus down on de ribber dat night, er floatin logs er cuttin timber er sum sich wuk es dat, when dese hear folks cum er stealin chillun. Delia en me wus de fust ones dat dey grab en de onliest ones dat dey git frum Old Marster, but dey sho got us. I 'members dat stealin good. Dem folks tuk us off ter de woods whar dey tied us up ter er tree fer er whole night en day, en tell us dat iffen we cry er holler dat dey gwine ter kills us sho. Den dey cum en tuk us er way en ganged us up wid er lot mo nigger boys en gals whut dey done stole sum whars else. Dey yoked us togedder en walked us clean ter Georgia whar dey sole us. Dey sho pushed dem chillun hard ober de rocks en de hard places till our feets wud bleed frum de sores whar de rocks en de thorns scratch.

"Dey sole me en Delia ter er young white man en he wife whut ain't been married long en ain't got no start er niggers yit. Us stayed dar fer mo dan er year I rekkin, en dem wus good white folks en wus good ter us. De Mis teach Delia ter be er house gal en de Marster teach me ter handle stock en plow wid him eber day. Us wus skeered ter tell dem white folks whut bought us whar us home wus en who us Marsters used ter be, kase we skeered dat de speckle-ladies mout cum bak en steal us sum mo, en tek us er way sum mo. I don't know how hit wus dat Old Marster Hodges Brown cum ter fine out whar we wus, but he sho learnt er bout hit sum sich er way, en one mornin early here cum Old Marster Hodges Brown wid two mo white mens cumin atter me en Delia. Atter dey thru dentifyin us, Old Marster tuk us on bak home wid him, en we sho wus glad ter go. Now Cap'n, dat is de truf I am tellin you bout dat stealin, when me en Delia wus stole.

"My pappy wus named, Jake, en he wus de wagoner fer Marster till he daid, den Marster tuk me en trained me fer de wagoner atter den. My Marster warnt no big, rich man lak er heap er de white folks in dem slabery times, yit en still, he sho hed er plenty er ebery-thing, en de bes of all he fed he niggers good en wus always good ter tem. Marster used ter peddle er heap in Columbia en Greenville bofe atter I git ter be de wagoner fer him. Us wud tek big loads er taters en truck ter dem towns whar Marster wud sell em ter de folks dar. Sumtimes he wud tek er bout twenty beeves ter one er dem towns en rent him er yard whar he wud butcher er bout one beef ebery day en peddle out de meat. Marster neber hed many niggers lak lots de white folks. He jes hed er bout er dozen in all. He sey dat all he want, er got eny use fer.

"Marster hed er big fruit orchard. Jes all kines er fruit wud be in dat orchard, en when dey ripe, Marster send loads dem apples en peaches down ter de still whar he had dem made up in ter Brandy en put in de kegs en barrels en brought bak home when hit done. Heap er times dat I 'members he call de folks up ter de bak gallery en sey, 'Cum on up here folks en git yo all er dram'. Dats whut he say.

"Whilst our Marster wus good ter all he niggers, dar wus heap er de marsters in dem slabery times whut wus mean, en dat whut mek de niggers run off en hide in de woods, en dats when dey git de nigger hounds on em en track em down jes lak ye do er coon. My pappy, Jake, he owned by er mean white man, fore old Marster bought him in. I 'members bout him tellin us chillun when he used ter run off en hide in de cane thickets fer days en days kase he marster so mean en beat him up so bad, en dat he git so hungry dat he slip bak in close ter de house in de night, en dat sum de wimmins slip him sum meat en bread. He sey dat he used ter sleep wid de dogs under de crib on cold nights so de togs cud keep him warm.

"Dar warnt none er de white folks in dem slabery times whut wud let dey niggers hab any learnin. Yo sho better not be cotch er tryin ter learn no readin er writin. Our Marster neber eben lowed dat, en iffen er nigger wus ter be foun whut cud write, den right straight dey wud chop his fore finger offen dat han whut he write wid. Dar warnt no sich er thing es no schools fer de niggers till atter de surrender.

"Endurin er de war, dar warnt no fightin tuk place roun whar us libed, en de onliest Yankees dat I eber seed wus in Greenville atter de surrender. I sho wus sprized when I seed dem Yankees, kase I neber knowed whut sort er lookin thing dat er Yankee wus. No Sir, Cap'n, I neber knowed dat er Yankee wus er man jes lak my white folks till I seed dem in Greenville, but yo know Cap'n er Yankee looks jes lak yo is, only he do talk funny en fast, mo so dan de kine er white folks dat I is always been er roun.

"Dar warnt nary one er old Marsters niggers whut lef him eben when dey set free, dat is dey did'n lebe him fer two er three years eny way, but atter den sum of em started ter driftin er roun en hirin er roun er bout. When de surrender cum, Old Marster tole em all dat dey free en kin go iffen dey want ter go, en effen dey want ter go dat he gib em sum grub ter go on. Marster wus er good man en iffen he war libin ter day, I wud sho quit dis place en go on wid him, whar-sum-eber he want me ter go.

"No Sir, Cap'n, de niggers dey did'n know what de war wus gwine on fer, en dey did'n know dat dey free till dere marsters tole em, whilst dey wus wantin ter be free all right. Atter us wus free, de white folks hab ter teach us jes lak yo teach er chile.

"Dem Klu Klux whut dey brought on atter de surrender wus sho pizen. Dey wus white mens. Dats whut dey wus, en all dressed up in dem long white garments wid er red cross on em en ridin er big hoss. Dey wus atter dem niggers whut dey claim is mean en zerted dey marsters en went en tuk up wid de Yankees. When dem Klu Klux fust cum in operation de niggers think dat dey is hants er spirits, till dey fine out dat dey warnt nuthin but white mens wid dem garments on em. Dem Klux wud cotch er nigger dat dey want en pin he haid down ter de groun wid er forked stick en one wud hold him whilst de others whip im wid er strop er a lash. Yes sir, Cap'n, dem Klu Klux sho did dis-encourage de niggers er heap.

"Plenty er de white mens whut wus mustered in ter de war wud tek er nigger wid em ter wait on em en ter tend ter de hosses en de sich eber whut dey want done, en I sho did want ter go wid Marse Hampton, en mebbe dat I cud tek care of im. Marse Hampton want me ter go wid him too en try ter swade Old Marster ter let me go, but Old Marster sey dat he hab ter hab me dar at home ter help mek de crops so's dat he kin send corn en meat ter de sojers. De day dat Marse Hampton lebe, he cum down ter de quarters fer ter tell all de niggers good-bye, en he sey ter me 'Abe,' he called me Abe, 'I gwine off ter dat war en kill out dat whole crowd er Yankees, en den I'se cumin bak en gwine ter Georgia en buy me er farm whar I kin git rich mekin cotton en terbakker. Yo know yo is my nigger en yo gwine ter Georgia wid me, when I goes'. Hit sho did hurt me when Marse Hampton got kilt kase I lubed dat white man. He wus good ter me.

"In my dreams at night I kin yit see Marse Hampton, en er heap er times in de day when I is by myself er hoein de cotton he talks ter me plain so's I kin understand, en he ax me iffin I is yit en still er good nigger, en tell me ter not be dis-encouraged. Cap'n de Bible is right when hit sey dat, 'De young mens dream dreams en de old uns see de visions'.

"I kin jes natchally feel spirits, Cap'n, I sho don't spute dat. I is skeered ter spute hit. When yo is gwine long de road en feel sum warm air, den dat is whar de spirits hes jes been. De wings er de daid has done fanned dat air till hits hot, en when I is gwine er long en hits dat hot air, den I knows dat sum spirit er hant hes been er long dat same route, kase hit sho is hants in dis worl, yit en still dey don't walk en act lak natchal people.

"Yes Sir, Cap'n, I kin tell yo sum er dem old songs whut de niggers used ter sing in de slabery times. Dis is sum of em:"

Black Judy wus er good gal,
En Black Judy wus er bad gal too.

Mus Jesus bear de cross alone
and all de worl go free?
Oh Brother don't stay away
Oh Blackslider, don't stay away.

My old Mistis promised me
dat when she died, she gwine set me free,
But she lived so long en got so po
dat she lef me diggin wid er garden ho.

Wheel er bout en do er bout
en jump Jim Crow.
Ebery time I do er bout
I do jes so.

Yo can't do wrong en git by
no matter how hard yo try.
Yo kin do lak you please
en feel at yo ease
But you can't do wrong en git by.

United States. Work Projects Administration

MAY 31 1938
Interviewer: Miss Irene Robertson
Person interviewed: Betty Harris
Brinkley, Arkansas
Age: About 45 or 50?

BETTY HARRIS

"My parents wus both in the Civil War. He was Levi Berthy and she was Misson Berthy. Mid Hill was mother's owner. She said he was better to them than most owners. He never whooped 'em. Mother was real light and father was dark. I was born in Pinola County, Mississippi. I had a stroke five years ago. I can't walk a step for two years now. My parents didn't let us hear them talk, they sent us out to play, then they died before they got old. I never heard much of their own lives. I live with my daughter and her husband. I don't get Welfare aid."

United States. Work Projects Administration

Interviewer: Mrs. Bernice Bowden
Person interviewed: Mary Harris
713 N. Plum Street, Pine Bluff, Arkansas
Age: 82

MARY HARRIS

"I was born right here in Arkansas and I remember they was havin' somethin'. I remember when they taken this town (Pine Bluff). The people what owned me was the parson of the Methodist church—Parson Walsh. Yes ma'm I knowed the Union soldiers was dressed in blue and the Secessors was called Greybacks. My father was with the Yankee soldiers. I don't know how he got with em but I know he was gone away from this town three years. He come back here after he was mustered out in Vicksburg.

"I remember the Yankee soldiers come and took the colored folks away if they wanted to go. That was after surrender. They carried us to the 'county band' and fed us.

"I know the day the Yankees taken Pine Bluff; it was on Sunday and Marse Jesse went to services. The Secessor soldiers left Pine Bluff. Of course I didn't understand what it was all about cause in them times people didn't enlighten children like they does now. They know everything now, ain't no secrets.

"Most work I've done is washin' and ironin' since I been a full-grown, married woman. I was twenty some odd when I was married. I know I was out of my teens.

"I went to school a good while after the war. My first teacher was Mr. Todd from the North.

"I used to do right smart sewing. I did sewing before machines come to this town. The frocks they used to make had from five to ten yards.

"We is livin' now in a time of worry. What they is doin' is told about in the scripture."

DEC 21 1937
Interviewer: Mrs. Bernice Bowden
Person interviewed: Rachel Harris
816½ E. Fifth, Pine Bluff, Arkansas
Age: 90

RACHEL HARRIS

"I reekolect when the war started. I was big enuf to be totin' water, sweepin', feedin' chickens. I was a big chap when it started. I went with the white chillun and watched the soldiers marchin'. The drums was playin' and the next thing I heered, the war was gwine on. You could hear the guns just as plain. The soldiers went by just in droves from soon of a mornin' till sundown. They said they was goin' to head off the Yankees. Dis fore the war ended I heered en say they was gwine to free the colored folks. That was in Mississippi.

"My old master was Jim Smith and old mistress' name was Louisa Smith.

"I had many a whip put on me. When they wasn't whippin' me the chillun was. They whipped my mother and everybody.

"My brother Lewis went plum through the war till surrender. He waited on a Rebel soldier—cooked and washed for him. I never did see no white Yankee soldiers but I seed the colored soldiers with the blue suits. I stood out many a night and day and heered them guns.

"Jim Smith had near bout a hundred head of colored folks on his place. He didn't go to war—he just seed that all the white women had plenty to eat while their men folks was away.

"My mother was sold away from my father long 'fore I was born. He used to come to visit, but a little while 'fore I was born they stopped him and wouldn't let him come no more.

"After surrender one of my brothers come home and say the war was over.

"We stayed there three years after surrender. They paid my mother and stepfather but they wouldn't pay us chillun nothin', so my mother sent me to town to live with my sister.

"I hired out as a nurse girl and them white folks just as good to me as could be. She paid me $3 a month and give me all my clothes. I was young and didn't have no sense, but all I didn't spend on candy I sent to my mother.

"In slavery times the white folks had a servant to comb the hair and lift up the dress. Yes ma'm, they had servants. I sho was glad they had that war and freed me.

"Yes, Jesus, I seen them Ku Klux. I member once we had a big ball. We was cuttin' a dash that night. The Ku Klux come and made out they was dead. Some of the folks run they was so scared, but one woman come out and said she knowed every one of the men. She knowed em by their hosses. Next mornin' we went by old Purvis Newman's house and it looked like they was a hundred saddles layin' out in the yard. I was a young woman then and sparkin' fit to kill. Yes ma'm I member all about it. I reekolect it just as well as I can walk out that door.

"My son wrote me bout eight years ago and say, 'Mama, you is might near a hunderd.' My daughter, my baby chile, is bout sixty-three.

"About this younger generation, I don't know what to think. Some say the devil loose 'for a season.' I say if he ain't loose, he tied mighty slack."

United States. Work Projects Administration

Name of Interviewer: Irene Robertson
Person Interviewed: Rachel Harris
Green Grove, Hazen, Arkansas
Occupation: Field.—Lives with her daughter.
AGE: 80

RACHEL HARRIS

When she was a child she remembered white children and colored playing "No Boogerman Tonight." One would catch the others as they ran from behind big trees. Then whoever he caught would be the boogerman, till he caught somebody else.

They made ash cakes and put black walnuts in it. It was just as good as crackling bread which was made from rendering lard. They made molasses candy and pulled it at the Master's house during Christmas.

Mothers combed their children's hair Sunday and wrapped it, sometimes had dyed string.

The Master had a mule named Beck. Only one on the farm could tend old Beck. He would buck and kick. Sometimes he would run and he would lope if you "hitched" him to a buggy. When freedom came the master studied who would tend old Beck so he gave him to Jack. Jack felt so free as he rode from the farm out into the big world all his own and no place to go. In about a year Jack sent a letter back by somebody to the Master. "I want you to send me $2.00 of your own money. My wife has gone raving destracted. My mule is dead. I am pestered and bothered. I bound you."

Will said there used to be witches when somebody got mad with somebody they would bewitch the cows. You couldn't get the butter to come no matter how long you churned and sometimes a bewitched cow would come up and give bloody milk. If you keep plenty salt around in the troughs the witches wouldn't come about so much.

If you carry a rabbit foot in your pocket it will bring you good luck. If you find anything pointed with point toward you, that is a sign of good luck. If you put your shirt or dress on wrong side out, don't change it. Thats good luck for the day.

Don't start to sew a piece of goods on Friday unless you are sure you can get it done before night for that is bad luck.

Interviewer: Miss Irene Robertson
Person Interviewed: William Harris
DeValls Bluff, Ark.
Age: 75 or 80

WILLIAM HARRIS

"I was born in Chetam County close to Nashville, Tennessee. Our master was named Joe Harris. His wife was Miss Sallie Harris. They had eight children. I knowed Newt, Tom and Kittie. My mother had nine children. Her name was Julia. My papa's name was Isom Harris. I think they belong to the same family of white folks. Granny was old woman looked after white children. See if any of em got sick. She seen after little nigger children too. Mama was a field hand like papa. After war Plummer Harris went on off. He was cruel to his wife and grown folks but good to the children. We had good houses and plenty wood but the feed was light.

"I seen the Yankees riding through the country. They looked pretty, 'specially them on white horses. My papa and mama left. Mama died with pneumonia. Papa died, too. We had a mighty hard time after freedom and before too. Papa worked about on shares—hired out on jobs.

"When freedom come on we went on and they didn't think to give us nothing. When the hands all left they had the land and nobody to work. They was land pore. It was tore up. Fences down, houses down, and nothing to be raised to eat in the winter.

"When I got bigger I helped build the North Western Railroad into Nashville. I made right smart of money. I was building up the track bed. I farmed, worked on the section. I delivered here till my feet got in bad fix.

"I got thirteen children in all. Some in Tennessee by my first wife and some here and some grandchildren.

"Folks won't work like I used to work. It ain't no use to be 'larmed bout the times—they been changing since the world started—still changing. If you able it is best to go hunt work and be at a job working.

"I heard about the Ku Klux, they never troubled us. I seen em. I was scared of em.

"I get commodities and a check for us three old folks. My wife washes and irons.

"I got a bunion on one foot and raw sores on top of my toes. It won't cure up. Both feet in bad shape. My wife had both her legs broke. We doing very well."

Interviewer: Miss Irene Robertson
Person interviewed: William H. Harrison
Forrest City, Arkansas
Age: Over 100

WILLIAM H. HARRISON

"I was born March 4, 1832 in Richmond, Virginia. Master Anderson Harrison was a cousin to Benjamin Harrison, the twenty-third President of the United States. Master Anderson Harrison was my owner. I was a personal attendant of his young son and when I reached manhood I was the carriage boy. I did all the driving on all the trips the young people of the family took. My memories of slave days was my easiest days. Slavery was pleasant for me. My owner's wife was named Ann. The son was Gummel L. Harrison. I went with him to war. I was his servant in the battle-field till we fought at Gettysburg and Manassas Gap. Then I was captured at Bulls Gap and brought to Knoxville, Tennessee and made a soldier. I was in the War three and one half years. They had us going to school. They had Yankee teachers in the army. All the schooling I ever got. I was mustered out at Chattanooga, Tennessee.

"My parents was Julia Ann Hodge and Cairo Hodge. I don't know my mother's last owners. When I was about eight years old I was sold to Ben Cowen. When I was thirteen years old I was sold to Master Anderson Harrison. My brothers Sam and Washington never were sold. Me and Sam Hodge, my brother, was in the War together. We struck up and knowed one another. A man bought mama that lived at Selma, Alabama. I never seen her ag'in to know her. After I was mustered out I went to Birmingham where she was drove and sold in search of her. I heard she was taken to Selma. I went there. I give out hunting for her. It was about dusk. I saw a woman standing in the door. I asked her to tell me where I could stay. She said, 'You can stay here tonight.' I went in, hung my overcoat up. I started to the saloon. I met her husband with a basket on his arm coming home. I told him who I was. We went to get a drink. I offered him sherry but he took whiskey. I got a pint of brandy, two apples, two oranges, for his wife and two little boys. I spent two nights there and two and a half days there, with my own mother but neither of us knew it then.

"Fourteen years later Wash wrote to me giving me the address. I told him about this and he said it was mama. He told her about it. She jumped up and shouted and fell dead. I never seen her but that one time after I was sold the first time. I was about eight years old then. She had eighteen of us boys and one girl, Diana, and then the half-brothers I seen at Selma. I had eleven brothers took off in a drove at one time and sold. They was older than I was. I don't know what become of them. I never seen my papa after I was sold. Diana died in Knoxville, Tennessee after freedom. I seen better times in slavery than I've ever seen since but I don't believe in slave traffic—that being sold.

"I was with my young master till my capture. That was my part in freedom. I was forced to fight by the Yankees then in the Union army. I was with General Grant when Lee surrendered at Appomattox. That was freedom. After the War I come to Arkansas and settled at Madison. My hardships started. I got married the first thing.

"This is how good my owners was to me. He sent me to Hendersonville, North Carolina (Henderson?) to learn to fiddle. I was so afraid of the old colored teacher I learned in a month about all he could play. I played for parties in eight states in slavery. All up in the North. They trained children to dance then. I took Martha Jane, Easter Ann, Jane Daniel, my young mistresses and their mother's sisters, Emma and Laura, to parties and dances all time. We went to Ashville, North Carolina to a big party. While they was having fine victuals after the dance they sent me out a plate of turnip greens and turnips, fat meat and corn bread. I took it and set it down. When Miss Martha Jane got in sight I took her to our carriage. She said, 'Empty it to the dogs,' and give me one dollar fifty cents and told me to go to town and buy my supper. I was treated same as kin folks. I et and drunk same as they had to use. After freedom I fixed up twice to move back to my young master. Once he sent me three hundred fifty dollars to move on. Betty fell off the porch and broke her thigh. That ended my hopes of going back. Betty was my first wife. I had seven children by her and one by my second wife and this wife ain't had none. She's been married twice though.

"I got one boy in Virginia seventy-three years old and one boy sixty-eight years old. My boys are scattered. One lives here. I don't hear from them now.

"After the War I come to Madison. It was a thriving little river town surrounded on all sides by wilderness. There were thousands of Indians camped in the neighboring woods. There was nothing but wooded hills where Forrest City now stands.

"When General Nathan Bedford Forrest built the cut between Forrest City and Madison for the road, I was his cook and the first fireman to make the run through the cut. I used to drive a stagecoach over the Old Military Road through Pine Tree on the stage run from Memphis to Little Rock.

"Game was the nicest thing the country afforded. I killed bear and other wild game on sites where Marianna, Wynn, and Jonesboro now stand. Where this house now is was a lake then. (West part of town on north side of the railroad track.) They caught fish in it then.

"When I heard Benjamin Harrison had been elected President of the United States, I asked Mr. George Lewis to write to him for me. I was working for him then. I handled freight at the depot for him. He was dubious of me knowing such a person but wrote it to please me. A few weeks a reply come to our letter and a ticket.

"I got my fiddle and went and visited two weeks. I et at the same table with the President. I slept in the White House. We et out of skillets together when I was a little boy and drunk out of the same cups. Me and him and Gummel raised up together. I played for the President and his Cabinet.

"Twice more I went and it cost me nothing. I played for big balls. My young master sent me my gold name plate. (It is heart shaped with his name, birth and birthplace—ed.) I been wearing it on my watch chain a long time. It is my charm. Mr. Lewis was so glad when I got my letter and ticket. He was good to me.

"I have voted. I voted a Republican ticket because it hope the party out that freed my race. Some white men told me they burnt up a lot of our votes. I never seen it done. I can't see to fool with voting.

"The colored folks are seeing a worse time now than in slavery times. There is two sides to it. The Bible say they get weaker and wiser. I did read before I got blind. I get a Federal pension of one hundred dollars a month. I'm thankful for it."

Interviewer's Comment

He has trouble talking. One lung is affected. He is deaf. He is blind. He said he was wounded caused his lung trouble. Seems to me old age. He isn't very feeble in the house. Their house was clean and he and his wife, also born in slavery, looked clean.

United States. Work Projects Administration

Interviewer: Bernice Bowden
Person Interviewed: Laura Hart
Eleventh & Orange St., Pine Bluff, Arkansas
Age: 85

LAURA HART

"I just can't tell you when I was born cause I don't know. My mother said I was born on Christmas Eve morning. I'm a old woman. I was big enough to work in slave times.

"Yes ma'am. I member when the war started. I was born in Arkansas. I'm a Arkansas Hoosier. You know I had to have some age on me to work in slave times.

"I pulled corn, picked cotton and drive the mule at the gin. Just walked behind him all day. I've pulled fodder, pulled cotton stalks, chopped down corn stalks. I never worked in the house when I was a child while I was under the jurisdiction of the white folks.

"My old master was Sam Carson and his wife was named Phoebe Carson, boy named Andrew and a daughter named Mary and one named Rosie.

"We had plenty to eat and went to church on Sunday. After the white folks had their services we went in. The church was on his place right across the river. That's where I was when freedom taken place.

"When the war started—I remember that all right—cause when they was gettin' started old master sent a colored man to take his son's place in the war.

"I was born up here at Fort Smith and brought here to Jefferson County and sold—my mother and three chillun.

"Now wait—I'm goin' to give you the full history. My father's mother was a white woman from the North and my father was a colored man. Her folks run her here to Arkansas and she stayed with her brother till my father was nine months old and then she went back North and my papa stayed with his uncle.

"When his uncle died he willed my papa his place. He had it recorded at the cotehouse in Little Rock that my papa was a free man. But he couldn't stay in Arkansas free, so he just rambled 'till he found old man Carson and my mother. He offered to buy my mother but old master wouldn't sell her so he stayed with old man Carson till they was all free.

"My white folks was tollable fair—they didn't beat up the people.

"My mother was as bright as you are. She could sit on her hair. Her mother was a Creole and her father was a Frenchman. After freedom they would a killed my father if it hadn't been for old Sam Carson, cause they thought my mother was a white woman, she was so bright.

"Ku Klux? The Lord have mercy! I remember them. They came and surrounded the house, hundreds of em. We had a loose plank in the floor and we'd hide under the floor with the dogs and stay there, too, till they'd gone.

"My father was a gambler. He gambled and farmed. My mother was a Christian woman. When I got big enough to know anything, she was a Christian woman.

"I married when I was fourteen. We lived at a place called 'Wildcat.' Didn't have no school. Nothin' up there but saloons and gambling.

"Then we moved to what they called the Earl Wright place. I had four chillun—three boys and one girl. Most of my work was in the field.

"I been here in Pine Bluff gwine on seventy-one years. You know—I knowed this town when they wasn't but one store and two houses. I'm a old woman—I ain't no baby.

"Honey, I even remember when the Indians was run out o' this town!

"Well, I done telled you all I know. In my comin' up, the colored people didn't have time to study bout the chillun's ages."

United States. Work Projects Administration

Interviewer: Mrs. Bernice Bowden
Person interviewed: Hatty Haskell
1416 W. Pullen, Pine Bluff, Arkansas
Age: 85

HATTY HASKELL

"Yes'm, I reckon I was about twelve when the Civil War ended. Oh, I could nurse a little.

"No ma'am, I wasn't born in Arkansas. I was born in Tennessee, but I was brought here when I was a baby. Come here before the war. The old master had sold 'em.

"We was bought by Will Nichols. You ever hear of this here Dick Lake? Well, that's the place.

"They taken my father and my sister to Texas and stayed till after freedom. My mother was sick and they didn't carry her and I was too little, so they left me. They was pretty good to us as far as I know.

"I remember when the Yankees come through. Oh, yes'm, I was scared. I used to hide under the bed. I wouldn't give 'em a chance to talk to me.

"Our folks stayed on the Nichols' place about two years. Then they farmed on the shares till he got able to buy him a mule, then he rented.

"After the war the cholera disease come along. My mother and sister died with it.

"Somebody said if you would hang up some beef outdoors between the road and the house, it would stop the disease. I know old master hung up about a half a quarter and it seemed to work. The meat would turn green.

"The Yankees took things to eat but the Rebels would take the women's clothes—and the men's too. I guess they just took 'em 'cause they could.

"Biggest work I've done is farm work.

"My daddy said I was sixteen when I married. I had thirteen children but they ain't all livin'.

"I remember when they said they was free. Some of the folks left the place and never come back and some of 'em stayed.

"Sometimes I had a pretty good time and sometimes pretty tough.

"I'm gettin' along all right now. I stay here with my son part of the time and then I go to the country and stay with my daughter."

Interviewer: Samuel S. Taylor
Person interviewed: Matilda Hatchett
424 W. Twenty-Fifth Street, North Little Rock, Arkansas
Age: Between 98 and 100

MATILDA HATCHETT

"I was born right here in Arkansas about nine miles from Dardanelles (Dardanelle) in Sevier County. I think it's Sevier. No, it was Yell County. Yell County, that's it. You put the Dardanelles there and if they get that they'll get the Yell part. Can't miss Yell if you get Dardanelles.

"I wish I could get holt of some of my old white folks. Maybe you can find 'em for me. There's one big policeman here looks like them but I don't know whether he is or not. The first white owners that I knowed was Jackie George in South Carolina. That is where I heard them talkin' about him comin' from. I wasn't born there; I was born here. I wasn't born when he come from South Carolina. His wife was named Nealie. He was just like a ole shoe. Never whipped me but one time in my life.

"I'll tell you about it. This is what they whipped me for. Me and my brother, Sam, had to water the horses. I didn't have to go with Sam, but I was big enough to do that. We had one ole horse named John—big ole horse. I would have to git up on a ten-rail fence to git on him. One day I was leading ole John back and I got tired of walking. So when I come to a ten-rail fence, I got up on ole John. I got up on 'im backwards and I didn't have hold of no bridle nor nothin' because I was lookin' at his tail.

"The others got back there before they did. Ole master said to them, 'Where's Tillie?'

"They said to him, 'She's comin', leadin' ole John.'

"Atter a while they saw me comin', an' one of 'em said, 'There's Tillie now.'

"An' 'nother one, 'Man, she's sittin' on the horse backwards.' And ole John was amblin' along nippin' the grass now an' then with his bridle draggin' and me sittin' up on his back facin' his tail and slippin' and slidin' with every step.

"Ole John was gentle. But they were scairt he would throw me off. Ole missis come out the gate and met him herself, 'cause she was 'fraid the others would 'cite him and make him throw me down. She gentled him and led him up to ole master. They was careful and gentle till they got me off that horse, and then ole master turned and lit into me and give me a brushin'.

"That's the only whippin' he ever give me. But that didn't do me no good. Leastwise, it didn't stop me from ridin' horses. I rode ole John ever chance I could git. But I didn't ride him backwards no more."

Dresses

"We used to wear homespun dresses. I have spun a many a yard and wove it. Did you ever see a loom? I used to have a wheel, and my children tore it up some way or 'nother. I still have the cards. We done our own knittin' and spun our own thread and knitted our socks and stockings."

Houses

"The white folks lived in pretty good houses and we did too. They lived in big log houses. The white folks' houses had piazzas between the rooms. That Haney didn't build them houses. His daddy, Tim Haney, built 'em. The Haneys come in by Tim bein' Thad's father. Thad married Jackie George's daughter—Louisa George. George was her daddy and Haney was her husband.

"There were four rooms besides the piazza. On one side, there was a big room built out of lumber. On the other side, there was a big room that a doctor lived in. There was a great big kitchen west of the piazza. The kitchen was about fifteen by fifteen. I know it was that large because we'd all eat at the same time. The old man, Tim, owned about thirty niggers. After he died they were all divided out among the boys. Every boy took his part of the land and his part of the niggers. But I wasn't at his house then. I was livin' with ole Jackie George. The white folks hadn't moved together then.

"But I went to ole Tim Haney's funeral. The old white woman fainted and they rubbed her with camphor and stuff and had her layin' out there. I wasn't old enough to cry over him and wouldn't anyhow because I didn't care nothin' much about him. But I would have cried for my ole master though, because I really loved him."

Soldiers

"I saw the soldiers when they come through our place. The first start of us noticin' them was this. I was always up to the white folks' house. Thad was goin' back to the Rebel army. Ole master tole my dad to go git 'im a hat. He'd got 'im one and was ridin' back with Thad's hat on on top of his'n. Before he could git back, here come a man jus' a ridin'.

"Thad was eatin'. He look out, and then he throwed his head back and said, 'Them's the Federals.'

"Thad finished his breakfast and then he ran on out and got with the Federals. He didn't join 'em. He jus' fooled 'em. The bridge was half a mile from our house and the Yankee army hadn't near finished crossing it when the head of it reached us.

"While they were at the house, pa came ridin' up with the two hats on his head. They took the hats and throwed pa's on the ground and tried Thad's on. They took the mare but they give it back.

"Them folks stood 'round there all day. Killed hogs and cooked them. Killed cows and cooked them. Took all kinds of sugar and preserves and things like that. Tore all the feathers out of the mattress looking for money. Then they put ole miss (Nealie Haney) and her daughter (Louisa Haney) in the kitchen to cookin'.

"Ma got scairt and went to bed. Dreckly the lieutenant come on down there and said, 'Auntie, get up from there. We ain't a goin' to do you no hurt. We're after helpin' you. We are freein' you. Aunt Dinah, you can do as you please now. You're free.'

"She was free!

"They stayed 'round there all night cooking and eatin' and carryin' on. They sent some of the meat in there to us colored folks.

"Next mornin' they all dropped off goin' down to take Dardanelles. You could hear the cannons roarin' next day. They was all night gettin' away. They went on and took Dardanelles. Had all them white folks runnin' and hidin'.

"The Secesh wouldn't go far. They would just hide. One night there'd be a gang of Secesh, and the next one, there'd come along a gang of Yankees. Pa was 'fraid of both of 'em. Secesh said they'd kill 'im if he left his white folks. Yankees said they'd kill 'im if he didn't leave 'em. He would hide out in the cotton patch and keep we children out there with him. Ole mis' made him carry us.

"We was freed and went to a place that was full of people. We had to stay in a church with about twenty other people and two of the babies died there on account of the exposure. Two of my aunts died, too, on account of exposure then.

"The soldiers didn't take anything that night but food. They left all the horses. What they took was what they could eat. But they couldn't catch the turkeys. The lieutenant stayed around all the time to make the soldiers behave themselves. The meals he made my ole mis' and her daughter cook was for the officers.

"Yes Lawd! I have been here so long I ain't forgot nothin'. I can remember things way back. I can remember things happening when I was four years old. Things that happen now I can't remember so well. But I can remember things that happened way back yonder."

Schooling

"I learnt to read a little after peace was declared. A ole lady, Aunt Sarah Nunly, learnt us how to spell and then after that we went to school. I went to school three weeks. I never went to school much.

"Didn't git no chance to learn nothin' in slavery. Sometimes the children would teach the darkies 'round the house their ABC's. I've heard of folks teachin' their slaves to read the Bible. They didn't teach us to read nothin'. I've heard of it, but I've never seen it, that some folks would cut off the first finger of a nigger that could write."

Father's Children Freed Before Emancipation

"My father had some children that were set free. They lived down on the river bottom. Their ole master was named ole Crow. He died and sot his niggers free. He had four slaves. He had five. If any of you know Philo Pointer, his father was one of 'em. They sot him free. His daughter—Crow's daughter—wanted the niggers and they would break the ole man's will. They furnished them a wagon and sot them free. They came by my father's place and he killed his hog and fed them and they put the rest of it in the wagon and went on to the free state. I've got an old piece of a dish them boys give my mama. It's done broke up to a piece now, but I saves that.

"Patsy Crow was the name of the girl that was freed, and one of the boys was named Joe Crow, and the others I don't know what it was. I guess it was Jim. Their old master had left a will givin' them the wagon and team because he knew it wouldn't be possible for them to stay there after he died. He said he didn't want his niggers to be under anybody after he died. Wills was wills in them days. His daughter wanted them niggers, but they didn't give them to her. They sot them free and sont them off."

Wants to See Her People

"I nursed three children for Thad Haney and Louisa, his wife. Them girls' names was: the oldest was Julia; the next one was named Emma; and the youngest one was named Virginia. If I can find them and see them again, I'll be so happy. I jus' want to meet them one more time—some of them—all of them if they're livin'; but I know they can't all be living.

"Matilda Haney was my name then, and I nursed Thad's children in slavery time."

Age

"I think I'm between ninety-seven and ninety-eight years old. They had an old-age contest in Reverend Smith's time. They had Reverend Coffee and another man here since Reverend Smith. The pastor we have now is Yates. Our church is Lee Chapel A. M. E. Church. The contest was in 1935 I think and the people all agreed that I was the oldest colored woman in North Little Rock. They said I was ninety-six years old then. That would make me about ninety-eight years old now. But I saw my children afterwards and they said I was a year older. I used to have my age in the family Bible and my husband's too, but it got burnt up. Accordin' to them I oughta be about ninety-nine or a hundred."

Occupation

"My folks didn't raise no cotton. They raised about two bales a year. Didn't have nobody to raise it. Thirty slaves were not enough for that. And they didn't care nothin' about it nohow. They had forty-six acres of land in wheat and lots in corn and potatoes. They raised cows, hogs, horses, turkeys, chickens, and everything else. Even had peafowls. The geese used to run me 'round many a day.

"They ran a cotton gin and my father managed it. That was his job all the time before the War.

"After the War, my father farmed. He worked on shares. They never cheated him that he knew about. If they did, he didn't know it. He owned his horses and cows."

Interviewer: Miss Irene Robertson
Person interviewed: John G. Hawkens
Biscoe, Arkansas
Age: 71

JOHN G. HAWKENS

"I was born in Monroe County, Mississippi December 9, 1866. My parents was Frances Hawkens. She was a half white woman. I was told my daddy was a white man, Mr. Young. Mother was a cook and house woman. Grandmother was a field woman. She was dark but had some Indian blood in her. I believe they said it was part Choctaw Indian. I don't remember a grandfather.

"Lamar County, Alabama was across the line from Monroe County, Mississippi. One of the Hawkens girls (white girl) married a man in Mississippi. The master had three boys and one or two girls. Grandmother was sold to the Hawkens and mother was born there in Alabama. There was another woman they owned called Mandy. They was all the slaves they owned that I knowd of.

"When the War come on, the old man Hawkens was dead. His widow had three sons but one was married and off from her home somewhere. All three boys went to war. Her married son died in the War.

"One son went to war but he didn't want to go. He ask his mother if she rather free the Negroes or go to war. She said, 'Go fight till you die, it won't be nothing but a breakfast spell.' He went but come back on a furlough. He spent the rest of the time in a cave he dug down back of the field. He'd slip out and come to the house a little while at night. It was in the back woods and not very near anybody else.

"Aunt Mandy, another old man, grandmother and my mother lived in a house in the yard, two of us was born in slavery. My sister Mandy was fifteen years old when slavery ended.

"The way we first heard about freedom, one of the boys come home to stay but no one knew that when he came. He told sister Mandy cook him a good supper and he would tell her something good. She cooked him a good supper and set the table. He set to eat and she ask him what it was. He told her, 'All the slaves are free now.' From that on it was talked. We left there. My mother and sister Mandy told me I wasn't born. We went to Mississippi then. I was born over there. Some sharecropped and some worked as renters.

"Sister Mandy told so many times about carrying fire in a coffeepot—had a lid and handle—to the son in the cave. She'd go across there, a meadow like and a field, calling the sheep for a blind so if the cavalry spied her they would think she had a little feed for the sheep. The cavalry was close about. It was cold and the young master would nearly freeze in his cave.

"Mother said they was good to them. They never touched them to beat them but they all went from early till late. They all worked and the old mistress too.

"Two of mother's children was slave born. Sister Mandy is dead but my brother George Hawkens is on 1114 Appenway, Little Rock. He can tell you more than I know. Two of us was born after slavery. We all had the same father—Mr. Young. He lived about two miles from Hawkens and had a white wife and family. I carried water to the field where he worked and talked a little with him. I saw him when he was sick. He had consumption. I heard when he died and was buried. He never did one thing for us children. Mr. Young and the Hawkens was partners some way in the farming. Mr. Young died young.

"When her son told my sister Mandy at supper table, 'All the slaves are free now', old mistress jumped up and said, 'It's not recorded! It's not recorded!'

"Mr. Wolf was a man, old, old man on a big plantation. He had one hundred slaves. He didn't know his slaves when he met one of them. He had overseers. He talked with his slaves when he met one about and they would tell him, 'You're my master.' They said during the War the old man had cotton seed boiled down for his slaves to eat. The War was about to starve them all out. Oil mills were unheard of at that time.

"The War brought freedom and starvation both to the slaves. I heard old people say they died in piles from exposure and hunger. There was no let-up to their work after freedom.

"All my family came from Mississippi to Forrest City, Arkansas together. I married the first time there. My wife died. Then I married at Brinkley, Arkansas. We have one boy living in Lee County. He's my only child."

Interviewer's Comment

J. G. Hawkens is the whitest Negro I have ever seen. He has blue eyes and straight hair. He was fishing two days I went to see him.

Interviewer: Miss Irene Robertson
Person interviewed: Lizzie Hawkens
Biscoe, Arkansas
Age: 65

LIZZIE HAWKENS

"I was born close to Magnolia, Arkansas.

"My mother was Harriett Marshal. Her old mistress was a Marshal. She was a widow woman and had let all her slaves go out to her children but mama. Mama was her husband's chile, what she tole mama. They come here from Atlanta, Georgia visiting her married daughter. They was the Joiners at Magnolia, Arkansas. She brought mama and on her way back home to Atlanta she died. Her daughter brought her back and buried her in Arkansas and kept mama.

"Mama said they was nice to her. They wouldn't let her keep company with no black folks. She was about as white as white folks. She was white as my husband. Her mother was light or half white. My own papa was a black man.

"The Joiners and Scotts visited down at Magnolia among themselves but they didn't want mama to marry in the Scott family (of Negroes). But the white folks was mighty good friends. Mama took care of the children. They was in the orchard one day. Papa spied mama. He picked up a plum and threw at her. She say, 'Where that come from?' He stooped down and seen her under the limbs. They was under another plum tree. Papa got to talk to her that day. The old mistress wouldn't let her out of sight. Papa never could have got her if Mistress Marshal had lived.

"Mama had three or four sisters and brothers in Atlanta, and her mother was in Atlanta. Her parents were Bob and Lucindy Marshal. Bob was Lucindy's master. Mama told old mistress to bring Harriett back and she promised she would. That was one thing made her watch after her so close. She never had been made a slave. She was to look after old mistress.

"After she died mama's young mistress let papa have her. He mustered up courage to ax for her and she said, 'Yes, L (for Elbert), you can have her.' That was all the marrying they ever done. They never jumped over no broom she said. They was living together when she died. But in slavery times mama lived on at Judge Joiner's and papa at Scott's place. One family lived six miles east of Magnolia and the other six miles north of Magnolia. Papa went to see mama twelve miles. They cut through sometimes. It was dense woods. Mama had one boy before freedom. In all she had three boys and four girls.

"The Scott and Joiner white folks told the slaves about freedom. Papa homesteaded a place one mile of the courthouse square. The old home is standing there now.

"Papa said during the Civil War he hauled corn in an ox wagon. The cavalry met him more than once and took every ear and grain he had. He'd have to turn and go back.

"He said when freedom come, some of the people tole the slaves, 'You have to root pig or die poor.'

"My great-grandpa was sold in South Carolina. He said he rather die than be sold. He went up in the mountains and found a den of rattlesnakes to bite him. They was under a stone. Said when he seen them he said, 'Uh-her! You can't bite me.' They commenced to rattle like dry butter-beans. He went on and dressed to be sold. Master Scott bought him and brought him on to Arkansas. He had to leave his wife. He never got back to see her.

"Grandpa had to come leave his wife. He married ag'in and had five sons and a girl. They was Glasco, Alex, Hilliard, Elbert, Bill, and Katherine. They belong to Spencers till the Scotts bought them but all these children was his Scott children.

"My uncle's wife belong to white folks not Scotts. Scotts wouldn't sell and her folks wouldn't part from her. They moved down in Louisiana and took her and one chile. Uncle run away to see her. The Scotts put the hounds after him and run him two days and two nights. He was so tired he stopped to rest. The dogs come up around him. He took a pine knot and killed the lead dog, hit him in the head and put him in a rotten knot hole of a hollow tree been burned out and just flew. The dogs scattered and he heard the horns. He heard the dogs howl and the hoofs of the man's horses. The old master was dead. He didn't allow the boys to slash in among his niggers. After he died they was bossy. Uncle said he made his visit and come back. He didn't ever tell them he killed the lead dog nor how close they come up on him. He said they was glad to see him when he come back. His wife was named Georgana.

"After freedom grandpa named himself Spencer Scott. He buried his money. He made a truck garden and had patches in slavery both in South Carolina and at Magnolia. He told me he had rusty dollars never been turned over since they made him came here. He left some money buried back there. We found his money on his place at Magnolia when he died. He tole us where it was.

"One night he was going across a bridge and taking a sack of melons to Magnolia to sell in slavery times. A bear met him. He jumped at the bear and said 'boo'. The bear growled and run on its way. He said he was so scared he was stiff. They let them work some patches at night and sell some things to make a little money. The ole master give them some money if they went to the city. That was about twice a year papa said. He never seen a city till years after freedom. His pa and grandpa got to go every now and then. Magnolia was no city in them days.

"It is hard to raise children in this day and time. When I went on the Betzner place (near Biscoe, Arkansas) my son was eight years old. He growed up along side Brooks (Betzner). I purt nigh talked my tongue out of my head and Brooks' (white boy) mother did the same thing. Every year when we would lay by, me and my husband (white Negro) would go on a camp. Brooks would ask me if he could go. We took the two of them. (The Hawkens boy is said to be a dark mulatto—ed.) He's a smart boy, a good farmer down in Lee County now. He married when he was nineteen years old. It is hard to raise a boy now. There is boxing and prize fighting and pool halls and that's not right! Times are not improving as I can see in that way. Worse than I have ever seen them."

Interviewer: Mrs. Bernice Bowden
Person interviewed: Becky Hawkins
717 Louisiana Street, Pine Bluff, Arkansas
Age: 75

BECKY HAWKINS

"Yes'm, I was born in slave times but my mammy was sucklin' me. Don't know much bout slavery but just come up free.

"My mammy's old master was Calvin Goodloe in Alabama, Pulaski County, near Tuscumbia. I heered my uncle say old master favored his niggers.

"Mammy told me bout em gettin' whippin's, but she never let the overseer whip her—she'd go to old master.

"My grandmama's hair was straight but she was black. She was mixed Indian. My mammy's father was Indian and she say he fought in the Revolution. She had his pistol and rocks. When he died he was the oldest man around there.

"I tell you what I remember. I 'member my mammy had a son named Enoch and he nussed me in slave days when mammy was workin' in the field. They didn't low em to go to the house but three times a day—that was the women what had babies. But I was so sickly mammy had Enoch bring me to the fence so she could suckle me.

"I went to school down here in Arkansas in Lincoln County. I got so I could read in McGuffy's Fourth Reader.

I member that story bout the white man chunkin' the boy down out of the apple tree.

"That was a government school on the railroad—notch house. Just had one door and one window. They took the nigger cabins and made a schoolhouse.

"After freedom my mammy stayed on old master's place—he didn't drive em away. My mammy spinned the raw cotton and took it to Tuscumbia and got it wove. Some of it she dyed. I know when I was a gal I wore a checked dress with a white apron. And my first Sunday dress was striped cotton. After she worked enough she bought me a red worsted dress and trimmed it and a sailor hat. We went to church and they led me by the hand. After church I had to take off my dress and hang it up till next Sunday. Had a apron made of cross barred muslin. Don't see any of that now. It was made with a bodice and had ruffles round the neck. Wore brass toed shoes and balmoral stockin's in my gal time. When my husband was courtin' me, my dress was down to my shoe top. He never saw my leg!

"My fust work was nussin'. I went to Hot Springs with the white folks. I nussed babies till I got against nussin' babies. I stayed right in the house and slep on a sofa with a baby in my arms. In my time they lowed you off half a day on Sunday.

"Chile, I washed and ironed and washed and ironed and washed and ironed till I married. I married when I was seventeen. My mother was dead and I'd rather been married than runnin' loose—I might a stepped on a snake.

"My daddy was a ex-soldier. I don't know what side he fought on but my mammy got bounty when he died. That's what she bought that land with down here in Lincoln County from her old master Goodloe.

"I tell you—I'm a old christian and I think this younger generation is growin' up like Christ said—they is gettin' weaker and wiser.

"My mother's sister, Patience Goodloe, lived in Pulaski County, Alabama and I went back there after I was married and stayed two months. I went up and down the fields where my daddy and mommy worked. I went out to the graveyard where my little brother was buried but they had cotton and corn planted on the old slavetime graveyard.

"I like that country lots better than this here Arkansas. Don't have no springs or nothin' here."

United States. Work Projects Administration

Interviewer: Samuel S. Taylor
Person interviewed: G. W. Hawkins
1114 Appianway, Little Rock, Arkansas
Age: 73

G. W. HAWKINS

"I was born in Lamar County, Vernon, Alabama, January 1, 1865. I was a slave only four months.

"My father was Arter Hawkins and my mother was named Frances. My grandmother on my mother's side was Malvina. I forget the name of my great-grandmother, but I believe it was Elizabeth. She was one hundred nine years old and I was twelve years old then. Her mind was just like a little sparrow floating in the air. That was my great-grandmother on my mother's side. My grandfather on my father's side was named Alec Young. My mother's father was named Eliza Wright.

"My mother's people were the Hawkins, and my father's were the Yanceys.

"My father and mother were farmers, and ran whiskey stills. There wasn't any revenue on whiskey then. The first revenue ever paid on whiskey was ten cents. The reason I remember that so well was that a fellow named John Hayman ran a still after the revenue was put on the stuff. Finally they caught him. They fined him.

"My folks farmed right after freedom and they farmed in slavery time. They didn't raise no cotton. They raised corn and wheat and such as that in Alabama. Alabama is good for cotton, corn, wheat, tobacco, or anything you want to grow. It is the greatest fruit country in the world.

"Right after freedom, my folks continued to farm till they all played out.

Insert on P. 9

"I came out here after I got grown. I just took a notion to go somewhere else. I have been in Arkansas forty-eight years. I first lived in Forrest City. Stayed there six years and did carpenter work. I have been a carpenter all my life—ever since I was about sixteen years old. I went to Barton, Arkansas and stayed there two years and then came here. I have supported myself by carpenter work ever since I came here. I helped build the Frisco Road from Potts Camp to the Alabama River. That is the other side of Jefferson County in Alabama.

"I haven't asked for the old folks pension—can't get no one to believe that I am old enough for one thing. Can't get it nohow. It is for destitute people. I can't get under the security because they say I am too old for that. I'm too much of a worker to get old age assistance and too old to be allowed to put up tax to become eligible for old age pension.

"I never went to school. I just got an old blue back speller and taught myself how to read and write with what I picked up here and there from people I watched. That's one way a man never fails to learn—watching people. That's the only way our forefathers had to learn. I learned arithmetic the same way. I never considered I was much at figuring but I took a contract from a man who had all kinds of education and that man said I could do arithmetic better than he could.

"I belong to the A. M. E. Church. I have been a member of it for forty-one years.

"I have three boys living and one stepdaughter. But she feels like she is my own. I don't make any difference. I never have whipped my children. I had one child—a girl—that died when she was eight months old. I taught all my boys the carpenter trade, and they all work and stay right here at home with me."

Living Conditions during and Immediately after Slavery

"There are two quarters that I used to visit with my grandmother when I was a little boy. The boss's house was built so that he could stand on the porch of his house and see anything on the place, even in the slave quarters. The houses were all built out of logs. The roof was put on with what they called rib poles. They built the cable and cut each beam shorter than the other. They laid the boards across them and put a big log on top of them to weight them down, so that the wind couldn't blow the planks off. They were home-made planks. They didn't have no nails. They had nothing but dirt floors.

"Where the men folks were thrifty when they wanted to, they would go out at night and split the logs into slabs and then level them as much as they could and use those for floors. All the colored folks' were split log floors if there were any floors at all. There was no lumber then. The planks were made with whipsaws and water-mills.

I was a grown man before I ever saw a steam mill. The quarters that I saw were those that were built in slave time.

"If cracks were too big, they would put a pole in the crack and fill up the rest of it with mud—that is what they called chink and dob. The doors were hung on wooden hinges. They would bore a hole through the hinge and through the door and put a wooden pin in it in place of screws. There wasn't a nail or a screw in the whole house when it was finished. They did mortise and tenon joints—all frame houses. Where we use nails now, if they had to, they would bore a hole and drive in a pin—wooden pin."

Furniture

"The colored folks would put a post out from the corner and bore a hole and put the other end in it. They wouldn't have any slats but would just lay boards across the side and put wheat or oat straw on the boards. The women made all the quilts. What I mean, they carded the rolls, spun the thread—spun it on an old hand-turned wheel—and then they would reel it off of the broach onto the reel and make hanks out of it. Then they would run it off on what they called quills. Then it would go 'round a big pin and come out with the threads separated. Then they would run through something like a comb and that would make the cloth.

"It was the rule in slave time to card one hundred rolls. Sometimes they would be up till after twelve o'clock at night. They carded that in one night and spun it the next night. Start with old cotton just like it come from the gin.

Card it one night and spin it the next. Done wool and cotton the same way. One hundred rolls carded gave enough threads to make a yard of cloth.

"In them days they tasked everybody to the limit."

Stoves

"For stoves they used an iron pot on a big fire. In the kitchen, they had a fireplace built ten feet wide. They had things they called pot racks hung down from the chimney, and they would hang pots on them. They put the pots on those hooks and not on the logs. When they baked bread they would use iron skillets—North Carolina people called them spiders. They would put an iron lid on them and put fire over the top and underneath the skillet and bake good bread. I mean that old-time bread was good bread. They baked the light bread the same way. They baked biscuits once a week. Sunday mornings was about the only time you ever got them."

Food in General (Slaves)

"In slavery times they had all kinds of meat—more than they have now—, vegetables and fruits too. They raised them themselves. There wasn't no food issued. Didn't need to be. One cook cooked it all in one kitchen and they all sat around the same big old long table long as a house. All the hands ate at the same table and in the same room and at the same time.

"The way they fed the children, they took pot-liquor or bean soup or turnip liquor or the juice from anything they boiled and poured it out in a great big wooden bowl and let all the children get 'round it like so many cats and they would just tip their hands in it and eat what they wanted. Of course they had all the milk they wanted because everybody raised cows. I didn't have to undergo this myself, but this was what they had to undergo at the places where my grandmother took me to visit."

Clothes

"A colored boy had to be more than twelve years old before he wore a pair of pants. He wore nothing but a long shirt that come down to his knees. The hands in slave time wore homemade shirts. All clothes were homemade—pants and coats and dresses and stockings and everything. The shoes were made out of harness leather. Tanned and made right by hand at home. I have seen tanning vats and yards two blocks square."

Patrollers

"You had to get a pass from owners to go out at night. If you had a pass and the pateroles found you, it was all right if you hadn't overstayed the time that was written on it. If you didn't have a pass or if you had overstayed your time, it was still all right if you could outrun the pateroles. That held before freedom and it held a long time after freedom. The pateroles were still operating when I was old enough to remember those old quarters. They didn't break them up for a long time. I remember them myself. I don't mean the Ku Klux. The Ku Klux was a different thing altogether. The Ku Klux didn't exist before the War. I don't know where they got the name from—I don't know whether they give it to themselves or the people give it to them. But the Ku Klux came after the War and weren't before it."

Ku Klux Influence on Negroes

"The Ku Klux Klan weren't just after Negroes. They got after white folks and Negroes both. I didn't think they were so much after keeping the Negro from voting as some other things.

"There was one colored fellow in Alabama—I think his name was Egbert Bondman—that wasn't influenced. He was a politician and they got after him one time. He lived about six miles south of Vernon in Lamar County, Alabama. He went down to the hole where they watered their horses and stretched an old cable wire across the road just high enough to trip up their horses. He hid in the woods and cut down on them with his shotgun when they came up. I hear there was one more scramble when those horses commenced stumbling, and those men started running through the forest to get away from that shot.

"I remember one night my mother woke me up, and I looked out and there was a lot of the Ku Klux riding down the road. They had on long white robes and looked like a flock of geese in the dark.

"The main thing the Ku Klux seemed to try to do, it seemed to me, was to try to keep the colored folks obedient to their former masters and to keep the white folks from giving them too much influence. And they wanted to stop the white men that ran after colored women.

"But they didn't last long. They whipped a fellow named Huggins in the early seventies, and he was a government man. After that government men camped on their trail, and they didn't amount to much."

Slave Breeding

"The thing they were fighting began in slavery. There were slave men kept that forced slave women to do what they wanted to do. And if the slave women didn't do it, the masters or the overseers whipped them till they did. The women were beat and made to go to them. They were big fine men, and the masters wanted the women to have children by them. And there were some white men, too, who forced the slave women to do what they wanted to. Some of them didn't want to stop when slavery stopped."

Slave Tasks and Hours of Work

"I've told you the slaves were tasked to the limit. The hours of the slave hands—if it was summer time—he must be in the field when the sun rose. And he must come home and eat his dinner and get back in the field and stay till the sun went down. In the winter time he must be out there by the time it was light enough to see the work and stay out till it was just too dark to see the work with just enough time out to stop and eat his dinner. This was just after slavery that I remember. But the hours were the same then. The average on cotton picking was two hundred pounds a day. Pulling fodder was a hundred bundles. Gathering corn and such as that was all they could do."

Wages just after Freedom

"The average wage that a man got for twenty-six days' work—twenty-six days were counted a working month—was eight dollars and board for the month. That was the average wage for work like that. That is the way they worked then."

This Matter of Slave Clothes Again

"Clothes!!! They didn't know nothing 'bout underclothes. They didn't wear them just after the War, and I know they didn't before the War—not in my part of Alabama. That's the reason why they say the Negro is cold natured. He didn't have anything on. I have seen many a boy picking and chopping cotton on a cold autumn day with nothing on but his shirt. In his bare feet too. He got one pair of shoes a year and he didn't get no more. When he wore them out, he didn't have any till the next year.

"When I was a boy I have seen many a young lady walk to church with her shoes flung over her shoulders and wait till she got nearly there before she would put them on. She didn't want to wear them out too soon.

"I didn't have to undergo this myself.

"When I was ten years old, my job was to drive a team twenty-six miles, and it took me two days to go and two days to come and one day to load and unload—five days.

The team was loaded with cotton going and anything coming back. We used to get salt from some place near New Orleans. We would drive ox teams down there, put in on order, wait till they dipped the water out of the lake, boiled the salt out of it, and packed it up. There was no such thing as mining salt like they do now. It would take from August first till about the middle of September to get it. Ox team won't make more than about twelve miles a day. The people would make up a wagon train and go and come together. People in those days didn't believe a horse would pull anything but a buggy, so they used steers mostly for heavy pulling. They ran all gins and thrashers by horse power and the running gear was all made out of wood. A lot of people say you couldn't make a wooden cotton press that would pack a bale of cotton. You can make a wooden press that will break a bale in two. Of course the gin was made out of metal. But they made the press out of wood."

Slave Schooling

"The slaves were not allowed to learn anything. Sometimes one would be shrewd enough to get in with the white children and they would teach him his a-b-c's, and after he learnet to spell he would steal books and get out and learn the rest for himself."

How Freedom Came

"The way I heard it the owners called their slaves up and told them they was free. They give them their choice of leaving or staying. Most of them stayed."

First Crop after Freedom

"In 1865, when the slaves were freed, they acknowledged they were free in May in Alabama. All that was free and would stay and help them make their crops, they give them one-tenth. That is, one-tenth went to all the hands put together. Of course if they had a lot of hands that wouldn't be much. Then again, it might be a good deal. I know about that by hearing the old people talk about it."

Opinions

"I'll tell you my opinions some other time. I think the young people are beyond control. I don't have any trouble with mine. I never have had any trouble with them."

Interviewer: Samuel S. Taylor
Person interviewed: Eliza Hays
2215 W. Twentieth Street, Little Rock, Arkansas
Age: 77 or more

ELIZA HAYS

"On the fourth of August, my birthday, and directly after the colored people were set free, all the white people gave a great big dinner to the slaves. All the white people at my home came together and gave a big dinner to us. It was that way all over the United States. My mother told me I was four years old at that big dinner. They went to a great big book and throwed it open and found my birthday in it. I never will forget that. You can figure from that exactly how old I am. (Seventy-seven or seventy-eight—ed.)

"My mother's name was Elizabeth Tuggle and my father's name was Albert Tuggle. My mother was the mother of sixteen children. They were some of them born in freedom and some born in slavery. They are all dead but three. My mother was married twice.

"Old Tom Owens was my mother's master. I just do remember him. My father's master was named Tom Tuggle. My mother and my father got together by going different places and meeting. They went together till freedom and weren't married except in the way they married in slavery. During slavery times, old master gave you to some one and that was all of it. My father asked my mother's old master if he could go with my mother and old man Owens said yes. Then father went to her cabin to see her. When freedom came, he taken her to his place and married her accordin' to the law.

"Aunt Mariny Tuggle was my father's mother. I don't know anything about his father. She has been dead! She died when I was young. I can remember her well, though.

"I can remember my mother's mother. Her name was Eliza Whitelow. Her husband was named Jack Whitelow. They was my grandfather and my grandmother on my mother's side. They old people. I can remember seeing them.

"I never saw my grandfather on my father's side. That was way back in slavery time. I used to hear them say he was a guinea man. He was short. My own father was small too. But my father's father was short as I am. I am about four and a half feet tall. (I stopped here and measured her, and she was exactly four feet six inches tall—ed.) I never heard nobody say where he came from. My father's sisters were part Indian. Their hair was longer than that ruler you got in your hand there. It came down on their shoulders. They was a shade brighter than I am.

"My father's mother was small too. His sisters were not whole sisters; their daddy was Indian."

Occupation

"My father and his father and mother were all farmers. My mother and her mother were farmers too. All my people were long-lived. Grandpa, grandma, and all of them. I reckon there about a hundred children scattered back there in Tennessee. Brother's children and sister's children. I believe my folks would take care of me if they knew about my condition. These folks here are mean. Them folks would take care of me if I were home."

Slave Houses

"The slaves lived in old log houses; just one room, one door, one window, one everything. They had any kind of furniture they could git. Some of them had old homemade beds and some of them one thing and another. You know the white folks wasn't goin' to give them no furniture.

"They had plenty of meat and bread and milk to eat. Coarse food—the commonest kind of food they could get 'hold of! When I knowed anything, I was in the big house eating the bes' with the white folks. Some of them could live well then. My mama gave me to the Owenses—her old mistress. I was raised on a pallet in the house. I was in the house from the time I was large enough to be taken from my mother. I didn't never do any work till I was married. Old mistress wouldn't let me work. Just keep by her and hand her a drink of water, and on like that. She's dead now—dead, dead, dead! They didn't leave but two children, they was 'round in the country somewheres then I left there.

"After I married I went to her husband's first wife's child. She had about nine or ten boys and one girl. I raised part of them. But most of them was great big children—

big enough for me to throw a glass of milk at their heads. I would fight. Sometimes they used to hear them hollering and come out, and I would be throwing a glass at one and jumping across the table at the other. But when them boys grew up, they loved me just the same as anybody. Nobody in town could touch me, right or wrong."

Mean Masters

"My mother's masters used to tie her down before the dairy door and have two men beat her. She has told me that they used to beat her till the blood ran down on the bricks. Some white people in slavery times was good to the niggers. But those were mean, that's the reason I ain't got no use for white folks. I'm glad I was not old in that time. I sure would have killed anybody that treated me that way. I don't know that my father's people beat him up. I think his people were kinder and sorter humored him because he was so small."

Marriage

"They tell me some of them would have a big supper and then they would hug and kiss each other and jump over the broomstick and they were supposed to be married."

Amusement and Recreation

"They used to go out and dance and carry on for amusement, and they would go to church too. It was just about like it is now. Dancing and going to church is about all they do now, isn't it? They got a gambling game down there on the corner. They used to do some of that too, I guess."

Breeders

"I have heard my mother say many times that a woman would be put up on the block and sold and bring good money because she was known to be a good and fast breeder."

Ku Klux, Patrollers, Robbers

"I've heard of the pateroles and Ku Klux. I thought they said the Ku Klux was robbers. I think the Ku Klux came after the War. But there was some during the War that would come 'round and ask questions. 'Where's yo' old master?' 'Where's his money hid?' 'Where's his silverware?' And on like that. Then they would take all the money and silver and anything else loose that could be carried away. And some of them used to steal the niggers theirselves 'specially if they were little childrens. They was scared to leave the little children run 'round because of that."

Opinions

"I don't know. I better keep my 'pinions to myself. You just have to go on and be thankful and look to the Lord."

Support and Later life

"I haven't done a day's work for seven years. I haven't been able. I have a son, but he has a family of his own to support and can't do nothin' for me. I have another son but he is now out of work himself. He can't get anything to do. I just have to git along on what little I can turn up myself, and what little I get from my friends.

"My husband died about seven years ago. I have lost two boys inside of seven years. After they died, I went right on down. I ain't been no good since. The youngest one, Mose, got killed on a Sunday night. I felt it on Saturday night and screamed so that people had to come 'round me and hold me and comfort me. Then on Sunday night Mose got shot and I went crazy. He was my baby boy and he and his brother were my only support. My other boy got sick and died at the hospital. When the man stepped on the porch to tell me he was dead, I knew it when I heard him step up before he could say a word. I can't git to see his wife now. She was the sweetest woman ever was. She was sure good to my son. She treated him like he was a baby. She was devoted to him and his last request to her was to see to me. I don't know just where she is now, but she's in the city somewheres. She would help me I know if I could get to her.

"My husband was a preacher. He pastored the St. John Baptist Church for fifteen years. He lived here over thirty years before he died. I left a good home in Brownsville, Tennessee. That's where we were married. I have been married twice. I lived with my first husband, George Shaver, a year. I married him about 1876. I was single for two years. After that I married Rev. Hays. I lived with Rev.

Hays about twenty-one years in Brownsville, Tennessee. We bought a house and lot there. We were gettin' along fine when we decided to come here. He was a shoemaker then. He made shoes after he came here, too. I ran a restaurant in Brownsville. I guess we lived together more then fifty years in all. He died seven years ago.

"I rent these two rooms in this little shack. They won't give me no help at the Welfare."

United States. Work Projects Administration

— 1- 1937
Interviewer: Mrs. Bernice Bowden
Person interviewed: Tom Haynes
1110 W. Second Street, Pine Bluff, Arkansas
Age:

TOM HAYNES

"I was six years old when the war ended—the day we was set free. My old mistress, Miss Becky Franks, come in and say to my mother 'Addie, you is free this morning' and commenced cryin'. She give my mother some jerked beef for us.

"I know I run out in the yard where there was eighty Yankee soldiers and I pulled out my shirt tail and ran down the road kickin' up the dust and sayin', 'I'm free, I'm free!' My mother said, 'You'd better come back here!'

"I never knew my mother to get but one whippin'. She put out her mouth against old mistress and she took her out and give her a breshin'.

"I can remember away back. I can remember when I was three years old. One day I was out in the yard eatin' dirt and had dirt all over my face. Young master Henry come out and say 'Stick out your tongue, I'm goin' to cut it off.' I was scared to death. He said 'Now you think you can quit eatin' that dirt?' I said 'Yes' so he let me go.

"One time the Yankee soldiers took young Master Henry and hung him up by the thumbs and tried to make him tell where the money was. Master Henry's little brother Jim and me run and hid. We thought they was goin' to hang us too. We crawled under the house just like two frogs lookin' out.

"Old master had about thirty-five hands but some of em run away to war. My father run away too, but the war ended before he could get into it.

"I went to school a little while, but my father died and my mother bound me out to a white man.

"When we was first freed I know those eighty soldiers took us colored folks to the county band in Monticello. There was forty soldiers in the back and forty in front and we was in the swing.

"I learned to read after I was grown. I worked for the railroad in the freight office fifteen years and learned to check baggage.

"I was a house mover when I was able, but I'm not able to work now. I own this house here and I'm livin' on the relief.

"My father was a blacksmith and shoemaker—made all our shoes. I've lived in town all my life.

"The people are better off free if they had any sense. They need a leader. When they had a chance if they had bought property, but no—they wanted to get in office and when they got in they didn't know how to act. And the young people don't use their education to help themselves."

Interviewer: Bernice Bowden
Person Interviewed: Joe Haywood
2207 West Eleventh Street, Pine Bluff, Arkansas
Age: 76

JOE HAYWOOD

"I was born the first day of January, 1862 Born in Mississippi, Yazoo County. My mother said I was a New Year's present. A. M. Payne was our owner.

"I just do 'member seein' the soldiers and that's all. I 'member the brim of slavery and that's all.

"I member Henry Dixon. He was a Klu Klux. He was Klu Klukin round breakin' up the benevolent societies. He was a real bad man. He just went round with his crowd and broke 'em up. My owner was a good man—good man. They all give him a good name.

"Our folks stayed there till I was plumb grown.

"I've farmed, carpentered, and all kinds of work on the plantation. I've been a engineer in a gin and gettin' out crops every year.

"After I left Mississippi I just roved around. Went through Louisiana to Texas. I lived in Texas. I reckon, from 1893 to '96. Then I started to rove again. I roved from Texas back home to Mississippi in 1902. Stayed there till 1932, then I roved over here to Arkansas. I done got too old to rove now.

"School? Oh Lord, I went to school all my days till I was grown. They kep' me in school. My mother kep' me in till she died and then my stepmother kep' me in. I got very near through the fifth grade. In my day the fifth grade was pretty good. Wilson's Fifth Reader was a pretty good book. They took me out of Wilson's Fifth Reader and put me in McGuffy's and there's where I quit. Studied the Blue Back Speller.

"I've had some narrow escapes in my life. I had a shot right through here in the breast bone—right over my heart. That was in ninety-six. Me and another fellow was projectin with a gun.

"Then I had a bad accident on the ninth of March, 1914. A 800-foot log came down on me. It near 'bout killed me. I was under a doctor 'bout six or eight months. That's how come I'm crippled now. It broke my leg and it's two inches shorter than the other one. I walked on crutches 'bout five years. Got my jawbone broke too. Couldn't eat? I ain't never stopped eatin'. Ain't no way to stop me from eatin' 'cept to not give it to me.

"I compressed after I got my leg broke. And I was a noble good bricklayer.

"I never have voted. Nobody ever pushed me up to it and I ain't never been bothered 'bout anything like that. Everythin was a satisfaction to me. Just whatever way they went was a satisfaction to me.

"I have never heard my folks give my white folks no 'down the hill'. My daddy was brought from Charleston, South Carolina. He was a ship carpenter. He did all of Payne's carpenter work from my baby days up.

"The last of the Paynes died since I came here to Arkansas. He was a A. M. Payne, too.

"I can 'member the soldiers marchin' by. They wore yellow shirts and navy blue coats. I know the coats had two little knobs right behind, just the color of the coat.

"I don't know what to think of the younger generation. I don't know why and what to think of 'em. Just don't know how to take 'em. Ain't comin' like I did. Lay it to the parents. They have plenty of leaders outside the family.

"I'm lookin' for a better time. God's got His time set for 'em on that.

"I belong to St. James Methodist Episcopal Church."

United States. Work Projects Administration

Interviewer: Samuel S. Taylor
Person interviewed: Marie E. Hervey
1520 Pulaski Street, Little Rock, Arkansas
Age: 62

MARIE E. HERVEY

"I have heard my father and mother talk over the War so many times. They would talk about how the white people would do the colored and how the Yankees would come in and tear up everything and take anything they could get their hands on. They would tell how the colored people would soon be free. My mama's white folks went out and hid when the Yankees were coming through.

"My father's white people were named Taylor's—old Job Taylor's folks. They lived in Tennessee.

"My mother said they had a block to put the colored people and their children on and they would tell them to tell people what they could do when the people asked them. It would just be a lot of lies. And some of them wouldn't do it. One or two of the colored folks they would sell and they would carry the others back. When they got them back they would lock them up and they would have the overseers beat them, and bruise them, and knock them 'round and say, 'Yes, you can't talk, huh? You can't tell people what you can do?' But they got a beating for lying, and they would uh got one if they hadn't lied, most likely.

"They used to take pregnant women and dig a hole in the ground and put their stomachs in it and whip them. They tried to do my grandma that way, but my grandpa got an ax and told them that if they did he would kill them.

"They never could do anything with him.

"My mother's people were the Hess's. They were pretty good to her. It was them that tried to whip my grandma though.

"You had to call everybody 'Mis'' and 'Mars' in those days. All the old people did it right after slavery. They did it in my time. But we children wouldn't. They sent me and my sister up to the house once to get some meal. We said we weren't goin' to call them no 'Mars' and 'Mis'.' Two or three times we would get up to the house, and then we would turn 'round and go back. We couldn't make up our minds how to get what we was sent after without sayin' 'Mars' and 'Mis'.' Finally old man Nick noticed us and said, 'What do you children want?' And we said, 'Grandma says she wants some meal.' When we got back, grandma wanted to know why we took so long to go and come. We told her all about it.

"People back home still have those old ways. If they meet them on the street, you got to get off and let them by. An old lady just here a few years ago wouldn't get off the sidewalk and they went to her house and beat her up that night. That is in Brownsville, Tennessee in Hayeard (Haywood) County. That's an old rebel place.

"White people were pretty good to the old colored folks right after the War. The white folks were good to my grandfather. The Taylors were. They would give him a hog or something every Christmas. All the old slaves used to go to the big house every Christmas and they would give them a present.

"My husband ran off from his white people. They was in Helena. That's where he taken the boat. He and a man and two women crossed the river on a plank. He pulled off his coat and got a plank and carried them across to the other side. He was goin' to meet the soldiers. He had been told that they were to come through there on the boat at four o'clock that afternoon. The rebels had him and the others taking them some place to keep them from fallin' into the hands of the Yankees, and they all ran off and hid. They laid in water in the swamp all that night. Their bosses were looking for them everywhere and the dogs bayed through the forest, but they didn't find them. And they met some white folks that told them the boat would come through there at four o'clock and the white folks said, 'When it comes through, you run and get on it, and when you do, you'll be free. You'll know when it's comin' by its blowin' the whistle. You'll be safe then, 'cause they are Yankees.'

"And he caught it. He had to cross the river to get over into Helena to the place where the boat would make its landin'. After that he got with the Yankees and went to a whole lot of places. When he was mustered out, they brought him back to Little Rock. The people were Burl Ishman and two women who had their children with them. I forget the names of the women. They followed my husband up when he ran off. My husband's first name was Aaron.

"My husband had a place on his back I'll remember long as I live. It was as long as your forearm. They had beat him and made it. He said they used to beat niggers and then put salt and pepper into their wounds. I used to tell daddy that 'You'll have to forget that if you want to go to heaven.' I would be in the house working and daddy would be telling some white person how they 'bused the slaves, and sometimes he would be tellin' some colored person 'bout slavery.

"They sold him from his mother. They sold his mother and two children and kept him. He went into the house crying and old mis' gave him some biscuits and butter. You see, they didn't give them biscuits then. That was the same as givin' him candy. She said, 'Old mis' goin' to give you some good biscuits and some butter.' He never did hear from his mother until after freedom. Some thought about him and wrote him a letter for her. There was a man here who was from North Carolina and my husband got to talking with him and he was going back and he knew my husband's mother and his brother and he said he would write to my husband if my husband would write him a letter and give it to him to give to his mother. He did it and his mother sent him an answer. He would have gone to see her but he didn't have money enough then. The bank broke and he lost what little he had saved. He corresponded with her till he died. But he never did get to see her any more.

"Nothin' slips up on me. I have a guide. I am warned of everything. Nothin' happens to me that I don't know it before. Follow your first mind. Conscience it is. It's a great thing to have a conscience.

"I was born in Tennessee. I have been in Arkansas about forty-six years. I used to cook but I didn't do it long. I never have worked out much only just my work in the house. My husband has been dead four years this last April. He was a good man. We were married forty years the eleventh of December and he died on the eighth of April."

United States. Work Projects Administration

MAY 11 1938
Interviewer: Miss Irene Robertson
Person interviewed: Phillis Hicks
Edmondson, Arkansas
Age: 71

PHILLIS HICKS

"My mother's owner was Master Priest Gates. He had a son in Memphis. I seen him not long ago. He is an insurance agent. They was rosy rich looking folks. Mama was a yellow woman. She had fourteen living children. Her name was Harriett Gates. Papa named Shade Huggins. They belong to different folks. They was announced married before the War and they didn't have to remarry.

"She said the overseers was cruel to them. They had white men overseers. She was a field hand. I heard her say she was so tired when she come to the house she would take her baby in her arms to nurse and go to sleep on the steps or under a tree and never woke till they would be going to the field. She would get up and go on back. They et breakfast in the field many and many a time. Old people cooked and took care of the children. She never was sold. I don't know if my father was. They come from Alabama to Mississippi and my mother had been brought from Georgia to Alabama.

"She picked geese till her fingers would bleed to make feather beds for old master I reckon. They picked geese jus' so often. The Gates had several big quarters and lots of land. They come to be poor people after the War—land poor. Mother left Gates after the War. They didn't get nothing but good freedom as I ever heard of. My father was a shoemaker at old age. He said he learned his trade in slavery times. He share cropped and rented after freedom.

"I heard 'em say the Ku Klux kept 'em run in home at night. So much stealing going on and it would be laid at the hands of the colored folks if they didn't stay in place. Ku Klux made them work, said they would starve and starve white folks too if they didn't work. They was share cropping then, yes ma'am, all of them. I know that they said they had no stock, no land, no rations, no houses to live in, their clothes was thin. They said it was squally times in slavery and worse after freedom. They wore the new clothes in winter. By summer they was wore thin and by next winter they had made some more cloth to make more new clothes. They wove one winter for the next winter. When they got to share croppin' they had to keep a fire in the fireplace all night to warm by. The clothes and beds was rags. Corn bread and meat was all they had to eat. Maybe they had pumpkins, corn, and potatoes. They said it was squally times.

"I got a place. I rented it out to save it. My brother rents it. I can't hardly pay taxes. I'd like to get some help. I could sew if they would let me on. I can see good. I'm going to chop cotton but it so long till then.

"I washed and ironed in Memphis till washing went out of style. Prices are so high now and cotton cheap. I'm counting on better times.

"Times is close. Young folks is like young folks always been. Some are smart and some lazy. None don't look ahead. They don't think about saving. Guess they don't know how to save. Right smart spends it foolish. I'm a widow and done worked down."

United States. Work Projects Administration

Interviewer: Pernella Anderson
Person interviewed: —Will Hicks.
Hicks, Will

WILL HICKS

"I was born in Farmerville, La., I don't know what year. I was about three or four years at surrender. I lived with my mother and father. The first work I ever did was plow. I did not work very hard at no time but what ever there was to do I went on and got through with it. All of our work was muscle work. There were no cultivators.

"I stayed at home with my father and mother until I was 32 years of age. I was thirty years old when papa died and mother lived two years longer. About a month after mother died I married. We lived in a real good house. My father bought it after slavery time. We had good furniture that was bought from the hardware. The first stove that we used we bought it and father bought it just after surrender. Never used a homemade broom in my life. Now, Ma just naturally liked ash cakes so she always cooked them in the fireplace. We wore all homespun clothes, and we wore the big bill baily hats. We chaps went barefooted until I was 16 years old then I bought my first pair of shoes. They were brass toe progans. I never been in the school house a day in my life. Can't read neither write nor figure. I went to church. Our first preacher was name Prince Jones. The biggest games I played was ball and card. I was one of the best dancers. We danced the old juland dance, swing your partner, promonate. Danced by fiddling. The fiddlers could beat the fiddlers of today. Get your partners, swing them to the left and to the right, hands up four, swing corners, right hands up four promonate all around all the way, git your partners boys. I shoot dice, drink, I got drunk and broke up church one Sunday night. Me and sister broke up a dinner once because we got drunk. Whiskey been in circulation a long time. There have been bad people ever since I been in the world."

Interviewer: Mrs. Bernice Bowden
Person interviewed: Bert Higgins
611 Missouri Street, Pine Bluff, Arkansas
Age: 88

BERT HIGGINS

"I was born in slavery times. I was thirteen when peace declared. I was workin' in the field.

"No ma'am, I wasn't born in Arkansas. I was born in Macon, Mississippi.

"Marcus Higgins was my old master. He was good to me. He treated me all right.

"He had a good big plantation—had two plantations. One in North Carolina and one in Mississippi.

"Sold? Yes'm, I was put up on the block, but they couldn't quite make it. Had six of us—boys and girls—and he sold one or two I 'member. But that's been a long time.

"Yes'm, I can 'member when I was a boy in slavery. Run off too. Old master ketch me and switch me. Look like the switch would sting so. 'Member the last switchin' I got. Dr. Henderson—I think he was old master's son-in-law. Me? Well, he whipped me 'cause I'd steal his eggs. I don't reckon I would a been so bad but I was raised up a motherless child. My mother died and my stepmother died.

"I can 'member pretty well way back there.

"He'd send me off on a mule to carry the mail to his people around. And I used to tote water. He had a heap a darkies.

"I could do very well now if I could see and if I wasn't so crippled up. I was a hard worker.

"We had a plenty to eat and plenty to wear in slavery times.

"Old master would whip me if I went any further than the orchard. If I did happen to go outside the field, I come in 'fore night. But I hardly ever went outside. Sometimes I run off and when I come back to the house, he'd give me a breshin'.

"I seen the Yankees durin' of the War. I run from 'em and hid. I thought they was tryin' to carry me off. White folks never did tell me nothin'. They'd come in and throw things outdoors and destroy 'em—old master's provisions. And they'd take things to eat too.

"My father belonged to Marcus Higgins when I first could remember.

"After freedom we stayed there till I was grown. I don't never 'member him payin' me, but I got somethin' to eat and a place to stay.

"I never went to school; I had to work. I farmed all my life till I come to the city of Pine Bluff. I worked here 'bout thirty years.

"I've always been well treated by my white folks. I never sassed a white person in my life as I remember of—never did. I think that's the reason I was so well took care of 'cause I never sassed 'em. I've always tried to do what was right.

"I think these here government people have treated us mighty well. They have give us money and other things.

"When we got free old master read it to us out of the paper. We was out in the field and I was totin' water. Some of 'em struck work and went to the house and set around a while but they soon went back to the field. And a few days after that he hired 'em.

"Old master was good. He'd let you stop and rest. He hired a overseer but he didn't do no work. The time run out 'fore he got started.

"I think this younger generation is havin' a heap harder time than the old folks did. Their disbehavior and the way they carry theirselves now'days. So many of 'em will pick up things don't belong to 'em.

"I don't believe in these here superstitions. I tried carryin' a rabbit foot and I know it never brought me no good luck. If you serve the Lord and try to live right, pray and serve the Lord, and whatever you need you'll get it."

Circumstances of Interview

STATE—Arkansas
NAME OF WORKER—Samuel S. Taylor
ADDRESS—Little Rock, Arkansas
DATE—December, 1938
SUBJECT—Ex-slave

Name and address of informant—Annie Hill, 3010 Izard

Street, Little Rock.

Date and time of interview—

Place of interview—3010 Izard Street, Little Rock.

Name and address of person, if any, who put you in touch with informant—

Name and address of person, if any, accompanying you—

Description of room, house, surroundings, etc.—

Personal History of Informant

STATE—Arkansas
NAME OF WORKER—Samuel S. Taylor
ADDRESS—Little Rock, Arkansas
DATE—December, 1938
SUBJECT—Ex-slave
NAME AND ADDRESS OF INFORMANT—Annie Hill, 3010 Izard Street, Little Rock.

Ancestry—father, Richard Hill; mother Hulda Bruce.

Place and date of birth—Nashville, Arkansas in 1877.

Family—

Places lived in, with dates—Nashville, Benton and Little Rock. No dates.

Education, with dates—

Occupations and accomplishments, with dates—Laundry work.

Special skills and interests—

Community and religious activities—

Description of informant—

Other points gained in interview—

Text of Interview (Unedited)

STATE—Arkansas
NAME OF WORKER—Samuel S. Taylor
ADDRESS—Little Rock, Arkansas
DATE—December, 1938
SUBJECT—Ex-slave
NAME AND ADDRESS OF INFORMANT—Annie Hill, 3010 Izard Street, Little Rock

"My mother lived to be one hundred years old. She died in 1920. Her name is Hulda Bruce. She belonged to a man named Leslie during slavery. I forget his name—his first name. She come from Mississippi. She was sold there when she was eleven years old. That is where all her people were. There might be some of them here and I don't know it. She said she had three sisters but I don't know any of them. The folks raised her—the Leslie white folks. It was the Leslies that brought her and bought her in the old country. I don't know the names of the people that sold her. She wasn't nothing but a kid. I guess she would hardly know.

"The Leslies brought her to Arkansas when she was eleven. That is what she always told us kids. She was eleven years old when they sold her. Just like selling mules.

"I don't know what is the first place they come to here. Benton, Arkansas was the first place I knowed anything about. That is where her folks were and that is where the young generation of them is now. The old ones is dead and gone.

"I was born in Nashville. And she had come from Benton to Nashville. She was living In Benton, Arkansas when she died. She was never able to send me to school when I was young. When the white folks first turned them loose they weren't able to do for them as they are now. Children have a chance now and don't appreciate it. But when I was coming up my folks weren't able. Mother knew she was one hundred eight years old because her white folks told her what it was. When her old white folks died, the young ones hunted it up for her out of the old family Bible and sent it to me. The Bible was so old that the leaves were yellow and you could hardly turn them. They were living in Benton, Arkansas and I guess they are still living there because that is the old home place. That is the kids is still there, 'cause the old folks is dead and gone. One girl is named Cora and one of the boys is called Bud, Buddy. Leslie is the last name of them both.

"I got one of her pictures with her young master's kids—three of 'em—in there with her. Anybody that bothered that picture would git in it with me, 'cause I values it.

"Mother farmed right after the surrender. She married after freedom but went back to her old name when her husband left. He was named Richard Hill. He was supposed to be a bishop down there in Arkadelphia. But he wasn't no bishop with mama. All them Hills in Arkadelphia are kin to me. She had four children—one boy and three girls. The boy died before I was born. She was just married the one time that I know about.

"Her white folks were good to her. You know there was so many of them that weren't. And you know they bound to be because they were always good to her. They would be looking for her and sending her something to eat and sending her shoes and clothes and things like that, and she'd go to them and stay with them months at a time so they bound to 've been good to her. All the young kids always called her their Black Mammy. They thought a heap of her. That is since freedom. Since I been born. That is somethin' I seen with my own eyes.

"I spect my mother's white folks is mad at me. They come to see her just before she died and they knew she couldn't live long. They told me to let them know when there was a chance.

"That was about three days before she died. There come a storm. It broke down the wire so we couldn't let them know. My boy was too small; I couldn't send him. He was only nine years old. And you know how it is out in the country, you can't keep them long. You have to put them away. You can't keep no dead person in the country. So I had to bury her without letting 'em know it.

"I do laundry work for a living when I can get any to do. I am living with my boy but I do laundry work to help myself. It is so good, and nice to kinda help yourself. I'll do for self as long as I am able and when I can't, the children can help me more. I have heard and seen so many mothers whose children would do things for them and it wouldn't suit so well up the road. You see me hopping along; I'm trying to work for Annie.

"My mother told me about seein' the pateroles before the War and the Ku Klux Klan afterwards. She knowed them all right. She never talked much about the pateroles. It was mostly the Ku Klux. Neither of them never got after her. She said the Ku Klux used to come in by droves. She said the Ku Klux were dressed all in white—white caps and white hoods over their faces, and long white dresses. They come out mostly at night. They never did bother her, but they bothered others 'round her that she knowed about. Sometimes they would take people out and beat them and do 'round with them. But she never did know just what it was they did and just what they did it for. You see, her white folks was particular and didn't talk much before her. So many colored folks learnt things because they eavesdropped their white folks, but mother didn't do that. She didn't learn nothin' but what they talked before her, and they were careful. But they protected her. They never did allow nobody to bother her no way.

"She was a Baptist. She belonged to the white folks' church before she was freed. Then she joined the Methodist church at Benton because there wasn't no other church there. But she was a full-blood Baptist."

Interviewer: Mrs. Bernice Bowden
Person interviewed: Clark Hill
715 E. 17th Street, Pine Bluff, Arkansas
Age: 82

CLARK HILL

"Good morning. My name is Clark Hill. My name goes by my white folks. I was born in Georgia—in Americus, Georgia. My old master was Will G. Hill and they called my young master Bud. I never did know what his name was—they just called him Bud.

"It was my job to sweep the yard, keep smoke on the meat and fire under the kiln. Yes mam! Old master had a big orchard and he dried all the fruit in the kiln—peaches, apples, and pears. Then he had lots a watermelons too. When they got ripe they'd get all the childun big enough to tote a melon and we'd carry 'em to the house. I would like to be with my white folks now.

"Old master raised pigeons too and it used to be my job to go down to the pigeon house and ketch the squalls (squabs).

"I used to go to church with my white folks too. I was the gate opener. They put me on the little seat at the back of the carriage. When we got there they'd let us childun sit in the back. The preacher would tell us to obey our master and not take anything that belonged to him.

"Oh, my white folks was good to me. He never hit me but once and that was one time when my brother went into the kitchen, went into some peas the cook had and she told on him. Old master come down and told my brother to eat the whole dish full. He never hit him or nothin' but just stood there and made him eat 'em. I thought I'd help him out a little and said to my brother, 'Give me some.' Old master just took his walking stick and hit me over the head, and that's the onliest time he ever hit me.

"When you got big enough to marry and was courtin' a woman on another plantation, you couldn't bring her home with you. Old master would marry you. He'd say 'I give this man to you' and say 'Clark, I give this woman to you and now you is man and wife.' They never had no book of matrimony—if they did I never seen it. Then you could go over to see her every Saturday and stay all night.

"I used to work in the field. They didn't farm then like they do now. They planted one row a cotton and one row a corn. That was to keep the land from gettin' poor.

"I remember when the Yankees was comin' through I got scared because some of the folks said they had horns. I know old master took all his meat and carried it to another plantation.

"When freedom come old master give us all our ages. I think when they say we was free that meant every man was to be his own boss and not be bossed by a taskmaster. Cose old master was good to us but we wanted to have our own way 'bout a heap a things.

"I come to Arkansas the second year of surrender. Yes'm, I voted when Clayton was sheriff and I voted for Governor Baxter. I voted several tickets. I was here when they had the Brooks-Baxter War. They fit not far from where I was livin'.

"Well, that's 'bout all I can remember. My mind ain't so good now and I got the rheumatism in my legs."

United States. Work Projects Administration

Interviewer: Mrs. Bernice Bowden
Person interviewed: Clark Hill
818 E. Fifteenth Street, Pine Bluff, Arkansas
Age: 84

CLARK HILL

"I was workin' 'round the house when freedom come. I was eleven.

"Born in Georgia—Americus, Georgia. Used to go with my young master to Corinth after the mail. We'd ride horseback with me right behind him. He used to carry me to church too on the back seat to open the gates.

"They worked me in the loom room too. Had to hold the broche at the reel. I was glad when my young master called me out to go after the mail. Then they worked me in the smokehouse.

"I never had no schoolin' a tall. What little I know I learned since I married. My wife was a good scholar.

"I thank the Lord he spared me. Eighty-four is pretty old.

"I come here to Pine Bluff in '66. Wasn't no town here then. Just some little shacks on Barraque. And Third Street was called Catfish Street.

"They was fifty carloads come here to Arkansas when I come.

"I've farmed mostly. Then I've cooked four or five years in railroad camps, when they was puttin' in this Cotton Belt track. Then I've cooked on a steamboat.

"Yes ma'am, I've voted. I voted teeth and toe-nail for one man, and he got it and then they shot him down. He was about to get on to the fraud. He was 'testin' the election. That was John M. Clayton. They can do most anything in these here elections. I know 'cause I done been in so many campaigns."

"I heard a story 'bout a old colored man named Tony. It was in slave times and he was prayin' to the Lord to take him out of bondage. He was prayin', 'Oh Lord, come and take poor old Tony away.' Just then somebody started knockin' and Tony says, 'Who'd dat?' 'It's the Lord, I come to take you away.' Then Tony said, 'No! No! Don't take me away. I ain't ready to go.'"

"I've heard if a turkle dove, when the season first starts, comes to your house and starts moanin', it's a sign you is goin' to move out and somebody else goin' move in.

"If a squinch owl starts howlin' 'round your house and if you turn your shoe upside down at the door, they sure will hush. Now I know that's so.

"I used to run myself nearly to death tryin' to get to the end of the rainbow to get the pot of gold.

"And I've heard the old folks say if you start any place and have to go back, you make a circle on the ground and spit in it or you'll have bad luck."

Interviewer: Bernice Bowden
Person interviewed: Elmira Hill
1220 North Willow
Pine Bluff, Ark.
Age: 97

ELMIRA HILL

"I'm one of em. Accordin' to what they tell me, I think I'll be ninety-eight the ninth day of February. I was born in Virginia in Kinsale County and sold from my mother and father to Arkansas.

"The Lord would have it, old man Ed Lindsey come to Virginia and brought me here to Arkansas. I was here four years before the Old War ceasted and I was twelve when I come here.

"I was right there standin' behind my mistis' chair when Abe Lincoln said, 'I 'clare there shall be war!' I was right here in Arkansas—eighteen miles from Pine Bluff when war ceasted. The Lord would have it. I had a good master and mistis. Old master said, 'Fore old Lincoln shall free my niggers, I'll free em myself.' They might as well a been free, they had a garden and if they raised cotton in that garden they could sell it. The Lord bless His Holy Name! We didn't know the difference when we got free. I stayed with my mistis till she went back to Virginia.

"Yes, honey, I was here in all the war. I was standin' right by my mistis' chair. I never heard old master make a oaf in his life, but when they brought the paper freein' the slaves, he said, 'Dad burn it.'

"I member a man called Jeff Davis. I know they sung and said, 'We'll hand old Jeff Davis to the sour apple tree.'

"I been here a long time. Yes, honey, I been in Arkansas so long I say I ain't goin' out—they got to bury me here. Arkansas dirt good enough for me. I say I been here so long I got Arkansas 'stemper (distemper).

"My old master in Virginia was Joe Hudson. My father used to ketch oysters and fish. We could look up the Patomac river and see the ships comin' in. In Virginia I lived next to a free state and the runaways was tryin' to get away. At Harper's Ferry—that's where old John Brown was carryin' em across. My old mistis used to take the runaway folks when the dogs had bit their legs, and keep em for a week and cure em up. This time o' year you could hear the bull whip. But I was lucky, they was good to me in Virginia and good to me in Arkansas.

"Yes, chile, I was in Alexandria, Virginia in Kinsale County when they come after me by night. I was hired out to Captain Jim Allen. I had been nursin' for Captain Allen. He sailed on the sea. He was a good man. He was a Christian man. He never whipped me but once and that was for tellin' a story, and I thank him for it. He landed his boat right at the landin' on Saturday. Next day he asked me bout somethin' and I told him a story. He said, 'I'm gwine whip you Monday morning!' He wouldn't whip me on Sunday. He whipped me and I thank him for it. And to this day the Lindsey's could trust me with anything they had.

"I was in Virginia a play-chile when the ships come down to get the gopher wood to build the war ships. Old mistis had a son and a daughter and we all played together and slep together. My white folks learned me my A B C's.

"They come and got me and carried me to Richmond—that's where they sold em. Sold five of us in one bunch. Sold my two brothers in New Orleans—Robert and Jesse. Never seed them no more. Never seed my mother again after I was sold.

"Yes, chile, I was here in Arkansas when the war started, so you know I been here a long time.

"I was here when they fit the last battle in Pine Bluff. They called it Marmaduke's Battle and they fit it on Sunday morning. They took the old cotehouse for a battery and throwed up cotton bales for a breastworks. They fit that Sunday and when the Yankees started firin' the Rebels went back to Texas or wherever they come from.

"When we heard the Yankees was comin' we went out at night and hid the silver spoons and silver in the toilet and buried the meat. After the war was over and the Yankees had gone home and the jayhawkers had went in—then we got the silver and the meat. Yes, honey, we seed a time—we seed a time. I ain't grumblin'—I tell em I'm havin' a wusser time now than I ever had.

"Yankees used to call me a 'know nothin' cause I wouldn't tell where things was hid.

"Yes, chile, I'm this way—I like everbody in this world. I never was a mother, but I raised everbody else's chillun. I ain't nothin' but a old mammy. White and black calls me mamma. I'll answer at the name.

"I was married twice. My last husband and me lived together fifty years. He was a preacher. My first husband, the old rascal—he was so mean to me I had to get rid of him.

"Yes, I been here so long. I think the younger generation is goin' the downward way. They ain't studyin' nothin' but wickedness. Yes, honey, they tell me the future generation is goin' a do this and goin' a do that, and they ain't done nothin'. And God don't like it.

"My white folks comes to see me and say as long as they got bread, I got it.

"I went to school the second year after surrender. I can read but I ain't got no glasses now. I want you to see this letter my mother sent me in 1867. My baby sister writ it. Yes, honey, I keeps it for remembrance.

"Don't know nothin' funny that happened 'ceptin stealin' my old master's company's hoss and runnin' a race. White chillun too. Them as couldn't ride sideways ridin' straddle. Better not ride Rob Roy—that was old master's ridin' hoss and my mistis saddle hoss. That was the hoss he was talkin' bout ridin' to the war when the last battle was fit in Helena. But he was too old to go to war.

"Well, goodbye, honey—if I don't see you no more, come across the Jordan."

Interviewer: Samuel S. Taylor
Person interviewed: Gillie Hill
813 Arch Street, Little Rock, Arkansas
Age: About 45

GILLIE HILL

"My grandmother told me that they had to chink up the cracks so that the light wouldn't get out and do their washing and ironing at night. When they would hear the overseers or the paterolers coming 'round (I don't know which it was), they would put the light out and keep still till they had passed on. Then they would go right on with the washing and ironing.

"They would have to wash and iron at night because they were working all day.

"She told me how they used to turn pots down at night so that they could pray. They had big pots then—big enough for you to get into yourself. I've seen some of them big old pots and got under 'em myself. You could get under one and pray if you wanted to. You wouldn't have to prop them up to send your voice in 'em from the outside. The thing that the handle hooks into makes them tilt up on one side so that you could get down on your hands and knees and pray with your mouth close to the opening if you wanted to. Anyway, my grandma said they would turn the pots upside down and stick their heads under them to pray.

"My father could make you cry talking about the way they treated folks in slavery times. He said his old master was so mean that he made him eat off the ground with the dogs. He never felt satisfied unless'n he saw a nigger sufferin'."

Interviewer's Comment

Gillie Hill is the daughter of Evelyn Jones already interviewed and reported. The few statements which she hands in make an interesting supplement to her mother's story. The mother, Evelyn Jones, remembered very few things in her interview and had to be constantly prompted and helped by her daughter and son who were present at each sitting. There was considerable difference of opinion among them over a number of things, especially the age of the mother, the daughter showing letters to prove the age of seventy, the mother saying she had been told she was sixty-eight, and the son arguing that the scattering of the ages of her nineteen children showed that she must be well over eighty.

Gillie Hill claims to be somewhat clairvoyant. She gave a brief analysis of my character, stating accurately my regular calling and a few of my personal traits even indicating roughly my bringing-up and where. She is not a professional fortune-teller, and merely ventured a few statements. My impression was that she was an unusually close and alert observer. Like her mother she is somewhat taciturn. I should have said that her mother was reserved as well as forgetful. The mother never ventured a word except in answer to a question, and used monosyllabic answers whenever possible.

Interviewer: Miss Irene Robertson
Person Interviewed: Harriett Hill
Forrest City, Ark.
(Visiting at Brinkley, Ark.)
Age: 84

HARRIETT HILL

"I was born in Lithonia, Georgia, at the foot of Little Rock Mountain, close to Stone Mountain, Georgia. I been sold in my life twice to my knowing. I was sold away from my dear old mammy at three years old but I can remember it. I remembers it. It lack selling a calf from the cow. Exactly, but we are human beings and ought to be better than do sich. I was too little to remember my price. I was sold to be a nurse maid. They bought me and took me on away that time. The next time they put me up in a wagon and auctioned me off. That time I didn't sell. John George (white man) was in the war; he wanted some money to hire a substitute to take his place fightin'. So he have Jim George do the sellin'. They was brothers. They talked 'fore me some bit 'fore they took me off. They wouldn't take me to Atlanta cause they said some of the people there said they wouldn't give much price—the Negroes soon be set free. Some folks in Atlanta was Yankees and wouldn't buy slaves. They 'cluded the best market to sell me off would be ten or twelve miles from home. I reckon it was to Augusta, Georgia. They couldn't sell me and start on back home. A man come up to our wagon and say he'd split the difference. They made the trade. I sold on that spot for $1400. I was nine or ten years old. I remembers it. Course I do! I never could forget it. Now mind you, that was durin' the war.

"Master Jake Chup owned mammy and me too. He sold me to John George. Jim George sold me to Sam Broadnax. When freedom come on that was my home. Freedom come in the spring. He got some of the slaves to stay to finish up the crops for 1/10 at Christmas. When they got through dividin' up they said they goin' to keep me for a bounty. I been talkin' to Kitty—all I remembers her name Kitty. She been down there at the stream washin'. Some children come told me Kitty say come on. She hung out the clothes. I lit out over the fence and through the field with Kitty and went to Conniars. She left me at the railroad track and went on down the road by myself to Lithonia. I walked all night. I met my brother not long after Kitty left me. He was on a wagon. He knowed me and took me up with him to Mr. Jake Chup's Jr. He was the young man. Then Chups fed me till he come back and took me to mammy. Master Chups sold her to Dr. Reygans. I hadn't seen her since I was three years old. She knowed me. My brother knowed me soon as ever he saw me. I might a not knowed them in a gatherin' but I hadn't forgot them. They hear back and forth where I be but they never could get to see me. I lived with my folks till I married.

"The first man I lived with ten years. The next one I lived with fifty years and some days over. He died. They both died. The man I married was a preacher. We farmed long with his preachin'. We paid $500.00 for forty acres of this bottom land. Cleared it out. I broke myself plum down and it got mortgaged. The Planters Bank at Forrest City took it over. I ain't had nothin' since. I ain't got no home. I ain't had nothin' since then. My husband died two years ago and I has a hard time.

"My folks was livin' in Decatur, Georgia when the Ku Klux was ragin'. We sure was scared of em. Mighty nigh to death. When freedom come on the niggers had to start up their churches. They had nigger preachers. Sometimes a white preacher would come talk to us. When the niggers be havin' preachin' here come the Ku Klux and run em clear out. If they hear least thing nigger preacher say they whoop him. They whooped several. They sure had to be mighty particular what they said in the preachin'. They made some of the nigger preachers dance. There wasn't no use of that and they knowed it. They must of had plenty fun. They rode the country every night for I don't know how long and that all niggers talked bout.

"My mammy had eleven children. I had one boy. He died a baby.

"My pa come and brought his family in 1873. He come with a gang. They didn't allow white men to take em off so a white man come and stay round shy and get nigger man to work up a gang. We all come on a train to Memphis, then we got on a big boat. No, ma'am, we didn't come on no freight train. We got off at White Hall Landing. They got off all long the river. We worked on wages out here. Pa wanted to go to Mississippi. We went and made eighteen bales cotton and got cheated out of all we made. We never got a cent. The man cheated us was Mr. Harris close to Trotter's Landing.

"Mr. Anderson, the poor white man we worked for, jumped in the river and drowned his self. The turns (returns) didn't come in for the first batch we sold at all, then when the turns come they said we done took it up—owed it all. We knowed we hadn't took it up but couldn't get nothin'. We come back to Arkansas.

"I been to Detroit, short time, and been way, but I comes back.

"I forgot to say this: My mammy was born in South Carolina. Marbuts owned her and sold her. My pa lived to be 114 or 115 years old. He died in Arkansas. She did too.

"Of course I don't vote! Women ain't got no business runnin' the government!

"I nursed, worked in the field. When I was a slave they raised a little cotton in Georgia but mostly corn. I chopped cotton and thinned out corn.

"The present times is too fast. Somethin' goin' to happen. The present generation too fast. Folks racin'. Ridin' in cars too fast. They ain't kind no more.

"I rent a house where I can and I get $10.00 from the government. That all the support I got. I farmed in the field mighty hard and lost all we had."

MAY 11 1938
Interviewer: Mrs. Bernice Bowden
Person interviewed: Hattie Hill
Route 2, Main Street, Pine Bluff, Arkansas
Age: 85

HATTIE HILL

"Yes ma'am, I was raised a house gal. Me and another cousin and I was borned in Georgia. My old master's name was Edward Maddox. Yes ma'am.

"I had a good master but I didn't have such a good missis. Her name was Fannie Maddox. We belonged to the old man and he was good to his niggers. He didn't 'low 'em to be cut and slashed about. But when he was gone that's when old mis' would beat on us.

"I've seen a many a one of the soldiers. They used to march by our place.

"I can remember one of my old missis' neighbors. Her name was Miss Phipps. Old mis' would send me there to borry meal. Yes ma'am, I'd go and come. She'd always send me. I met the soldiers a many a time. I'd hide behind a tree and as they'd go by I'd go 'round the tree—I was so scared.

"But thank the Lawd, we is free now.

"I heered old master pray a many a prayer that he would live to see his slaves sot free. And he died the same year they was sot free. He sent for all his hands to come and see him 'fore he died. Even the little chillun. I can remember it jus' as well as if 'twas yesterday. Old mis' died 'fore he did.

"Our folks stayed on the place two years. Old master told 'em he wanted 'em to take care of themselves and said, 'I want you to get you a place of your own.' He said, 'I raised you honest and I want you to stay on the place as long as you live or as long as the boys treat you right.'

"I seed the patrollers all right. I 'member that old song 'Run Nigger Run' and a heap of 'em run too.

"Them Ku Klux was hateful too, but they never bothered my father's house. They beat one man—Steve McLaughlin—till he couldn't get back to the house. They beat him from the soles of his feet to the top of his head.

"We had a plenty to eat in slave times. They fed us good. I never did work in the field—I was raised up a house gal.

"After freedom my father had me in the field.

"I used to cut and split a many a hundred rails in a day and didn't mind it neither.

"I used to like to work—would work now if I was able. And I'd rather work in the field any day as work in the house. The people where I lived can tell you how I worked. I didn't make my living by rascality. I worked like my father raised me. Oh, I haven't forgot how my old father raised me.

"Never went to school but one day in my life. I can't read.

"I didn't come to Arkansas till after I was free. I been livin' here so long I can't tell you how many years.

"I married young and I'm the mother of six chillun.

"I think a heap of the colored folks is better off free, but a heap of 'em don't appreciate their freedom.

"Heap of the younger generation is all right and then they's a heap of 'em all wrong.

"I can't remember nothin' else 'cause I was too young then and I'm too old now."

United States. Work Projects Administration

OCT 18 19—
Interviewer: Mrs. Bernice Bowden
Person interviewed: Oliver Hill
1101 Kentucky Street, Pine Bluff, Arkansas
Age: 94

OLIVER HILL

Oliver Hill is ninety-four years old, erect, walks briskly with the aid of a cane, only slightly hard of hearing and toothless.

He was born and lived in the state of Mississippi on the plantation of Alan Brooks where he said his father was an overseer and not a slave. Said his mother was a full-blooded Indian. (I have never talked to a Negro who did not claim to be part Indian.) He cannot read or write and made rather conflicting statements about the reason why. "White folks wouldn't let us learn." Later on in the conversation he said he went to school about one month when his "eyes got sore and they said he didn't have to go no more."

"I was nineteen years old when de wa' begun. De white folks never tole us nothin' 'bout what it was fo' till after de surrender. Dey tole us then we was free. They didn't give us nothin'."

After the surrender most of the slaves left the plantations and were supported by the Bureau. In the case of Oliver Hill, this lasted five months and then he went back to his former master who gave him one-fifth of what he made working in the field. Alan Brooks grieved for the loss of his slaves but at no time were they under any compulsion to remain slaves. After a long time about half of them came back to work for pay.

The Ku Klux Klan was "de devil", but about all they wanted, according to Oliver, was to "make a Democrat" of the ex-slaves. They were allowed to vote without any trouble, but "de Democrats robbed de vote. Yes'm I knowed they did."

Concerning the present restricted suffrage, he thinks the colored people should be allowed to vote. In general, his attitude toward the white people is one of resentment. Frequent comments were:

"Dey won't let de colored people bury in de same cemetery with de white people."

"Dey don't like it if a colored man speak to a white woman."

"Dey kill a colored man and de law don't do nothin' 'bout it."

"Old Man Brooks" when referring to his former master.

He lived with the Brooks family for five years after freedom, and seems to have been rather a favored one with not much to do but "ride around" and going to dances and parties at night. When Alan Brooks died he left Oliver $600 in cash, a cow and calf, horse, saddle and bridle and two hogs. He went to live with his father taking his wife whom he had married at the age of twenty-one.

As soon as the inheritance was gone, the scene changed. In his words, "I thought it gwine last forever." But it didn't and then he began to hold a succession of jobs—field hand, sorghum maker, basket weaver, gardener and railway laborer—until he was too old to work. Now he is supported by the Welfare Department and the help a daughter and granddaughter can give.

About the younger generation—"I don't know what gwine come of 'em. The whites is as bad as the blacks." He thinks that present conditions are caused by the sinfulness of the people.

There were no slave uprisings but sometimes when they did not work fast enough or do the task right, they were "whupped" by the overseer and given no food until it was done right.

Oliver came to Arkansas in 1910. He has had two wives and "de Lawd took both of 'em." His second wife was "'ligious" and they "got along fine." All in all he had a good time during his active days "and didn't have no trouble with de white folks". He does not believe God ever intended some of the people to be slaves.

MAY 31 1938
Interviewer: Miss Irene Robertson
Person interviewed: Rebecca Brown Hill
Brinkley, Arkansas
Age: 78

REBECCA BROWN HILL

"I was born October 18, 1859 in northeast Mississippi in Chickasaw County. It was close to the Fulton Road to Houston, Mississippi. My folks belong to C. B. Baldwin. After 'mancipation papa stop calling himself Jacob Baldwin and called himself Jacob Brown in his own pa's name. Mama was named Catherine Brown. The same man owned them both. They had twelve children. They lost a child born in 1866. I had two brothers sent to Louisiana as refugees. The place they was sent to was taken by the Yankees and they was taken and the Yankees made soldiers out of them. Charlie died in 1922 in Mobile, Alabama and Lewis after the War joined the United States army. I never saw any grandparents. Mama was born in Baltimore and her mother was born there too as I understood them to say. Mama's father was a white Choctaw Indian. He was a cooper by trade. His name was John Abbot. He sold Harriett, my grandma, and kept mama and her brother. Then he married a white woman and had a white family. Her brother died. That left her alone to wait on that white family. They cut her hair off. She hated that. She loved her long straight black hair. Then her papa, John Abbot (Abbott?), died. Her brother run off and was leaving on a ship on the Potomac River. A woman lost her trunk. They was fishing for it and found mama's brother drowned. He had fell overboard too.

"Mama took a bucket on her arm to keep the stealers from gagging her. She knowed if she had a bucket or basket they would not bother, they would know she went out on turn (errand) and would be protected. They didn't bother her then. She went down to the nigger trader's yard to talk awhile but she was making her way off then. Sometimes she went down to the yard to laugh and talk with some she knowed down there. She said them stealers would kill 'em and insect (dissect) 'em. But they didn't get her. But might as well, Jim Williams owned that nigger yard. He put her on a sailboat named Big Humphries. She was on there hard sailing, she said, twenty-four days and nights. Jim Williams stole her! On that sailboat is where she seen my papa. When they got to New Orleans a white man from Baltimore was passing. He seen my mama. He ask her about her papers. She told him she had been stole. He said without papers Jim Williams couldn't sell her. He told Jim Williams he better not sell that woman. Jim Williams knowed she was crazy about my papa. He hired him out and ask her if she wanted to go with him. He got pay for both of them hired out. It was better for him than if he owned her. When they had two children, Jim Williams come back out to Chambers County, Alabama where he had them hired out. He ask her if he would agree to let him sell her. He was going to sell papa and the two children. She said she had seen them whooped to death in the yards because they didn't want to be sold. She was scared to contrary him. She had nobody to take her part. So she let him sell her with papa and the two children. Jim Williams sold her and papa and the two children to

Billy Gates of Mississippi. Jim Williams said, 'Don't never separate Henry and Hannah 'cause I don't have the papers for Hannah.' Then they lived in the prairies eighteen miles from Houston, where Billy Gates lived. Mama done well. She worked and they treated her nice. Eight of us was born on that place includin' me.

"I was raised up in good living conditions and kept myself so till twelve years ago this next August this creeping neuritis (paralasis) come on. I raised my niece. I cooked, washed and ironed, and went to the field in field time.

"Master Billy Gates' daughter married Cyrus Brisco Baldwin. He was a lawyer. He give mama, papa and one child to them. Master Billy Gates' daughter died and left Miss Bessie. Mr. C. B. Baldwin married again. He went to war in the 'Six Day Crowd.' Miss Bessie Baldwin married Bill Buchannan at Okolona, Mississippi. Mama went and cooked for her. They belong to her. She was good as she could be to her and papa both. One time the overseer was going to whip them both. Miss Bessie said, 'Tell Mr. Carrydine to come and let us talk it over.' They did and she said, 'Give Mr. Carrydine his breakfast and let him go.' They never got no whippings.

"Mama was white as any white woman and papa was my color (light mulatto). After freedom they lived as long as they lived at Houston and Okolona, Mississippi. She said she left Maryland in 1839.

"Some blue dressed Yankees come to our shack and told mama to bake him some bread. I held to her dress. She baked them some. They put it in their nap sacks. That was my first experience seeing the Yankees.

"They come back and come back on and on. One time they come back hunting the silverware. They didn't find it. It was in the old seep well. The slaves wasn't going to tell them where it was. We washed out of the seep well and used the cistern water to drink. It was good silver. They put it in sacks, several of them, to make it strong. Uncle Giles drapped it down in there. He was old colored man we all called Uncle Giles. He was no kin to me. He was good as could be. I loved him. Me and his girl played together all the time. Her name was Roxana. We built frog houses in the sand and put cool sand on our stomachs. We would lie under big trees and watch and listen to the birds.

"When Mr. Billy Gates died they give Henry, my youngest brother, to his son, John Gates. Henry, a big strong fellow, could raise a bale of cotton over his head.

"One time the Yankees come took the meat and twenty-five cows and the best mules. They left some old plugs. They had two mares in fold. Uncle Giles told them one mare had buck-eye poison and the other distemper. They left them in their stalls. We had to tote all that stuff they give out back when they was gone. All they didn't take off they handed out to the slaves. There was some single men didn't carry their provisions back to the smokehouse. Everybody else did. They kept on till they swept us all out of victuals. The slaves had shacks up on the hill. There was six or eight pretty houses all met. Mr. Gates' house was one of them.

"Freedom—Capt. Gehu come and sent for all the slaves to come to Mr. John Gates. We all met there. He said it was free times now. We lived on and raised peas, corn, pumpkins, potatoes. The Yankees come and took off some of it. That was the year of the surrender. Mama moved off the hill in a man's home what moved to town to look after the house for them. It was across the road from Master John Gates' house. We worked for the Gates a long, long time after that. We worked for the Baldwins and around till the old heads all dead. I come to Clarendon, Arkansas, eleven o'clock, eleventh of May 1890. I have no children. I raised my sister's baby. She died. I live wid her now. She's got grandchildren. I get ten dollars from the Welfare a month. I buy what I needs to eat with it. I helps out a sight. I had a baby girl. It died an infant.

"The place they refugeed Charlie and Lewis was to Opelousas, Louisiana. It was about the first part of the country the Yankees took.

"Ku Klux—They never bothered us but in 1876 I seen them pass. My nephew was a little boy. He said when they passed there was Jack Slaughter on his horse. He knew the big horse. They went on. The colored men had left their wives and children at home and went up to Red Bud Church (colored). We seen five pass but others joined on. They had bad times. A colored man killed a Ku Klux named Tom Middlebrook. One man got his foot cut off wid a ax. Some called them 'white caps.' I was scared of whatever they called theirselves.

"The younger set of folks seems more restless than they used to be. I noticed that since the last war (World War). They ain't never got settled. The women is bad as the men now it seems. Times is better than I ever had them in my life."

United States. Work Projects Administration

Interviewer: Miss Irene Robertson
Person interviewed: Tanny Hill
Brinkley, Arkansas
Age: 56? No record of age

TANNY HILL

"Uncle Solomon" we all called him but he wasn't no kin to us, he was the funniest old man I ever heard tell of. He was a slave. He belong to Sorrel Crockell I heard him say. He didn't go to no war.

"When the War ended he was a fisherman in Arkansas. He used to tie his own self to a tree keep the fish from pulling him in the river. He caught big fish in the early times. He'd come to our house when I was nothing but a child and bring 'nough fish for all our supper. Ma would cook 'em. Pa would help him scale 'em. We'd love to see him come. He lived thater way from house to house.

"One time he made me mad. I never had no more use for him. We'd give him tomatoes and onions. He told us to go bring him thater watermelon out of the garden. He cut and eat it before us. Never give us a bite. He was saying, 'You goiner get your back and belly beat black and blue.' I didn't know what he was saying. Grandma found the watermelon was gone. I owned up to it. Ma got switches and whooped us. I was singing what he was saying. Grandma tole me what he meant. From that on we had no more of his good fish."

Interviewer's Comment

Large, medium black.

Interviewer: Samuel S. Taylor
Person interviewed: Elizabeth Hines
1117 W. Fourteenth Street, Little Rock, Arkansas
Age: 70

ELIZABETH HINES

"I was born January 10, 1868, in Baton Rouge, Louisiana. I came here. I can't read or write. My brother-in-law told me that I was born three years after the War on January tenth.

"My mother's name was Sara Cloady. My father's name was Square Cloady. I don't remember the names of any of my grand people. Yes I do; my father's mother was named Bertha because I called my daughter after her. She must have been in the Square family because that was his name.

"I had four brothers and sisters. Three of them I don't know anything about. I have never seen them. My sister, Rachael Fortune, suckled me on her breast. That is her married name. Before she was married her name was Rachael Bennett. Her father and mine was not the same. We was just half-sisters. We have the same mother though. My father was half Indian and hers was pure-blooded Indian. They are all mean folks. People say I am mean too, but I am not mean—unless they lie on me or something. My mother died when I was three years old. Children three years old didn't have as much sense then as they do now. I didn't know my mother was laid out until I got to be a woman. I didn't have sense enough to know she was dead. My sister was crying and we asked her what she was crying about.

"I don't know the name of my mother's old master. Yes I do, my mother's old master was named Laycock. He had a great big farm. He was building a gas house so that he could have a light all night and work niggers day and night, but peace came before he could get it finished and use it. God took a hand in that thing. I have seen the gas house myself. I used to tote water home from there in a bucket. It was cool as ice-water. The gas house was as big 'round as that market there (about a half block).

"My father served in the army three years and died at the age of one hundred ten years about twenty years ago as near as I can remember. That is the reason I left home because he died. He served in the War three years. He was with the Yankees. Plenty of these old white folks will know him by the name of Square Cloady. The name of his company was Company E. I don't know the name of his regiment. He got his pension as long as he lived. His last pension came just before he died. I turned it back to the courthouse because it is bad to fool with Uncle Sam. They wrote for my name but when I told them I was married they wouldn't send me anything. I didn't know to tell them that my husband was dead.

"I was married when I was about twenty-seven and my husband died more than three years before my father did. My father lived to see me the mother of my last child; my husband didn't. When my husband was dying, I couldn't see my toes. I was pregnant. My husband died in the year of the great tornado. The time all the churches were blown down. I think it was about 1915. (Storm time in Louisiana.)

"I don't know what my mother did in slavery. I don't think she did anything but cook. She was fine in children and they buys women like that you know. My sister was a water toter. My father raised cotton and corn and hogs and turkeys. His trade was farming before the War. I don't know how he happened to get in the army but he was in it three years. *cf. p. 3*

House, Furniture and Food

"Laycock's farm was out in the country about four miles from Baton Rouge, Louisiana. Some of the slaves lived in log houses and some in big old boxed houses. Most of them had two rooms. They had nothing but four post beds and chairs like this I am settin' down in (a little cane chair). I reckon it is cane—looks like it is. They had homemade chairs before the War, boxes, and benches. The boards were often bought. But nothing else.

"They et greens and pickled pork. My father got tired of that and he would raise hogs. Pickled pork and corn bread!

"My father never told me what his master was to him, whether he was good or mean. He got free early because he was in the army. He didn't run away. The soldiers came and got him and carried him off and trained him. *cf. p. 2* I just know what my father told me because I wasn't born. He served his full time and then he was discharged. He got an honorable discharge. He had a wound in the leg where he was shot.

"I got along all right supporting myself by planting cotton until last year when the doctor stopped me.

"I took care of my father and the Lord is taking care of me. I am weak and still have that giddy head but not as bad as I used to have it."

Opinions

"Some of the young people do very well but some of them ain't got no manners and don't care what they do. I am scared for them. The Man above ain't scared and he is going to cut them down."

Name of interviewer: Martin—Barker
Information by: Charles Hinton
  Place of residence: RFD 5 Old riv. Rd.
Age: 83

CHARLES HINTON

"Son of Martha and Peter Hinton. Came from N.C. about 12 years ago, at close of Civil War. Mother had nine children, she belonged to Mr. Sam Hinton.

"At close of war mistis called us to her, said we were free and could go. So we went away for about a year, but came back. Sorry we were free.

"We saw about 2000 soldiers. Never went to school. Went to white church on plantation. White preachers said, servants, obey your marster. I was valued at $800.00.

"When I was a small boy I lay at marsters feet and he would let us play with his feet. He always had shiny shoes and we niggers would keep rubbing them so they would shine more. As I grew older, I cleaned the yard, later helped pick cotton.

"I am a Baptist. Have behaved myself. Have prayer meeting at my home.

"During the war we had prayer meetings at the different houses on the plantations. We prayed to be set free. Turned wash pots down in the house to keep the sound down so white folks wouldn't hear us singing and praying to be set free.

"Overseer would whip neggers when out of humor. Miss Mary would always tell them not to mistreat her help.

"Times were so hard during slave times, white marster took them into the bottoms and hid them, so they wouldn't run off with the Yankee soldiers.

"Talk of war got so hot, brought us out of the woods and put us in wagons and took us and de older people off to Texas.

"We got up at 4 AM, work all day until 9 or 10 at night. On Sunday we worked if it was necessary.

"I was tough and strong. I could outrun a wild animal, barefooted and bare headed.

"We would have a country dance once in awhile. Someone would play the banjo.

"Miss Mary, white mistis called us all in one day and opened a large trunk. She showed us money, gold and silver, saying that we had all helped to make it for them. Thats the first money I ever saw.

"Before Christmas we killed hogs.

"Our white folks didn't like any one wearing blue clothes. Thought they were Yankees, and that meant freedom for us niggers. Men in blue clothes came and put a rope around my marsters neck, took him all around the nigger cabins and asked where he hid them. He told them, Texas. They said, get them and free them or they would hang him.

"He sent after them and everything was alright.

"I though my white marster was God. He took sick and died.

"I heard the other slaves saying he committed suicide because he had lost all his money.

"In those times my father saw my mother, decided he wanted her for his woman. He tol his white folks and they fixed up a cabin for them to live in together. Was no ceremony. Had nigger midwives for babies.

"I knows every lucky silver pieces of money. I believe in lucky pieces of silver. I is a dreamer, always been dat way. I have seen my bright days ahead of me, in dreams and visions. If I hears a woman's voice calling me, a calling me in my sleep I is bound to move outa dat house. I dont keer wher I goes, I is got to go some whars."

United States. Work Projects Administration

Interviewer: Bernice Bowden.
Person interviewed: Charlie Hinton (c)
Age: 89
Home: Old River Road—Pine Bluff, Ark.

CHARLES HINTON

"Oh Lordy, lady, I was pickin' cotton durin' the war. I was here before the first gun was fired. When the war came they sent my mother and father and all the other big folks to Texas and left us undergrowth here to make a crop.

"My mother's name was Martha and my father was named Peter Hinton. Now I'm just goin' to tell you everything—I'm not ashamed. I've got the marks of slavery on me. My old marster and Miss Mary, they was good to me, but the old cook woman throwed me off the porch and injured my back. I ain't never been able to walk just right since.

"Now, here's what I remember. Our marster, we thought he was God.

"They pretty near raised us with the pigs. I remember they would cook a great big oven of bread and then pour a pan full of buttermilk or clabber and we'd break off a piece of bread and get around the pan of milk jest like pigs. Yes mam, they did that.

"Let's see now, what else occurred. Old marster would have my father and Uncle Jacob and us boys to run foot races. You know—they was testin' us, and I know I was valued to be worth five hundred dollars.

"But my folks was good to me. They wouldn't have no overseer what would be cruel. If he was cruel he would have to be gone from there.

"One time old marster say 'Charlie how come this yard so dirty?' You know there would be a little track around. I said, will you give me that old gray horse after I clean it and he said 'Yes'. So I call up the boys and we'd clean it up, and then the old gray horse was mine. It was just the old worn out stock you understand.

"I want to tell you when the old folks got sick they would bleed them, and when the young folks got sick they give you some blue mass and turn you loose.

"I remember when old marster's son Sam went to war and got shot in the leg. Old marster was cryin' 'Oh, my Sam is shot'. He got in a scrummage you know. He got well but he never could straighten out his leg.

"When freedom come, I heard 'em prayin' for the men to come back home. Miss Mary called us all up and told us our age and said, 'You all are free and can go where you want to go, or you can stay here.'

"Oh yes, the Ku Klux use to run my daddy if they caught him out without a pass, but I remember he could outrun them—he was stout as a mule.

"I been here so long and what little I've picked up is just a little fireside learnin'. I can read and write my name. I can remember when we thought a newspaper opened out was a bed-cover. But a long time after the war when the public school come about, I had the privilege of going to school three weeks. Yes mam, I was swift and I think I went nearly through the first reader.

"I am a great lover of the Bible and I'm a member of Mount Calvary Baptist Church.

"I'm glad to give you some kind of idea 'bout my age and life. I really am glad. Goodbye."

United States. Work Projects Administration

Interviewer: Mrs. Bernice Bowden
Person interviewed: Ben Hite
1515 Ohio Street, Pine Bluff, Arkansas
Age: 74

BEN HITE

"Well, I didn't zactly live in slavery times. I was born in 1864, the 4th of July. They said it was on the William Moore place four miles from Chattanooga but I was in Georgia when I commenced to remember—in Fort Valley—just a little town.

"I been in Arkansas sixty-five years the first day of January. Come to the old Post of Arkansas in 1873. I been right here on this spot forty-three years. Made a many a bale of cotton on the Barrow place.

"Went to school three weeks right down here in 'Linkum' County. I could read a little but couldn't write any much.

"I been married to this wife forty years. My fust wife dead.

"I lived in 'Linkum' County eight years and been in Jefferson County ever since.

"Three years ago I was struck by a car and I been blind two years. I can just 'zern' the light. When I was able to be about I used to vision what it would be like to be blind and now I know.

"Yes'm, I just come here on the eve of the breakin' up. I seed the Yankees in Georgia after freedom. They called em Bluejackets.

"All my life I have farmed—farmed."

Interviewer: Miss Irene Robertson
Person Interviewed: Betty Hodge
Hazen, Ark.
Age: 63

BETTY HODGE

"Uncle Billy Hill used to visit us. He was Noah's uncle. He was a slave and one thing I remembers hearing him tell was this: He was the hostler for his old master. The colored folks was having a jubilee. He wanted to go. He stole one of the carriage horses out—rode it. It started snowing. He said he went out to see bout the horse and it seemed be doin' all right. After a while here come somebody and told him that horse he rode was dead. He didn't believe it, but went out there and it was sho dead. He said he took that horse by the tail and started runnin' up the road. They drug that horse home and put him in the stable where he belong at. It was snowing so hard and fast they couldn't see their hands 'fo em he said. It snowed so much it covered up where they drug the horse and their tracks. He said the snow saved his life. They found the horse dead and never thought bout him having him out at the jubilee. He said none of em ever told a word bout it but for long time he was scared to death fear the old master find out bout it.

"Grandma Frances was born in West Virginia. She was papa's mama. She purt nigh raised us. Mama and papa went to the field to work. She cooked and done the housework. She had a good deal of Indian blood in her. I heard em say. She had high cheeks and the softest, prettiest hair. She told about the stars falling. She said they never hit the ground, that they was like shooting stars 'cepting they all come down like. Everybody was scared to death. She talked a good deal about Haywood County—I believe that was in Tennessee—that was where they lived durin' of the war. Papa made her a livin' long as she lived. When she got old noises bothered her, so then we growed up and she lived by herself in front of our house in a house.

"Grandma Frances and our family come to Arkansas 'reckly after the Civil War. They come with Mr. John and Miss Olivia Cooper. Miss Olivia was his wife, but Miss Presh was a old maid. Folks used to think it was sort of bad if a woman didn't marry. Thought she have no chances. It sort of be something like a disgrace if a woman was a old maid. Don't seem that-a-way no more. I never heard much about Miss Presh but I heard mama tell this: Grandma Mary Lea come on a visit to see mama and she brought her some sweet potatoes in a bag. Had nothing else and wanted to bring her something. Miss Olivia picked out the biggest ones and took em. Said she was mean. Said she had a plenty of everything. Just left mama the smallest ones. She said Miss Olivia was stingy. Mama was the house girl and nurse and they had a cook. Mama was a girl then she belong to the Coopers, but mama belong to somebody else. She hadn't married then.

"One day Miss Olivia called her and she didn't get there soon as Miss Olivia wanted her to. Miss Olivia say, 'You getting mean, Lucy. You like your ma.' She said, 'I just like you if I'm mean.' But Miss Olivia didn't understand it. She ask the cook and the cook told her she was talking to her. She told Mr. John Cooper to whoop em but he didn't. He kind of laughed and ask the cook what Lucy said to Miss Olivia. Miss Olivia told him if he didn't whoop em both she was going back home. He told her he would take her and she wouldn't come back neither when she left. He didn't whoop neither one of em and she never left him till she died, cause I been over to Des Arc and seen all of em since I come in this world.

"Mama was Lucy Lea till she married Will Holloway, my papa. Then she married Isarel Thomas the preacher here at Hazen. He come from Tennessee with old Dr. Hazen (white man). Mama's mama was Mary Lea; she lived out here at Green Grove. I don't know where she was born, but she was owned by the Lea's round Des Arc. She come and stay a month or two with us on a visit.

"Old folks was great hands to talk bout olden times. I forgot bout all they told.

"In old times folks had more principal, now they steal and fight and loud as they can be. Folks used to be quiet, now they be as loud as they can all the time. They dance and carouse all night long—fuss and fight! Some of our young folks got to change. The times have changed so much and still changing so fast I don't know what goin' to be the end. I study bout it a lot."

United States. Work Projects Administration

Interviewer: Miss Irene Robertson
Person interviewed: Minnie Hollomon
R.F.D., Biscoe, Arkansas
Age: 75

MINNIE HOLLOMON

"My parents was Elsie and Manuel Jones. They had five children. The Jones was farmers at Hickory Plains. Auntie was a cook and her girl, Luiza, was a weaver and a spinner and worked about in the house.

"I heard auntie talk about the soldiers come and make them cook up everything they had and et it up faster 'en it took 'er to fix it ready for 'em to guttle down. Dems her very words. They took the last barrel er flour and the last scrap er meat they had outen the smokehouse.

"Uncle Sebe Jones was Massa Jones' boss and wagoner (wagon man and overseer). Auntie said Uncle Sebe drunk too much. He drunk long as he lived 'cause old Massa Jones trained to that.

"Uncle Whit Jones was more pious and his young massa learned him to read and write. He was onliest one of the Jones niggers knowed how er had any learning er tall.

"The women folks spun and wove all winter while the nights be long.

"Pa said Massa Jones was pretty fair to his black folks. He fed 'em pretty good and seen they was kept warm in rainy bad weather. He watch see if the men split plenty wood to keep up the fires. Jones didn't allow the neighbors to slash up his black folks. He whooped them if he thought they needed it and he knowed when and where to stop. Mama didn't b'long to the same people.

"Grandma was a native of South Ca'lina. Her name was Malindy Fortner. She died over at Alex Hazen's place. She come to some of her people's after the War. I think ma come with her. Her own old mistress come sit on a cushion one day. The parrot say, 'Cake under cushion, burn her bottom.' Grandma made the parrot fly on off but the cake was warm and it was mashed flat under the cushion when she got up. She took it to her little children. She said piece of cake was a rarity. They had plenty corn bread, peas and meat.

"Grandma said after they had a baby it would be seben weeks b'fore they would let them put their hands in a washtub. They all had tasks in winter time. They sit by the fire and talk and sing. Ma said in slavery a girl had a baby and her hugging around a tree. Said her mistress come to the cabin to see about her and brought corn bread and pea pot-liquor. Said that would kill folks but it didn't hurt her.

"Pa b'long to the Jones and Whitlocks both but he never told us about ever being sold. He told us about it took nearly two weeks one time in the bad weather to meet the boat and get provisions. His wagon was loaded and when the rain and freeze set in it caught him. He like never got back. His white folks was proud when he got back."

United States. Work Projects Administration

Name of Interviewer—S. S. Taylor
Person interviewed—H. B. Holloway (Dad or Pappy)
1524 Valentine Street, Little Rock, Arkansas
Occupation: Formerly railroader and drayman—Pension now.
Age: 89

H. B. HOLLOWAY

Birth, Parentage

"I never lived in the country. I lived in town. But sometimes my father would go into the country to hunt and I would go with him.

"I was born in Austin County, Fort Valley, Georgia, 105 miles below Atlanta one way, and by Macon it would be 140. I was thirteen years old when the war began and seventeen when it ended. I was born the fifteenth day of February, 1848.

"My mother was a nurse and midwife. My father was a finished mechanic. I never had to do any work until after the Civil War, but I was just crazy about railroading and went to railroading early. I railroaded all my life. I did some draying too and a lot of concreting too.

"I was born free. There weren't so many free Niggers in Georgia. None that I knew owned any slaves. I never heered of any owning any slaves. My mother was a full blooded Cherokee woman, and my father was a dark Spaniard." ("Dad" or "Pappy" Holloway is a fine looking old white man and shows evidence of White and Indian blood; however, Negro blood shows.)

"I am the only one out of twelve children that can't talk my mother's language and don't know my father's. I remember the Indian war whoop, and the war dance—used to do that myself. When they run the Indians out of Georgia into Florida, my mother never did go. She was one hundred seven years old when she died."

Marriage, Breeding, Weddings, Separations

"You know, there weren't no marriages like now with Niggers—just like if you and your wife owned a man and I owned a woman, if your man wanted to marry, he got consent from you and my woman would get consent from me. And then they would marry, and I either got to buy your slave or you got to buy mine. Sometimes the white folks wouldn't want you to marry.

"They didn't force nobody to marry. They might force you to marry if both of you had the same master, but not if they belonged to different masters. They were crazy about slaves that had a lot of children.

"Niggers didn't separate in slave times because they never was married except by word of mouth. There was a lot of old souls that came out of slavery times that lived together and raised children that never was married (except by word of mouth), just got together. But they made out better and were better husbands and wives and raised better families than they do now.

"Sometimes folks would get separated when the slave traders would sell them, and sometimes families would get separated when their white folks died or would run into debt."

Slave Sales

"They had a slave block in Georgia. You see they would go to Virginia and get the people that they would bring across the water—regular Africans. Sometimes they would refugee them four or five hundred miles before they would get the chance to sell them. Sometimes a woman would have a child in her arms. A man would buy the mother and wouldn't want the child. And then sometimes a woman would holler out: 'Don't sell that pickaninny.' (You know they didn't call colored children nothin' but Pickaninnies then.) 'I want that little pickaninny.' And the mother would go one way and the child would go the other. The mother would be screaming and hollering, and of course, the child wouldn't be saying nothin' because it didn't know what was goin' on.

"They had a sale block in my home (Fort Valley, Georgia), and I used to go and see the Niggers sold often. Some few wasn't worth nothin' at all—just about a hundred dollars. But they generally ran about five or six hundred dollars. Some of them would bring thousands of dollars. It depended on their looks. The trader would say, 'Look at those shoulders; look at those muscles.'

"Someone would holler out, 'A thousand dollars.'

"Then another would holler out, 'Fifteen hundred.'

"They went like horses. A fine built woman would bring a lot of money. A woman that birthed children cost a heap.

"Virginia was where the slaves would be brought first. The slave traders would go there and get them and take them across the country in droves—just like you take a drove of cattle. They would sell them as they would come to sale blocks. The slaves would be undressed from the shoulders to the waist."

Houses, Food, Clothes

"The slaves lived in log huts on the plantations. Some men would weatherboard them. They didn't put any ceiling in. You could lay back in your bed and see the moon and stars shining through.

"Some got good food and some of the owners would make the Niggers steal their food from other folks. Old Myers Green would make his Niggers steal and he would say, 'If you get caught, I'll kill you.' One or two of them let themselves get caught, and he would whip them. That was to save him from paying for it. They couldn't do anything to you but whip you nohow. But they could make him pay for it.

"They used homemade clothes made out of homemade cotton cloth. They would spin the cotton to a thread. When they would get so many broaches of it, they would make it into cloth. A broach was just a lot of thread wound around a stick. They would take it to the wheel and make the cloth, them women used to have tasks:—spinning, weaving, dressmaking, and so on. Sometimes they would have five and six spinning wheels running before they would get to the weaving.

"I don't know who made the clothes. But you know them Niggers made them. They used to learn some slaves how to do some things,—the right way. Jus' like they learned themselves. There was plenty of nice seamstresses. The white folks used to make them make clothes for their children. The white folks wouldn't do nothin'. They wouldn't even turn down the bed to get in it."

Ages

"Colored folks in slavery times didn't know how old they was. When you would buy a drove of darkies, you would go by what they would tell you, but they didn't know how old they was. Some of those Niggers they bought from Africa wouldn't take nothin' neither.

"They would say: 'Me goin' do what you say do, but me aint goin' to get no whipping.' And when they whipped them, there was trouble.

"The masters kept records of ages of those born in their care. Some of them did. Some of them didn't keep nothin'. Jus' like people nowadays. Raised them like pigs and hogs. Jus' didn't care."

Amusements

"There used to be plenty of colored folk fiddlers. Dancing, candy pulling, quilting,—that was about the only fun they would have. Corn shucking, too. They used to enjoy that. They would get on top of that pile and start singing—the white folks used to like that—sometimes they would shuck corn all night long. And they would sing and eat too.

"They had what they called the old-fashioned cotillion dance—partners—head, foot, and two sides—four men and four women—each man danced with his partner. Music by the fiddlers. I used to dance that.

"At the quilting, they'd get down and quilt. The boys and young men would be there too and they would thread the needles and laugh and talk with the girls, and the women would gossip.

"The masters would go there too and look at them and see what they'd do and how they'd do and make them do. They would do that at the candy pullin' too, and anything else.

"The candy pulling—there they'd cook the candy and a man and a girl would pull candy together. Look to me like they enjoyed the corn shucking as much as they did anything else."

Christmas

"They'd give time to celebrate Christmas time. They'd dance and so on like that. But they worked them from New Year's day to Christmas Eve night the next year. The good white people would give them a pig and have them make merry. They'd make merry over it like we do now. That's where it all come from."

Run-Away Slaves

"I seen a many a runaway slave. I've seen the hounds catch them too. You could hear the hounds all hours of the night. Some Nigger was gone. Some of them would run away from the field. And some of them would slip out at night.

"I used to mock them hounds. The first hound would say 'Oo-oo-oo, He-e-e-e-re he-e-e-e-e G-o-o-o-oes.' The others would say, 'Put 'im up. Put 'im up. Put 'im up. Put 'im up. Put 'im up.' My mother would laugh at me. The lead-hound howled, and the catch dog wouldn't say nothin' but you could hear the sound of his feet. The lead hound didn't catch the Nigger, but he would just follow him. When he caught up with him, he would step aside and let the catch dog get him if he wasn't treed."

Pateroles

"The pateroles were for Niggers just like police and sheriffs were for white folks. They were just poor white folks. When a Nigger was out from the plantation at night, he had to have a pass. If the pateroles seen him, they would stop him and ask for his pass. If'n he didn't have it, he'd mos' likely get a beating. I was free and didn't have no pass. Sometimes they would stop me, but I never had no trouble with 'em. I was a boy then, and everybody knowed me."

Good Masters

"Men like Colonel Troutman, Major Holmes, and Preacher Russell—Thomas Russell—they didn't whip their Niggers and didn't allow no one else to whip them. They had a little guardhouse on the plantation and they would lock them up in it. You'd better not hit one of their Niggers. They'd take a pole or something and run you ragged."

Mean Masters

"White folks was cruel in slavery times. You see I was free and could go where I wanted too, and I see'd a lot. Old Myer Green would take a Nigger and tie his feet to one side of a railroad track and tie his hands to the other side, and whip him till the blood ran. Then he would take him down to the smoke house and rub him down with lard and red pepper. 'Rub plenty in,' he would say, 'Don't let him spoil.'

"Then I have seen them take up a ten-rail fence end set it down on a Nigger's neck and whip him. If he would rare and twist and try to jump up, he would break his neck.

Pateroles

"One night, when me and my mother was coming from town, my mother had a demijohn of whiskey. They (pateroles) tried to take it. And she snatched a palling off the fence and nearly beat them poor white trash to death. My mother was a good woman, strong as any man. I was sitting on the demijohn. I was a little fellow then. They didn't do nothin' to her neither, 'cause they knew what old Colonel Troutman would do." (Holloway's mother was midwife to Colonel Troutman's wife and nurse and 'mammy' to his boy, although a free Indian.)

Mixed Bloods

"I can carry you to Columbus, Georgia. There was ten mulatto Niggers born there and you would think they were all white; but they were all colored. They were slaves, but their master was their Daddy.

"I'll tell you somethin'. W. H. Riley and Henry Miller,—You know them don't you—they are blood brothers,—had the same mother and the same father. Riley's grandfather was a white man named Miller. Miller got mad at his son, Riley's father, and sold him to a white man named Riley. Riley took the name of his father's second master. After freedom, Henry and Josephine took the name of Miller, their real grandfather. They said, 'Miller had never done anything' for them."

Curious Beliefs and Slave Expectations of Freedom

"I was looking right in Lincoln's mouth when he said, 'The colored man is turned loose without anything. I am going to give a dollar a day to every Negro born before Emancipation until his death,—a pension of a dollar a day.' That's the reason they killed him. But they sure didn't get it. It's going to be an awful thing up yonder when they hold a judgment over the way that things was done down here."

Lincoln's Visit to Atlanta

"When the war was declared over, Abraham Lincoln came South and went to the capitol (of Atlanta), and there was so many people to meet him he went up to the tower instead of in the State House. He said, 'I did everything I could to keep out of war. Many of you agreed to turn the Negroes loose, but Jeff Davis said that he would wade in blood up to his neck before he would do it.'

"He asked for all of the Confederate money to be brought up there. And when it was brought, he called for the oldest colored men around. He said, 'Now, is you the oldest?' The man said, 'Yes Sir.' Then he threw him one of those little boxes of matches and told him to set fire to it and burn it up.

"Then he said, 'I am going to disfranchise every one of you (the white folks), and it will be ten years before you can even vote or get back into the Union.'"

Grant's Attitude

"Grant was the one that killed the Republican party. We ain't had but three real Republican presidents since the war—Garfield, McKinley and Teddy Roosevelt. They killed Garfield, and they killed McKinley, and they tried to kill Teddy Roosevelt. Well, they asked Grant if they could make state constitutions. Grant said, 'Yes, if they didn't conflict with the national constitution.' But they did conflict and Grant didn't do nothin' about it."

Schooling, Antebellum and Postbellum

"Northern teachers were sent down here after the war and they charged a dollar a month until the State set up schools. Some of the Niggers learned enough in the six months school to teach, and some white persons taught.

"In slave times, they didn't have any schools for Niggers. Niggers better not be caught with a book. If he were caught with a book they beat him to death nearly. Niggers used to get hold of this Webster's Blue Back Book and the white folks would catch them and take them away. They didn't allow no free Niggers to go to school either in slave times."

Share Cropping

"I used to see Niggers in Georgia share cropping. Nigger work all the year. Christmas eve night they would be going back to the plantation singing—done lost everything—sitting on the wagon singing:

'Sho' pity Lawd forgive
That ar' pentant rebel live.'

"Then they would have to get clothes and food against the next year's crop. Then you'd see 'em on the wagon again driving back to the plantation loaded down with provisions, singing:

'Lawd revive us agin

All our increase comes from thee.'

"I used to study how them people could live. They didn't give but ten dollars a month for common labor. They didn't give anything to the share cropper. They took all of it. They said he spent it, borrowed it, and on like that."

Didn't Want To Be Free

"Some that didn't know any better didn't want to be free. Especially them that had hard taskmasters. When the Nigger was turned loose sho nuff, some of them didn't have a good shirt to their back. The master hated to lose them so bad, he wouldn't give them anything.

"But for twenty-five years after slave times, there ain't no race of people ever traveled as fast as the Nigger did. But when the young ones came up, they are the ones what killed the thing. An old white man said: 'We thought if you folks kept it up we or you one would have to leave this country. But when the young ones came on, and began begrudging one another this and that and working against one another, then we saw you would never make a nation.'"

Riots and KKK

"I have been in big riots. I was in the Atlanta riots in 1891. We lost about forty men, and I don't know how many the white folks lost, but they said it was about a hundred. I used to live there. I came here in 1892.

"We had a riot there when the KKK was raising so much Cain. The first Ku Klux wore some kind of hat that went over the man's head and shoulders and had great big red eyes in it. They broke open my house one night to whip me.

"I was working as a foreman in the shops. One night as I was going home, some men stopped and said 'Who are you.' I answered 'H. B. Holloway.' Then they said, 'Well we'll be over to your house tonight to whip you.'

"I said, 'We growed up together and you couldn't whip me then. How you 'spect to do it now. You might kill me, but you can't beat me.'

"And one of them said, 'Well we'll be over to see you at eleven thirty tonight, and we are going to beat you.'

"I went on home end told my wife what had happened. She was afraid and wanted me to leave and take her and the children with her.

"But I said, 'No, you must take the little children and go in the bedroom and stay there.'

"She did. I had three sons that were grown up, between twenty and twenty-eight years old, and I had a Winchester, a shotgun and a pistol. I gave the Winchester to the oldest, the shotgun to the next, and the pistol to the youngest. I took my ax for myself. I stationed the boys at the far end of the room—away from the door.

"The oldest said, 'Papa, let's kill them.'

"I said, 'No. You just stand there and do nothing till I tell you. When they break in, I'll knock the first one in the head with the ax. But don't you do nothin' till I tell you.'

"After a while, we heard a noise outside, and I took my stand beside the door. Then they gave a rush, and battered the door down. A man with a gray hood on jumped inside. I hit him side the head with the flat of the ax, and he fell down across the door.

"Then the others rushed up, and the boys cut loose with all three of the guns, and such another uproar you never heard. They high-tailed it down the street, and the boys took right after them, shooting at their legs. The Winchester shot sixteen times, and the pistol shot six, and the boy with the shotgun was shooting and breaking down and reloading and shooting again as fast as he could.

"I went outside and whistled for the boys to come back. They come. They would always obey me. I told them to carry the man I had hit out. He was still lying there. Through all the fuss and uproar, he had been lying there across the doorway. Carried him out, and threw him on the sidewalk. My eldest son said the man said, 'Holloway, don't hit me no more.'

"I didn't, but if I had known who he was then, I would have gone out and cut his throat. He was old Colonel Troutman's son. There was just two hours difference in our birth. Me and him both nursed from the same breast. We grew up together and were never separated until we were thirteen (beginning of the war). Many people thought we were brothers. I had fought for him and he had fought for me. When he wasn't at my house, I was at his, and his father partly raised me. That's the reason I don't trust white people.

"We had a big dog that everyone was scared of. We always kept him chained up. I unchained the dog, and took the boys and we went out in the woods. It was cold; so we made a fire under a tall sapling.

"Near daylight, I said, 'The dog sees something, but we can't see what it is.' The eldest son said, 'Pappy, if you get astride the dog, and look the way he's looking, you can see what he sees.'

"I got astride him and looked, and finally way off through the trees and the branches and leaves, I saw six men riding through the woods on horseback. I took the guns away from the boys and put the pistol and shotgun under the leaves at my feet. I made the boys separate and hide in the brush at a good distance from me and from each other. I made the dog lie down beside me. Then I waited.

"When the men came near me and were about to pass on looking for me, I hailed them. I told them to stop right where they were or I'd drop them in their tracks. It was Colonel Troutman and five other of the old men from town out hunting me.

"Colonel Troutman said, 'We just wanted to talk to you Holloway.'

"I said, 'Stand right where you are and talk.'

"After some talk, I let them come up slowly to a short distance from me. The upshot of the whole thing was that they wanted me to go back to town with them to 'talk' over the matter. They allowed I hadn't done nothin' wrong. But Colonel Troutman's man was hurt bad, and some of the young men in the mob had had their legs broke. And they were all young men from the town, boys that knew me and were friendly to me in the daytime. Still they wanted me to go to town in their charge, and I knew I wouldn't have a chance if I did that. Finally I told Colonel Troutman, that I was going home to see my wife that evening, and that if he wanted to talk to me, he could come over there and talk.

"When they left, I sent the boys along home and told them to tell my wife. That night when I got home, Colonel Troutman was in the house talking to my wife. I went in quietly. He said that they said I had forty Niggers hid in the house that night. I told him that there wasn't anybody there but me and my family, and that all the damage that was done I done myself. He said that well he didn't blame me; that even if it was his son, they broke in on me and I had a right to defend my family, and that none of the old heads was going to do anything about it. He said I was a good man and had never given anybody any trouble and that there wasn't any excuse for anybody comin' stirrin' up trouble with me. And that was the end of it."

Hoodoo

"My wife was sick, down, couldn't do nothin'. Someone got to telling her about Cain Robertson. Cain Robertson was a hoodoo doctor in Georgia. They there wasn't nothin' Cain couldn't do. She says, 'Go and see Cain and have him come up here.'

"I says, 'There ain't no use to send for Cain. Cain ain't coming up here because they say he is a "two-head" Nigger.' (They called all them hoodoo men 'two-head'

Niggers; I don't know why they called them two-head.) 'And you know he knows the white folks will put him in jail if he comes to town.'

"But she says, 'You go and get him.'

"So I went.

"I left him at the house and when I came back in, he said, 'I looked at your wife and she had one of then spells while I was there. I'm afraid to tackle this thing because she has been poisoned and it's been goin' on a long time. And if she dies, they'll say I killed her and they already don't like me and lookin' for an excuse to do somethin' to me.'

"My wife overheard him and says, 'You go on, you got to do somethin'.'

"So he made me go to town and get a pint of corn whiskey. When I brought it back, he drunk a half of it at one gulp, and I started to knock him down. I'd thought he'd get drunk with my wife lying there sick.

"Then he said, 'I'll have to see your wife's stomach.' Then he scratched it, and put three little horns on the place he scratched. Then he took another drink of whiskey and waited about ten minutes. When he took them off her stomach, they were full of blood. He put them in the basin in some water and sprinkled some powder on them, and in about ten minutes more, he made me get them and they were full of clear water and there was a lot of little things that looked like wiggle tails swimming around in it.

"He told me when my wife got well to walk in a certain direction a certain distance and the woman that caused all the trouble would come to my house and start a fuss with me.

"I said, 'Can't you put this same thing back on her.'

"He said, 'Yes, but it would kill my hand.' He meant that he had a curing hand and that if he made anybody sick or killed them, all his power to cure would go from him.

"I showed the stuff he took out of my wife's stomach to old Doc Matthews and he said, 'You can get anything into a person by putting it in them.' He asked me how I found out about it, and how it was taken out, and who did it.

"I told him all about it, and he said, 'I'm going to see that that Nigger practices anywhere in this town he wants to and nobody bothers him.' And he did."

Opinions of Young People

"The young Niggers aint got as much sense as the old ones had,—those that were born before the war. One thing, they don't read enough. They don't know history. I can't understand them. Looks like to me they had a mighty good chance; but it looks like the more they get the worse they are. Looks like to me their parents didn't teach them right—or somethin'. Young ladies—I look at them every day of my life—coarse, swearing, running with bootleggers, and running the hoodlums down, smoking, going half-naked, and so on. They don't care what they do or nothing."

Relatives

"My brother was in Collodiusville, Georgia, the last time I heard from him. That is in Monroe County, or Upton County,—I don't know what county it's in. I know he is there if he is living because he owns a home there.

"William always lived in Macon but he is dead. Bud,—I don't know where he is. Milton, Irving, and Zekiel, I don't know where they are. I used to keep up with them regular. But we ain't written to each other in a long time.

"The last time I heard from Mahala and Laura, their husbands were bricklayers and they were living in Atlanta, I think. They went some other place where there was plenty of work. I think it was to Cleveland, Ohio. There's Josephine, Mandy, and little Mary—five sisters and seven brothers.

"Outside of William, Crawford, and Milton, I haven't seen none of them since fifty years. I haven't seen Zekiel since the year of the surrender. I seen some of the white folks the year they had the re-union here. They seen me on the street, and came over and talked to me, and wanted me to go back to Fort Valley, and offered to pay my railroad fare. But I told 'em I was goin' to stay here in God's country."

366

— 29 1938
Interviewer: Miss Irene Robertson
Person interviewed: Pink Holly
Holly Grove, Arkansas
Age: 70

PINK HOLLY

"I was born in Anderson County, South Carolina. My papa was Abe Brown and my mama was Lizzie White. She died when I was a baby and Miss Nancy White took me up to her house and raised me. Her husband was Mars Henry White. They was good to me. Miss Nancy was the best. They treated me like their own boy. It was done freedom then but my papa stayed on the place. I learned to do up the night turns, slop the hogs and help bout the milkin'. They had young calves to pull off. I toted in the wood and picked up chips. She done everything for me and all the mother I knowed.

"When I was seven years old my papa pulled me off to Arkansas. We come on a immigration ticket, least I recken we did. I don't think my papa paid our way. We was brought here. The land was better they told em.

"We settled in the woods close to Mariana and commenced farmin'. I been farmin' and workin' in the timber and I carpenters a little. The timber is gone.

"I supports myself all I can. I own a little house at Clarendon I recken is the reason I don't get no Government help."

United States. Work Projects Administration

Interviewer: Samuel S. Taylor
Person interviewed: Dora Holmes
1500 Valentine St., Little Rock, Ark.
Age: 60?
Occupation: Housewife

DORA HOLMES

"My father's half brothers were white. They all fought in the army. They were Confederate soldiers. Once during the war when they came home, they brought my mother the goods for two dresses,—twenty yards of figured voile, ten yards for each dress. The cost of the whole twenty yards was fifty dollars ($50.00).

"I still have the dresses and some petticoats and pantaloons which are nearly as old. I have ironed these things many a time until they were so stiff they stand straight up on the floor."

Interviewer's Comments

Mary Ann King, mother of Dora Holmes, was the original owner of the dresses. She died at the age of ninety-eight two or three years ago. One of the dresses is still in the possession of the daughter. It has a skirt with nine gores and a twelve-inch headed ruffle.

The petticoat is of white muslin with a fifty-two yard lace ruffle in sixteen tiers of lace with beading at the top. It was worn just after the Civil War.

There are also a baby dress and a baby petticoat fifty-six years old.

MAY 31 1938
Interviewer: Samuel S. Taylor
Person interviewed: Elijah Henry Hopkins
1308½ Ringo Street, Little Rock, Arkansas
Age: 81

ELIJAH HENRY HOPKINS

"My father's master was old Tom Willingham, an awful big farmer who owned farms in Georgia and South Carolina, both. He lived in southwest Georgia in Baker County. Old man Willingham's wife was Phoebe Hopkins. Her mother was old lady Hopkins. I don't know what the rest of her name was. We never called her nothin' but old lady Hopkins or Mother Hopkins. She was one of the richest women in the state. When she died, her estate was divided among her children and grandchildren. Her slaves were part of her estate. They were divided among her children and grandchildren, too. Tom Willingham's family come in for its part. He had three sons, Tom, Jr., John, and Robert. My father already belonged to Tom Willingham, Sr., so he stayed with him. But my mother belonged to old lady Hopkins, and she went to Robert, so my daddy and mother were separated before I knew my daddy. My father stayed with old man Willingham until freedom.

"Robert Willingham was my mother's master. He never married. When he died he willed all his slaves free.

But his relatives got together and broke the will and never did let 'em go.

"When I saw my father to know him, I saw him out in Georgia. They told me that was my father. Then he had another wife and a lot of children. My mother brought me up and my father taken charge of me after she died and after freedom—about a year after. It was close to emancipation because the states were still under martial law.

"I was born May 15, 1856, in the Barnwell district, South Carolina. They used to call them districts then. It would be Barnwell County now. They changed and started calling 'em counties in 1866 or thereabouts. I was running around when they mustered the men in for the Civil War, and I was about nine years old when the War ended. I was about ten when my mother died and my father taken charge of me. I was taken from South Carolina when I was about four years old and carried into Georgia and stayed there until emancipation. My mother didn't tarry long in Georgia after she was emancipated. She went back into South Carolina; but she died in a short time, as I just said. Then my father taken charge of me. I got married in South Carolina in 1885, and then I came out here in 1886—to Arkansas. Little Rock was the first place I came to. I didn't stay here a great while. I went down to the Reeder farm on the Arkansas River just about sixteen miles above Pine Bluff. I started share cropping but taken down sick. I never could get used to drinking that bottom water. Then I went to Pine Bluff and went to work with the railroad and helped to widen the gauge of the Cotton Belt Road. Then the next year they started the Sewer Contract, and I worked in that and I worked on the first water plant they started. In working with the King Manufacturing Company I learned piping.

"I stayed in Pine Bluff sixteen years. My wife died August 1, 1901. A couple of years after that, I came back to Little Rock, and have been here ever since. I went to work on the Illinois Central Railroad just across the river, which is now the Rock Island Railroad. After it became the Rock Island, the bridge was built across the river east of Main Street. They used to go over the old Baring Cross Bridge and had to pay for it. The Missouri Pacific enjoined the Rock Island and wouldn't let it go straight through, so they built their own bridge and belted the city and went on around. I got stricken down sick in 1930 and haven't been able to do heavy work since. You know, a plumber and steam-fitter have to do awful heavy work.

"I get a little old age assistance from the state. They are supposed to give me commodities but my card got out and they ain't never give me another one. I went down to see about it today, and they said they'd mail me another one."

How the Little Children Were Fed

"My mother was always right in the house with the white people and I was fed just like I was one of their children. They even done put me to bed with them. You see, this discrimination on color wasn't as bad then as it is now. They handled you as a slave but they didn't discriminate against you on account of color like they do now. Of course, there were brutal masters then just like there are brutal people now. Louisiana and Alabama and

Mississippi always were tough states on colored people. South Carolina and Georgia got that way after people from those places came in and taught them to mistreat colored people. Yet in Alabama and Louisiana where they colored people were worse treated, it seems that they got hold of more property and money. Same way it was in Mississippi."

Patrollers

"The patrollers was just a set of mean men organized in every section of the country. If they'd catch a nigger out and he didn't have a pass, they'd tie him up and whip him and then they'd take him back. You had to have a pass to be out at night. Even in the daytime you couldn't go no great distance without a pass. Them big families—rich families—that had big plantations would come together and the niggers from two or three places might go to a church on one of them. But you couldn't go no place where there wasn't a white man looking on."

Reading and Writing in Slave Time

"Some of the white people thought so much of their slaves that they would teach them how to write and read. But they would teach them secretly and they would teach them not to read or write out where anybody would notice them. They didn't mind you reading as much as they minded you writing. If they'd catch YOU now and it was then, they'd take you out and chop off them fingers you're doing that writing with."

Slave Occupation and Wages

"My daddy was a builder. Old man Willingham gave him freedom and time to work on his own account. He gave him credit for what work he done for him. He got three hundred dollars a year for my father's time, but all the money was collected by him, because my father being a slave couldn't collect any money from anybody. When my father's master died, he may have had money deposited with him. But he was strictly honest with my father. No matter how much he collected, he wouldn't take no more'n three hundred dollars and he put all the rest to the credit of my father. He said three hundred dollars was enough to take."

How Freedom Came

"The owners went to work and notified the slaves that they were free. After the proclamation was issued, the government had agents who went all through the country to see if the slaves had been freed. They would see how the proclamation was being carried out. They would ask them, 'How are you working?' 'You are free.' 'What are you getting?' Some of them would say, 'I ain't gettin' nothin' now.' Well, the agent would take that up and they would have that owner up before the government. Maybe he would be working people for a year and giving them nothin' before they found him out. There are some places where they have them cases yet. Where they have people on the place and ain't paying them nothin'."

Memories of Soldiers and the War

"I have seen thousands and thousands of soldiers. Sometimes it would take a whole day for them to pass through. When Sherman's army marched through Atlanta, it took more than a day. I was in Atlanta then. He sent word ahead that he was coming through and for all people that weren't soldiers to get out of the town. I saw the Rebels, too; I saw them when they stacked their arms. Looked like there was a hundred or more rifles in each stack. They just come up and pitched them down. They had to stack their arms and turn them over.

"I was taken to Georgia when I was four years old, you know. I recollect when all the people came up to swear allegiance, and when they were hurrying out to get away from Sherman's army. They fit in Atlanta and then marched on toward Savannah. Then they crossed over into South Carolina. They went on through Columbia and just tore it up. Then they worked their way on back into Georgia. They didn't fight in Augusta though.

"Jeff Davis was captured not far from my father's place[7]. Jeff Davis had a big army, but the biggest thing he had was about a thousand wagons or more piled up with silver and other things belonging to the Confederacy. He was supposed to be taking care of that. He had to turn it over to the North."

'Shin Plasters'

"They had a kind of money right after the Civil War—paper money gotten out by the United States Government and supposed to be good. The Confederate money was no good but this money—these 'shin plasters' as they were called—was good money issued by the government. They did away with it and called it all in. You could get more for it now than it is worth. The old green back took its place but the 'shin plaster' was in all sizes. It wasn't just a dollar bill. It was in pinnies, five cents, ten cents, twenty-five cents, and then they skipped on up to fifty cents, and they didn't have nothin' more till you got to a dollar."

Schooling

"I haven't had a great deal of schooling. I have had a little about in places. Just after the emancipation, my mother died and my father married again. My stepmother had other children and they kept me out of my education. Since I have been grown, I have gotten a little training here and there. Still I have served as supervisor of elections and done other things that they wanted educated people to do. But it was just merely a pick-up of my own. The first teachers I had were white women from the North."

Politics

"I have never taken a great deal of interest in politics. Only in the neighborhood where I lived there was a colony of colored people at Bentley, South Carolina. They chose me to represent them at the polls and I did the best I could. I got great credit for both the colored and the white people for that. But I never took much interest in politics.

"My father spent a fortune in it but I never could see that it benefited him. I never did care for any kind of office except a mail contract that I had once to haul mail. I went through that successfully and never lost a pouch or anything but at the end of the year I threw it up. I couldn't trust anyone else to handle it for me and I had to meet trains at all hours. The longest I could sleep was two or three hours a night, so I gave it up at the end of the year."

Care of Old People

"Some of the masters treated us worse than dogs and others treated us fine. Colonel Robert Willingham freed his slaves but his sisters and brothers wouldn't stand for it. They went and stole us off and sold us. My mother being a thrifty colored woman and a practical nurse, everywhere she went, a case gave thirty dollars and her board and mine. My father paid his master three hundred dollars a year. He built these gin houses and presses. The old man would write him passes and everything and see that he was paid for his work. Some years, he would make as much as three or four thousand dollars. His master collected it and held it for him and gave it to him when he wanted it. That was during slavery times."

Opinion of the Present

"Slavery days were hard but in the same time the colored people fared better than now because the white folks taken up for them and they raised what they needed to eat. You couldn't go nowhere but what people had plenty to eat. Now they can't do it.

"I know what caused it too. The Jews didn't have much privilege till after the Negro was emancipated. They used to kill Jews and bury them in the woods. But after emancipation, he began to rise. First he began to lend money on small interest. Then he started another scheme. People used to not have sense. They went to work and got in with the Southern white folks and got a law passed about the fences.

"The Greeks and Italians are next to the Jews. They don't make much off the white man; they make it off the Negro. They come 'round and open up a place and beg the niggers to come in; and when they get up a little bit, they shut out the niggers and don't want nothin' but white folks. It's a good thing they do, too; because if somebody didn't shut the Negro out, he'd never have anything.

"The slaveholders were hard, but those people who come here from across the water, they bring our trouble. You can't squeeze as much out of the poor white as you can out of the darkey. The darkey is spending too much now—when he can get hold of it. Everywhere you see a darkey with a home, he's got a government mortgage on it. Some day the government will start foreclosing and then the darkeys won't have anything, and the biggest white man won't have much.

"A hundred years from now, they won't be any such thing as Negroes. There will be just Americans. The white people are mixed up with Greeks, Germans, and Italians and everything else now. There are mighty few pure Americans now. There used to be plenty of them right after the War.

"The country can't hold out under this relief system.

"They're sending the young people to school and all like that but they don't seem to me to have their minds on any industry. They have got to have backing after they get educated. Now, they'll bring these foreigners in and use them. In the majority of states now the colored man ain't no good unless he can get some kind of trade education and can go into some little business.

"In slavery times, a poor white man was worse off than a nigger. General Lee said that he was fighting for the benefit of the South, but not for slavery. He didn't believe in slavery."

Occupation and Present Support of Hopkins

"I came to Arkansas in 1886. I got married in 1885 in South Carolina. I never had but the one wife. I have done a little railroading, worked in machinery. I have planted one crop. Did that in 1887 but got sick and had to sell out my crop. For forty-six years, I worked as a plumber and piper. I worked in piping oil, gas, water, and I worked with mechanics who didn't mind a colored man learning. They would let me learn and they would send me out to do jobs.

"Nothing hurts me but my age. If I were younger, I could get along all right. But the work is too heavy for me now.

"I get old age assistance from the state. They pay me eight dollars. I have to pay four dollars for the use of this shack. So that don't leave much for me to live on. I'm supposed to get commodities too, and I am waiting for my order now."

FOOTNOTES:

[7] Jeff Davis captured May 10, 1865, outside Irwinsville, Ga.

United States. Work Projects Administration

Interviewer: Miss Irene Robertson
Person interviewed: Nettie Hopson
Helena (home—Poplar Grove), Arkansas
Age: ?

NETTIE HOPSON

"I don't know how old I is. I am old. I been here so long. I feel my age now right smart. I want to do things and give out. I know I'm old. I look old. I was born in Alabama.

"Mother was sold to Bud Walls at Holly Grove. Papa bought her and brought us to this state. My father died seven months before I was born my mother told me. She married ag'in. She was the mother of ten children. We all lived and do better than we do now. Mother was light. She worked in the field ever since I come to know 'bout things. Her name was Martha Foster. I don't know my father's name but Foster. The rest of the family was called Walls. Whether they wanted to be called that, they was called Walls' niggers 'fore and after freedom both.

"My husband is living. My daughter died first day of March. It sorter addled me."

United States. Work Projects Administration

Interviewer: Miss Irene Robertson
Person interviewed: Molly Horn
Holly Grove, Arkansas
Age: 77

MOLLY HORN

"My ma and pa belong to the same white folks. I was born in North Carolina. Ma and pa had six children. I don't know how many owners they ever had in North Carolina. Ma and pa was named Sarah and Jad Nelson.

"When I was a baby Rubin Harriett bought me and mama. His wife was Becky Harriett. Ma was too old to sell without me. They didn't want to sell me but they couldn't sell her widout me. I am the baby of our family. Papa didn't get to come to Arkansas. That parted them. After freedom her other children came. I heard ma say how they kept papa dodged round from the Yankees. The white folks kept him dodged round. He was a field hand. Ma was a cook and house girl. She never did work in the field till she come out here. She said white folks didn't whoop him; he wouldn't take it. I don't know why they thought he wouldn't be whooped.

"I could walk when I first seed the Yankees. I run out to see em good. Then I run back and told Miss Becky. I said, 'What is they?' She told ma to put all us under the bed to hide us from the soldiers. One big Yankee stepped inside and says to Miss Becky, 'You own any niggers?'

She say, 'No.' Here I come outen under the bed and ask her fer bread. Then the Yankee lieutenant cursed her. He made the other four come outen under the bed. They all commenced to cryin' and I commenced to cry. We never seed nobody lack him fore. We was scared to deaf of him. He talked so loud and bad. He loaded us in a wagon. Mama too went wid him straight to Helena. He put us in a camp and kept us. Mama cooked fer the Yankees six or seven months. She heard em—the white soldiers—whisperin' round bout freedom. She told em, 'You ain't goiner keep me here no longer.' She took us walkin' back to her old master and ax him for us a home. Then she married man on the place. He was real old. I had five half brothers and sisters then. I was a good size girl then.

"They had run him and some more men to Texas. They went in a wagon and walked. They made one crop there. He said fifteen or sixteen families what belong to different owners went out there. They heard some people talking—overheard it was free times. They picked up and left there at night. They dodged round in the woods and traveled at night. When he got back he made terms to work as a share cropper.

"Master, he didn't give us nuthin'. I didn't hear they would give em anything. Truth of it was they didn't have much to keep less givin' the niggers something. We all had little to eat and wear and a plenty wood to burn and a house to shelter us. The work didn't slack up none. The fences down, the outhouses had to have more boards tack on. No stock cept a scrub or so. We had no garden seed cept what be borrowed round and raised. Times was hard. We had biscuits bout once a week, lucky if we got that.

"The Ku Klux got after our papa. They fixin' to kill him. He hid in the gullies. They come to our house once or twice but I never seed em. Papa come once or twice and took us all and hid us fore sundown. They quit huntin' him.

"We farmed wid Mr. Hess. Mr. Herrin wouldn't let nobody bother his hands.

"We had good times. I danced. We had candy pullings bout at the houses. We had something every week. I used to dance in the courthouse at Clarendon—upstairs. Paul Wiley was head music man. All colored folks—colored fiddlers.

"I was married over fifty years. Bunt Sutton's mother helped bout my weddin' supper. (Bunt Sutton's mother was a white woman.) She and her family all was there. She had then two boys and two girls. Mama bought me a pure white veil. I was dressed all in white. We had a colored preacher to marry us. We married at night, borrowed lamps and had em settin' about. There was a large crowd. Ann Branch was the regular cake-cooker over the country. She cooked all my cakes. They had roast pork and goose and all sorter pies. Then I went on to my new home on another man's place bout one-fourth mile from mama's house. Bunt Sutton's mama was a widow woman.

"My husband voted some but I don't pay no tention to votin'.

"I own a place but it don't do no good. My son is cripple and I can't work. I done passed hard work now. My husband bought this place before he died. I don't get help from nowhere.

"This is hardest times in my life. Well, education doin' a heap of good. The papers tell you how to do more things. It makes folks happier if they can read.

"Now I don't be bothered much wid young folks. You heard em say flies don't bother boilin' pots ain't you? I does nough to keep me going all the time and the young folks shuns work all they can cept jes' what it takes for em to live on right now. Their new ways ain't no good to me."

Interviewer: Samuel S. Taylor
Person interviewed: Cora L. Horton
918 W. Ninth Street, Little Rock, Arkansas
Age: Between 50 and 60?

CORA L. HORTON

"My grandfather on my mother's side was a slave. After my mother had been dead for years, I went to Georgia where he was. I never had seen him before and I would always want to see him, because I had heard my mother speak of him being alive and he would write to her sometimes. I said if I ever got to be grown and my grandfather stayed alive, I was going to Georgia to see him. So the first opportunity I got I went. That was a long time ago. If I'd waited till now he'd a been dead. He's been dead now for years. He lived a long time after I visited him. His name was John Crocker. He lived in Marshallville, Georgia.

"I couldn't tell how he and my mother got separated. I don't know. I don't believe I ever heard her say. In Georgia when she was quite a girl, I think she said some of her people left Georgia and went to Covington, Tennessee. Some of the white people that was connected with them in slavery were named Hollinsheds and my auntie went in that name. That is, her husband did. My mother's name was Adelaide Crocker. She was never a slave. Her mother was.

"My mother and father had children—twelve of them. I don't know how many children my grandparents had. I know three uncles—William, Harmon, and Matthew. They were all my grandmother's children and they were Flewellens. She married a Flewellen. Those were my father's brothers. My auntie's husband was named Dick Hollinshed. They all come from Georgia.

"It comes to me now. I remember hearing my mother say once that her father was sold. I think she said that her father was sold from her mother. She didn't seem to know much about it—only what she heard her father say.

"A man came through the country when I was a girl before my mother died. She died when I was young. He came to our house and he said he was a relative of my mother's and he went on to tell what he knew of her folks in slave times. By him telling so much about her folks, she thought he really was related to her. But after he left, she found out that he was just a fraud. He was going 'round throughout the country making it by claiming he was related to different people. I don't know how he found out so much about the different people he stopped with. I suppose there was a lot of people made it that way.

"I don't know what my grandparents did in slavery time. When I did see my grandfather, he wasn't able to do anything. He didn't live so long after I seen him. My mother's mother was dead and he had married another woman. I never did see my grandmother. I do remember seeing one of my granduncles. But I was so small I don't remember how he looked.

"I used to hear my grandma say that they weren't allowed to have a church service and that they used to go out way off and sing and pray and they'd have to turn a pot down to keep the noise from going out. I don't know just how they fixed the pot.

"I had one auntie named Jane Hunter. When she died, she was one hundred and one years old. She married Rev. K. Hunter over here in North Little Rock. She had been married twice. She was married to Dick Hollinshed the first time. She's been dead ten years. She was thirty-eight years old when Emancipation came. She baked the first sacrament bread for the C. M. E. Church when it was organized in 1870.

"My grandmother lived a hundred years too. That was my father's mother. I knew both of them. My grandmother lived with us. That is, she lived with us a while when my mother died. She lived here a while before she died, and then she went back to Georgia because she had a son there named William Flewellen. He is a presiding elder in the C. M. E. church, in Georgia.

"My father was a railroad man and when my mother did anything at all, she worked in the field. My father farmed during the time when he was working on the railroad.

"I have heard my grandmother talk about slaves being put on the block and sold and then meeting way years after and not knowing one another. She told me about a woman who was separated from her son. One day, years after slavery, when she had married again and had a family, she and her husband got to talking about old slave times. She told him about how she had been sold away from her baby son when he was a little thing. She told him how he had a certain scar on his arm. Her husband had a similar scar and he got to talking about slave times, and they found out that they were mother and son. He left her and went on his way sad because he didn't want to stay on living as husband with his mother. I don't think those people were held accountable for that, do you?"

Omit
Interviewer's Comment

Cora Horton is the first president of the Woman's Missionary Society composed of the societies of the three Arkansas C. M. E. Conferences. She has been president of the Annual Conference division of the Woman's Home Missionary Society of the Little Rock Conference for about seven years. She visits all meetings of the General Conference and the General Board of the C. M. E. church as well as all connectional meetings of the Little Rock Conference, and such meetings of the Arkansas and Southwest Conferences as relate to the discharge of her duties as president of the State Woman's Home Missionary Society organization.

She has been president of the N. C. Cleves Club of Bullock Temple C. M. E. Church of Little Rock for seven years and is a most active church worker as will be seen from this comment. In her worship she represents the traditional Negro type, but she buys the current issue of the C. M. E. Church Discipline and is well acquainted with its provisions relating to her specific church work as well as to all ordinary phases of church work and administration.

There is a lot of drama in her story of the mother who unwittingly married her son.

There is an interesting sidelight on slavery separations in this interview. Never had it occurred to me that imposters among Negroes might seize upon the idea of missing relatives as the basis for a confidence scheme.

There is also an interesting sidelight on C. M. E. Church history in the naming of Jane Hunter as the woman who baked the first sacrament bread at the organization of that Church in 1870.

United States. Work Projects Administration

Name of interviewer: Thomas Elmore Lucy
Person interviewed: Laura House
Russellville, Arkansas
Age: 75?

LAURA HOUSE

"No sir, I don't remember hearing my parents ever tell me just when I was born, the year or the month, but it was sometime during the War. My parents' master was named Mentor—spelled M-e-n-t-o-r. We come to Pope County several years after the War, and I have lived here in Russellville forty years and raised our family here. Father passed away about fifteen years ago.

"Mother used to tell me that the master wasn't overly kind to them. I remember she used to talk of some money being promised to them after they were freed, but I don't know how much. But I do know that none was ever paid to them.

"No sir, I cannot read or write.

"I have been a member of the A. M. E. Church ever since I was a little girl."

NOTE: Mrs. House is very neat in her dress and general deportment, is industrious, and keeps busy working here and there at odd jobs, but her memory is very uncertain as to many important details about her ancestry.

United States. Work Projects Administration

NOV 30 1936
Mrs. Mildred Thompson
Mrs. Carol Graham
El Dorado District

Ex-Slave—Hoodoo—Haunted Houses

AUNT PINKEY HOWARD

Aunt Pinkey Howard, an old negress of slavery days, can't "comember" her age but she must be about 85 or 86 years old as she was about fourteen or fifteen when the war closed. In speaking of those days Aunt Pinkie said:

"Oooh, chile, you ought to been there when Mr. Linktum come down to free us. Policemen aint in it. You ought ter seen them big black bucks. Their suits was so fine trimmed with them eagle buttons and they wuz gold too. And their shoes shined so they hurt your eyes. I tell yo ah cant comember my age but it's been a long time ago.

"My ole Marsa Holbrook lived at Hillsboro and he wuz a good marsta. I never went hungry or wid out cloes in them days. Slavery days was good old days. These days is hard days. Po' ole neeger caint git enough to feed herself. Them days weuns made our cloth and growed our food and never paid for it. Never did want for nothin' and Marster had heaps of slaves. Use to bring them across Moro Bay and them neegers always fighting and running off. They'd run off and go across Moro Bay trying to get back home. Marsta neva went after em. Said: 'Let 'em go. Aint no count no ways.'

"I wooden take $100 for living in slavery days and I member when they all parted out. Mr. Linktum come down. Yasum, Mr. Abe Linktum and his partner Horace Greeley, comed down. Lieutenants and 'Sarges' all comed. And some big yaller buck niggers all dressed up fine. I served Mr. Linktum myself wid my own hands. Yasum I did. I fetched cold water from the spring on a waiter and I stood straight an held it out just like dis in front of me. Yasum and his partner, Mr. Horace Greeley too. And them big yaller buck niggers went in the kitchen where my mammy was cookin and tole her: 'Git out er here nigger. You don have to wait on dese white fokes no more.' Yasum dey did. And they done said: 'You aint got no more marster and no more missus. Yo don' have to work here no more.' But my mother said: 'I'se puttin old marster's victuals on to cook. Wait till I gets em on.' An they tole her again that she didn't have no more marster and no more missus. I tole my mammy to kick him down the step but she said she was afeard he would shoot her. All I hates about them 'Sarges' and Lieutenants is they never did shave. Them days all wore whiskers. I 'comember' when I was a little chap standin on the block with my mammy and being sold. But Ah always had a good marster.

"Ah members standin on nuther block to cook. Tables wuz high to keep nothin from draggin things off. Grandma Aiken learnt me to cook an I stood on a block and made out biscuits with a spoon. Ah neber put my scratchers in the dough in my life. And I could cook good too. Wuz knowed as the drummers cook. Drummers would come through fum New Orleens and et at ole marsters and bragged on my cookin and tried to git me ter go wif them to New Orleans and cook fuh they wives.

"Mah fust name was Pinkie Dixon. I was married on ole mistesses front gallery and mah name wuz Cook then. Next time ah married mah name wuz Howard.

"Ah can count but not to member hit. Ah don' know the number of my chilluns but ah kin name em. There's Alec, Henry, Winnie, Ellen, Mary, Gola, Seebucky, Crawford, Sarah and Ruby. Seebucky wuz named fer Sears and Roebuck. Cause at that time weuns ordered things fum them and ordered Seebuckys clo'es fore she cum fum thar. That why we named 'er that.

"Ah deednt git no book larnin. Ah larnt enough to keep out of devilment and ah knowed how to cook. Now these fools aroun here don' know nothin. They never did see Linktum or Horace Greeley. Ah wishes it wuz work time agin but ah caint hold out now."

"Ah never gits hot nor cold lak yo does. Ah takes mah cold bath ever mornin and ah feels good."

Thus old aunt Pinkey rambled on and on talking of this and that and especially the good days—slavery days. She evidently thought that some of the army officers were Lincoln and Greeley. She probably heard her master or mistress talk about these men and got them confused with the army officers who visited in the home.

Old Marion Johnson was seven years old when the war closed. Is 79 now. "Chillun let me tell you ah don want to go over what I done been over. Not agin. In slavery days we had plenty to eat and plenty to wear but since then Oh,

Lordy. My old Mawster's name was Alex Anderson and he lived in Jackson Parrish, Louisiana. Yuh say youh wants me to tell you some tales about ole times, ghostes and the like. Well ah sure can if ah gits started but somehow I jest don' seem wound up this mawnin.

"One time there was a man what had a house full of daughters and his girl Janie wanted to git married. Her lover asked her father's permission to wed. He said: 'Well Mr. have you got any objection to me and your daughter Janie maryin'?' The old man didn't want the young one to see how anxious he was to get rid of his daughter so he said: 'You wantin to marry my daughter, Janie? Janie don't want ter git married.' The girl was behind the door listening and when her father said that she spoke up and said: 'Yes I do pappa, bad.' The young man said: 'See there now we both wants to git married.' The ole man spoke then and said: 'Well, damn you, dash you take her.'

"You know what the clocks says? The big old mantle clocks we used to have ticked along real slow and they said: 'Take your time. Take your time. Take your time.' The little alarm clocks of today say: 'Get together. Get together. Get together.' And that is jes like the young folks. When I was young the young folks them days young folks took their time and went together a long time and they married they stayed married. The young folks today rush around and get married in a week and fust thing you knows they is done duvoced and married agin. They is jest as diffunt as the clocks is diffunt.

"You knows if you makes up yo mind to do somethin and asks the Lord to help you he will. I was comin along that path in June 12 years ago. I chewed Brown Mule tobacco and wanted a chaw. I had been plowing all day and when I pulled the tobacco outen my pocket it was wet where I had sweated on hit and the outer leaves wuz all curled up so I said 'Lord help me' and throwed it out in the weeds and havn't taken a chew since.

"Youns notice how the younguns cuss this day. The womens too. In the olden days the women didn't cuss out loud but they did 'wooden cussin.' Now I bet you girls is done wooden cussin lots o times. Loose your temper and want to say things and don't dare so you slams chairs around on the floor when you is movin them to sweep. That is wooden cussin.

"You says you is interested in buried treasure? Well near Strong where the CCC Camp is was a place of buried treasure. Madam Hartline and three other white folks and myself went down there in a car. With a finding rod (divining rod) we located the treasure. Then I took this here proving rod you sees here and drove it down in the groun till hit struck somethin hard. A voice from somewhere said: 'What you all doing here? What you after?' Ever body lit a shuck to the car and nobody ever did go back to see about the treasure. You says why did I run? Dese feets wuz made to take care of this body and I used em is all.

"When ah was a young man and livin down in Louisiana below Farmerville ah went with a bunch of white fellows to dig fer buried gold. They didn't begin diggin until after dark. Six men were on guard. We dug by a light made by a big pine torch. Dug and dug and dug. Finally we struck hit. Got hit all uncovered and sure nuff there hit was. Jest then the torch blew out and we heard the quarest noises and ever' body run to camp. Hit jest poured down rain that night and the next mornin, we went back to get the money and hit was gone.

"And you says you is interested in spooks and ghosties. Down in Louisiana Dr. Fred Hodge (white) had me to hitch up his buggy and go with him on my horse to make a call many miles away from home one night. Hit must have ben bout nineteen miles. I was ter go on some other place with him but the patient was so bad that he had ter stay and sent me on in the buggy an kept my horse to ride back. I was glad to git the buggy sos I could take my gal for a ride. The doctor stayed till bout four o'clock in the mornin. He had to go home by a graveyard. There was a big white oak tree growin by the side of the road and when the doctor passed there every limb fell off the tree and left the naked tree standin there. The doctor rode back to the house where he had been and he rode so fast that the horse was winded when he got there. The man went on back with him and there stood the tree just as hit was before ever a limb fell ofn it.

"Nother man I knew went to town on horseback and bought a bolt of domestic for his wife and tied it on the back of his saddle. He had to pass a cemetery. Jest as he passed he noticed a flapping sound and looked back to see sumpin white wavin behind. He whipped his horse and made him run and the faster he ran the more the flapping sounded and it got longer and longer behind him. At last he got home and found that the domestic had got unwrapped and was flappin in the wind. The man was plumb weak and the horse died he had run him so hard.

"An talk of hainted houses. This here one that ahm livin in is hainted. Frank Thompson a yaller nigger died here before me and mah wife moved here. Before mah wife died, weuns would hear things and mah wife said hit was Frank Thompson come back. We would be in bed and would hear fokes walkin aroun and the door would come unlatched and come open. Mah wife would say that hit wes Frank Thompson's sperit come back and as soon as he got through ramblin aroun she would git up and bolt the door agin. One Satiday night me and her went to town. On our way back as we wuz comin acrost that little ditch out thar she said to me step aside Marion and let Frank Thompson pass. Don' you see him comin? And we stepped aside an she said he passed and we come on home. Ah hears him now at times walkin aroun and goin in and out the doors but ah aint never done seen him like she has.

"Now ah'll tell you about a curious happenin'. One time down in Louisiana a brown skin girl died. When they started to the graveyard with her the sun was shinin as purty as hit is right now they lowered the coffin in the grave and it 'come-inced' to rain hard and ever'body run in the church and stayed till it quit raining. The rain stood in holes and puddles and ever'body expected the grave to be full but when we went out there was not a bit of water in the grave. How come if it wasn't hoodooed?

"Ah jes aint wound up right this mawnin to tell youns what you wants to know but if you all will come back ahm sure ah can member some more ah knows."

And Uncle Marion kept working with the chair in which he was weaving a new bottom of white-oak splits. Before we left he showed us baskets that he had woven.

Old Della Benton can neither read nor write and doesn't know her age she must be near seventy. Della was my washwoman several years ago and I remembered hearing her tell something about hoodoes so we went to see Della to get all we could about it.

"Honey don' you know that if you make a hole in a tree and put a hair from the head of the person you want to hoodoo in the tree and seal it up in there the person will go crazy. Yas mam and ifn you puts pins and needles in with the hair before you seals the hole they will die. Why my neighbor Angelina Thompson was hoodood by a woman and Ah'll jest take you all ovah and let her tell you for herself.

"And ifn you all wants to drive somebody away fum home sos they'll nevah come back take one of their hairs and put hit in a steam of runnin water so hit'll run off and they will leave home and nevah come back.

"An somebody can git your track and run you slam crazy. Yasum they kin too. Where you steps in the clay or mud they gits hit and takes hit up with sumpin and does things to you and you goes crazy.

"Now you chillun come with me ovah to Sister Thompson's and she kin tell you fer herself what was done done to her when she wuz hoodooed."

We went to a nearby house and Della called Angelina out. She told us that she was truly hoodoed and what she said was as follows:

"Sister Thompson tell these ladies about bein hoodooed. Oh they is alright. This is some of my white folks I used to work fuh long time ago."

Then Angelina told the following:

"Yasum, I sholey wuz hoodooed. How hit come about I loaned my clothes to a woman. A dress and shoes. She put something on them that looked like snuff. It was brown lookin and I jes though she had spilled snuff on em. That wuz 18 years ago and she done hit outa jealousy. She wanted my ole man and she thought she would hoodoo me and ahd die and she'd get him. And she woulda too ifn hit hadn a been for Mother Dye. You all know she's a doodoo doctor who lived at Newport. An I went to her fer bout two years and she cured me. Mother Dye is daid now but Jess Rogers, a man thar does the docterin now.

"You all ask how hit fected me when ah was hoodooed. I tole you bout the brown stuff bein in my shoes and on mah dress. Well ah put em on and in a little while mah feet itched lak an could claw the bones out. Ah nevah was in such misery. Then ah tuk somethin like the dry rot. The meat come off my fingers and toes. Jest look at them scars. And look at these scars in mah hair. See how mah haid is all scarred up. At times ah had a mind that ah wanted to go and didn' know where. They had to watch me all the time. But ole Mother Dye cured me and that woman didn' git mah ole man aftah all."

Della and Angelina talked among themselves for a moment and Della said "Ah believe ah will." Then she said: "Does you all know Phil Green? He lives about two miles and a half down the Junction City Highway and he is a hoodoo man. He can tell you all things efn you all cares to go ahll go with you. He can tell you what is gwianter happen and what has happened and he can hoodoo." Of course we were in for going right then while we had a car so Della crawled in the back seat and we were away to Phil Green's. Went out the highway about two miles and turned off on a country road. Up hill and down, around this field and that and through a big gate, winding around through a field and orchard. At last we arrived. Phil Green looked to be a prosperous farmer. We drove up to the back of the house and around front. Some negro had just killed a chicken for dinner. Several cars were parked in the yard. One bore a Louisiana license. The porch was full of negroes. Della called and asked if Phil was there. They replied that he was but that he was busy. Della said, "We wants to see him" and a black negro woman came out to the car. My, but she was furious. We had never seen a negro so angry before. The first thing she did was to tell us that they didn't serve white people but the way she expressed it was a scream she said: "We don' use white people. No suh! We don' use em. Hits too dangerous. Ah don't care who tole you Phil used white people. He don'. He is may husban and ah won't let him."

We soon pacified her by telling her that we appreciated her point of view and that it was perfectly alright with us. Della crawled out of the car right now and said: "You all knows the way back to town don' you? Ah's going ter stay."

The next morning we went back to Della's. She told us that the people on Phil's front porch were from Marion Louisiana and they had come to get him to tell them how to get one of the men of the family out of the penitentiary. She apologized for taking us out there and declared that she believed that he once served white people.

Aunt Dilcie Raborn and all her family declared that she would be a hundred this August. She is an ex-slave and Mr. John Wright of Louisiana was her master.

"Yas'm chillun I'se a hunnerd years ole. Ah was one of the las' young niggers on marster's plantation. Mah job was nusin the chillun. Ole Marster's father was livin in them days and he fought in the Resolution War. Yasum he did. He was rail old and my mother chawed fer him jes like she did fer her baby. I'se seen more hardness since I got old than ah ever did in mah life. Slavery wuz the easiest time of all. Mah muthas name was Charity and she wuz the family cook, yasum an ah wuz the nuss girl. I tuk care of the chilluns. Ole marster's wife lost her mind and they had to watch her all the time. Did you ask they send her to the sylum? No man Thar warn't no sylums in them days and anyway ole marster had plenty of niggers to wait on her and take care of her and watch her sos she wouldn't git out and git hurt. She did slip out one time and ah was totin the flour from mill from the gate to the kitchen and she grabbed hit away fum me and throwed hit all ovah me and rubbed hit in mah face good and then laughed at me. Then she run and got in the creek and set down in the watah and the niggas had to git in thar and git her out. Hit made her sick and old marster sho did git them niggers fer lettin her git out.

"I sho wish all times could be slavery times. Ah had everything nice then.

"I had some chillun. Ah cant count em but ah can name em. Joe, Habe, Abram, Billy, Johnny, Charity and Caline. Ah makes mah home here with Charity, she is mah baby chile and she is fifty.

"You asks is ah afeard of haints? Ah'v never taken no frightment off'n em. Ah'v lived in houses other folks couldn't live in but ah'v never lived that way that I had to run from haints.

"Ah lived jes like a millionaire when ah lived in slavery times, seed more hardness since I got old than I ever did in mah life."

Then we left aunt Dilcie with her snuff and went to find Aunt Jane Carter.

After rambling around in Rock Island quarters we at last found Jane Carter. She was living with her grand daughter and was sitting out in the yard with a bunch of her great-grand-children. She was so deaf that we were not able to talk to her, much to our disappointment. The granddaughter told us that she was 106 years old and that Mrs. Roscoe Taunton's granfather was Jane's old master.

We later saw Mrs. Taunton and she told us that Jane had belonged to her grandfather Stephen Manning and was her mother's nurse. Jane was grown when Mrs. Taunton's mother was born.

We were told about old Bill who lives in Barton Quarters and went to find her. She was sitting out on the porch of her cabin and we sat on the edge of the porch much to the dismay of Bill who could not walk because of a sore foot which she told us was caused by the bite of a rattlesnake years ago in slavery time.

"Ah don' want mah white folks to sit on the floo'. Honey go in dah and git dat sheet and spred hit on the floo'. Ole Bill would go herself efn she could walk. Honey you all is gwianter git blistered out in de sun like you is widout no hats on. Don you all know you had orter take keer of thet purty white skin of yourn? My ole missus never would git out in the sun widout somethin on her haid. Ole Mawster thought she was purty and she aimed to stay purty.

"You all says you wants ter heah ole Bill tell about slavery days, lawsy chillun Ah pray ter God ah'll be with mah white chillun agin and play mah harp with em. We'll have plenty to eat and plenty to wear jes as we did when we had our good mawster in slavery days. Marster's grown son used to say: 'Bill she's ruint to death.' Why I used ter git my young mistesses dresses and put em on and git out in the yard and flounce and flip. The young mistess would scole me but young marster would say 'Leave Bill erlone, ah lack to see her dance. Dance some moah Bill.' Mah white folks use ter teach me. Now when white folks taugh me ahm a nigger done taughted.

"Honey ah jes don' like ter see mah white folks sit on the floo' ah wishes ole Bill cud foch some cheers fer yo all ter set on.

"How ole is ah? Ah jes don' member but ah's powerful ole.

"Yas'm ah' wuz nurse girl for marsters chillun. I nevah had ter wuk hard a tall, all ah had ter do was play wid the chillun and take keer of em. Oncet a circus show comed thru and mawster bought a rattle snake fum em fer a pet. Hit nevah did have hits teeth pulled (fangs). Hit wuz a plum pet too, allus followin us about. We would have to knock hit back outn de way sometimes. One time ah wuz comin down de stairs wid a chile in each arm and de snake wuz crawlin erlong sides me. Jest as we got ter the bottom hit crawled roun front of me and ah didn see hit cause of havin the chillun in mah arms and ah stepped slambang on that snake an hit turnt aroun and bit mah foot. Ah nevah drapped them chillun though. My ole man said ifn hit had been him he'd a throwd them chillun down and run but not ole Bill. Marster and Mistess trusted Bill to take keer of them chillun and ole Bill sho did take keer of em. But mah foot nigh bout kilt me and thet foot is whut is the mattah wid me terday.

"You ask haint ah got no folks? No'm. Ah nevah had but one youngun and hit died wid the croup. The man next doo' owns this heah house and lets ole Bill live heah. The guvment lady send me a check ever' month (pension) and Joe Lyons gits hit and fetches hit out ter me.

"You ask does ah know erbout any hainted houses? No'm when ah fin's a house is hainted ah aint gwian in. No'm not ole Bill. But sumpin happened not long ergo that give me a big fright. Hit waz long bout dusk ah seed two women, white as anybody gwian down de road and when they got along thar they quit the road and come aroun the path. Ah said: 'Howdy' and they never even speak jus kep' a goin'. Ah say: 'Whar is you all a goin' and they nevah say a word. Then ah say to em: 'Won't you all come by and set with ole Bill a while.' An still they nevah say nothin. Jus kep' on a goin' roun' that house and down the road. Then ah got skeered and went in the house an ah doan set out late no moah. Efn them ghost had uh come in th house ah would a gone undah the house.

"You all chillun ain goin is you? Come back ter see ole Bill. Ah sholey hates to have mah white folks sit on the floor but mebby ole Bill's foot will be bettuh next time an she can git her white fokes some cheers."

Aunt Sally Fields said to be 106 years old lived in Mack Quarters about two and a half or three miles south of El Dorado. She is blind and lives with Hattie Moseley. During slavery days she belonged to the Patterson family and came with them from Alabama to Louisiana and later to Caledonia where she was living at the close of the Civil War. Her mind was wandering to such an extent that we could not get very much from her and when asked about slavery times she said:

"Slavery time is gone. The stars are passed. The white folks that raised me said: 'I want you all to get up in the morning and tell me about the stars.' Oh Lordy! The stars fell. Ole Missus would come say: 'Ah want to be standing up behind the door. Ah don' want to be buried.' My ole missus was good to all the niggers.

"There was a big spring on marsters plantation. When we would start to the spring mistress would say: 'Don't go on the left hand side of the spring, go up the right hand side to the chinquapin tree.'"

It took Sally about twenty minutes to say that much so we didn't stay longer.

United States. Work Projects Administration

Interviewer: Carol Graham
Person Interviewed: Pinkie Howard (Add)
El Dorado, Ark.
Age: ?

PINKIE HOWARD

"Mornin', honey! Here you is to see Aunt Pinkie again. What did you bring me? Didn't you bring old Aunt Pinkie somethin' good to eat?

"Lawsy, honey, its been so long I can't member much bout plantation days. But I members the children on the plantation would ring up and play ring games. And we used to have the best things to eat back in them days. We used to take taters and grate them and make tater pudding. Made it in ovens. Made corn bread and light bread in ovens too and I used to bake the best biscuits anybody ever et and I didn't put my scratchers in them neither. Old Miss taught me how. And we had lasses pone corn bread and them good old tater biscuits. We used to eat parched corn, and cornmeal dumplings was all the go back there.

"I worked all my life and hard, too, but I still is a pretty good old frame.

"He! He! He! Look at that black boy passing, will you? Them brichie legs is half way his thighs. He needs to put sugar in his shoes to sweet talk his brichie legs down. And did you notice he didn't speak to old Aunt Pinkie. Young folks ain't got no manners these days. Now when I was young back there on that plantation at Hillsboro old Miss Aiken taught all her niggers manners. She would say to us, 'Now, you all don' clean your noses, or years, or fingernails before folks; it's ill manners. And don' make no 'marks bout folks. Don' eat onions and go out in company, if you does, eat coffee to kill the taste. Don't talk with yo' mouth full of sumpin' to eat; that ill manners too. Don' eat too fast cause you is liable to git strangled. And don' wear yo' welcome out by staying too long.'

"Ain't it warm and nice today missy? Jus like a spring day. An see that bee after my flower? Wasn't it a bee? You know, bees used to swarm in the springtime back on the plantation. The way they would catch em was to ring a bell or beat on a old plow and keep beatin' and ringin' till they settled on a tree limb. Then they made a bee gum and covered it and left a hole at the bottom of the gum for them to go in and out, then they sawed the limb off and put the bees in the gum and put some sweetened water made from molasses so they can start to makin' honey. Sometimes the bees would sting some of us and we would put a little snuff on it and cure it right up."

Interviewer: Miss Irene Robertson
Person interviewed: Josephine Howell
Brinkley, Arkansas
Age: 72

JOSEPHINE HOWELL

"My mother was Rebecca Jones. She was born in Nashville, Tennessee. Grandma was a cook and a breeding woman. The Jones thought she was very valuable. They prized her high. She was the mother of twenty-one children. Mother was more than half Indian. She was bright color. The Jones wanted to keep her, thought she would be a fine cook and house woman and a fine breeder. She had such a terrible temper they sold her to McAlways, some of their relations close to Augusta, Arkansas.

"Mama said she was eight years old when Gabe McAlway come to Nashville, Tennessee and got her. He bought her. He was a young man and a saloon-keeper at Augusta, Arkansas. He put her out on the farm at his father's. She was a field hand. She was part African and a whole lot Indian. She was fractious and high tempered. The old man McAlway and the overseers would drop her clothes down in the field before all the hands and whoop her. Gabe never even slapped her. His aunt Mrs. Jones didn't want them to put her in the field. She wanted to keep her but couldn't she was so fractious, and she didn't know how bad old man treated her.

"When mother was sold she was brought from twenty brothers and her mother and never saw none of them no more. She left them at Wolf River. They took the boat. Wolf River is close to Memphis. They must have brought them that far but I don't know. This is what all she told me minua and minua time. Her own papa bought her when she was eight years old, Gabe McAlway. When she got to be a young maid he forced motherhood up on her. I was born before freedom. How old I am I don't know. Gabe McAlway was sort of a young bachelor. He got killed in the Civil War. He was a Scotch-Irishman. I never seen my father.

"Mother married then and had five children. She lived in the back yard of Mrs. Will Thompson. Dr. Goodridge stopped her from having children, she raved wild. She had such a bad fractious temper. She suckled both Mrs. Will Thompson's children, old man Nathan McGreggor's grandchildren. She lived in Mrs. Thompson's back yard but she slept in their house to help with the babies.

"Judge Milwee's wife and auntie, Mrs. Baxter, raised me from a baby (infant). Judge Milwee was in Brinkley but he moved to Little Rock. Them is my own dear white folks. Honey, I can't help but love them, they part of me. They raised me. They learned me how to do everything.

"My son live with me and I raising my little great-grandson. We can't throw him away. My baby's mother is way off in St. Louis. He is three years old.

"Mother never talked much about slavery other than I have told you. She said during of the War women split and sawed rails and laid fences all winter like men. Food got scarce. They sent milk to the soldiers. Meat was scarce. After she was free she went on like she had been living at John McAlway's. She said she didn't know how to start doing for herself.

"Some of our young generation is all right and some of them is too thoughtless. Times is too fast. Folks is shortening their days by fast living. Hurting their own bodies. Forty years ago folks lived like we ought to be living now."

United States. Work Projects Administration

Interviewer: Miss Irene Robertson
Person interviewed: Pauline Howell Nickname Pearl
Brinkley, Arkansas
Age: 65 or 70?

AULINE HOWELL PEARL

"I was born in Paris, Tennessee and come to Arkansas when I was a child. I don't know how old I am but my mama knowed 'bout when I was born. It warnt long after the war. I past sixty-five and it is nearer seventy from what she said. She ain't been dead long. She was about a hundred years old. I. C. switch killed her. She was going cross there to Fisher Body and the switch engine struck her head. She dropped something and stooped to pick it up or the engine wouldn't touched her. She lived in Memphis.

"She was born at Oaks, Tennessee. She took me down to see the cabin locks where she was born. They had rotted down and somebody lived in the big house. It had gone to rack then pretty bad. My father's master was George Harris. He was Governor of Tennessee. My mother's mistress at Oaks was Miss Ann LaGuion (or maybe Gwion). I never heard her husband's name. They had several farms and on each farm was the cabin locks (little houses all in a row or two rows). The houses was exactly alike. Grandma cooked for the white folks and mama nursed. The baby was a big fat heavy sort, a boy, and it was so heavy she couldn't hardly pick it up. She had to carry it around all day long. When night come she was wore out.

There was several of them. When she go to their houses in Memphis they honor her. They take her down town and buy her shoes and dresses. Buy her whatever she say she want. They say they was proud of her. She was a little black guinea woman (low and stocky). Not long go Mr. (white man) in Brinkley asked me when my ma coming back here. Said he ain't seed her for so long. I tole him she was dead. He said he have to go tell Mrs. _____ (his wife). She come out here and stay and piece quilts. She sewed so nice. Made pretty little stitches. She'd take the most time and pains fixing the pieces together to look pretty. She'd set there and sew and me over there and tell me bout how she was raised and I'd cry. Cry cause she had so hard a time when she was a girl.

"The old master sent my father to Liverpool, England to bury his money. He was his own son anyhow. Sent him with his money to keep the Yankees from taking it. My aunt, my father and Uncle Jesse all his own children. Course old mistress love them little children like her own. She couldn't help herself.

"Mariah Steed went in Governor Harrises name after freedom. So did Randall Travis Harris.

"My mama said she was never sold but her sister and her children were. She was put upon the auction stile and all her little children. A man in Mobile, Alabama bought her. They never did see nor hear tell of her no more. The reason they sold her was she killed two men overseers. They couldn't manage her. The last one was whipping her with a black snake whip and she grabbed him. Grabbed his privates and pulled 'em out by the roots. That the way she killed both the overseers. Cause she knowed that was show death. My mama said that was the nicest little soft man—the last man she killed. She said he just clum the walls in so much misery that night.

"She said they would whisper after they go to bed. They used pine torches for lights. They had to cover up the fire—cover up fire in the ashes so it be coals to kindle a fire in the morning—put out the light pretty early. Old master come stand round outside see if they all gone to bed.

"When freedom—my mama said old master called all of 'em to his house and he said: 'You all free, we ain't got nothing to do wid you no more. Go on away. We don't whoop you no more, go on your way.' My mama said they go on off then they come back and stand around jess lookin' at him an' old mistress. They give 'em something to eat and he say: 'Go on away, you don't belong to us no more you been freed.'

"They go way and they kept coming back. They didn't have no place to go and nothing to eat. From what she said they had a terrible time. She said it was bad times. Some took sick and had no 'tention and died. Seemed like it was four or five years before they got to places they could live. They all got scattered.

"She said they did expect something from freedom but the only thing old master give Jesse was a horse and bridle and saddle. It was new. Old master every time they go back say: 'You all go on away. You been set free. You have to look out for your selves now.'

"The only way I know this is I remembers from hearin' my dear old mama tell me when she come here to see me. I was too little. I guess I wasn't born till two or three years, maybe longer than that, after freedom.

"After my son died here I get $2.50 a month, just my house rent. I work out when I can get something to do. Work is so scarce I hardly get a living.

"If you could see my brother in Little Rock he could tell you a heap he remembers. He is white headed, keeps his hair cut close and goes dressed up all the time. They say he is a good old man. He does public work in Little Rock. Henry Travis is his son. His phone is 4–5353. His street is 3106 Arch. My brother is really born a slave, I ain't. Ask for E. K. Travis, that is his name. He can tell you bout all you want to know."

JAN 29 1938
Interviewer: Miss Irene Robertson
Person interviewed: Molly Hudgens
DeValls Bluff, Arkansas
Age: Born in 1868

MOLLY HUDGENS

"I was born in Clarendon in 1868. My mother was sold to Judge Allen at Bihalia, N. C. and brought to Arkansas. The Cunninghams brought father from Tennessee when they moved to this State. His mother died when he was three months old and the white mistress had a baby three weeks older en him so she raised my father. She nursed him with Gus Cunningham. My father had us call them Grandma, Aunt Indiana, and Aunt Imogene.

"When I was seven or eight years old I went to see them at Roe. When I first come to know how things was, father had bought a place—home and piece of land west of Clarendon and across the river. I don't know if the Cunninghams ever give him some land or a mule or cow or not. He never said. His owner was Moster John Henry Cunningham.

"My father was a medium light man but not as light as I am. My mother was lighter than I am. I heard her say her mother did the sewing for all on her owner's place in North Carolina. My mother was a house girl. The reason she was put up to be sold she was hired out and they put her in the field to work. A dispute rose over her some way so her owner sold her when she was eighteen years old. Her mother was crying and begging them not to sell her but it didn't do no good she said. After the war was over she got somebody to write back and ask about her people. She got word about her sister and aunt and uncle. She never seen none of them after she was sold. Never did see a one of her people again. She was sold to Judge Allen for a house girl. His wife was dead. My mother sewed at Judge Allen's and raised two little colored children he bought somewhere cheap. He had a nephew that lived with him.

"Mr. Felix Allen and some other of his kin folks, one of them made me call him 'Tuscumby Bob.' I said it funny and they would laugh at me. Judge Allen went to Memphis and come home and took smallpox and died. I heard my mother say she seen him crying, sitting out under a tree. He said he recken he would give smallpox to all the colored folks on his place. Some of them took smallpox.

"We have been good living colored folks, had a right smart. I farmed, cooked, sewed a little along. I washed. I been living in DeValls Bluff 38 years. I got down and they put me on the relief. Seems I can't get back to going agin.

"Don't get me started on this young generation. I don't want to start talking about how they do. Times is right smartly changed somehow. Everybody is in a hurry to do something and it turns out they don't do nuthin'. Times is all in a stir it seem like to me.

"I don't vote. I get $8 and demodities and I make the rest of my keepin'."

Interviewer: Miss Irene Robertson
Person interviewed: Charlie Huff
Brinkley, Arkansas
Age: Born 1864

CHARLIE HUFF

"I was born close to Charlotte, North Carolina. Alex Huff owned my parents and me. My pa was a dark man. He was named Alex Huff too. Ma was named Sarah Huff. She was ginger cake color they called it. Both her parents was part Creek Indian. I seen the block at Richmond, Virginia where they sold pa. They kept him three weeks away from me before he was sold. They sold him at the last of slavery for $1,500. Ma never seen him no more. After freedom she brought me and immigrated to Arkansas. My sister wouldn't come, she was fixing to marry. We come on the train, paid our own way. We heard it was a fine country and ma heard somebody out here bought pa. We kept inquiring till after she died. I heard where he was. I went to see him. He told me what I told you. He was sold and brought to Louisiana. He was a cross-eyed man and named Alex the best way I found him. My ma never was sold as she remembered.

"Master Alex Huff owned a turpentine factory and pa worked at it. Ma washed and cooked. Master Alex Huff raised Palmer Christy beans. I think he sold the seed to keep moles out of the land. Moles was bad in new cleared land. When they found a mole hill they opened it and put in a few beans so the mole would eat them and die. He sold the beans.

"The Ku Klux never bothered us.

"We come to Arkansas as soon as we could after freedom. We wanted to find pa. When we first come I worked on a steamboat, then I mined at Pratt City, Tennessee—coal mines—a year and a half. Then for forty-five years I worked on the railroad section as a hand. I made two crops in all my life. The first year I did fine and not so bad the next. But since three years ago I had these two strokes. I am here and not able to work. My wife draws $12 from the Welfare Order.

"It has been a long time since I voted. I voted last time for President McKinley. I didn't like the strict franchise laws."

Interviewer: Miss Irene Robertson
Person interviewed: Louvenia Huff
Brinkley, Arkansas
Age: 64

LOUVENIA HUFF

"I was born third year after the surrender. There was thirteen children in my family when I was a child. We was different sizes and the grown children helped look after the little ones. My parents was field hands. My parents belong to Dr. Hatch. He lived in Aberdeen, Mississippi. We lived in the country on his place. He had five or six children. Ben and Needham come out to the farm. He was an old man and we stayed on the son's place—same place—till I come to Arkansas. We come in 1885. We heard it was a better country and open stock range. Dr. Hatch was very good to my folks.

"I don't think the Ku Klux bothered my folks but we was afraid of them.

"My father voted a Republican ticket. I never voted.

"My grandmother was real light skin. Mother was mixed with white. She told us she was sold away from her mother when she was a little bitter of a girl and never seen her no more till she was the mother of six children. They didn't know one another when they met. Her mother knowed who bought her and after freedom she kept asking about her and finally heard where she was and come to her. There was no selling place at Aberdeen so I don't know where she was bought. Dr. Hatch lived to be an old man. He owned a lot of slaves and lots of land.

"Father's old master was Whitfield. He sold him to Dr. Hatch when he was a young man. Father was a driver in the Civil War. He hauled soldiers and dumped them in the river. The Union soldiers wouldn't give them time to bury the other side. He took rations all but the times he hauled dead soldiers. He got shot in his arm above the wrist. He died before they give him a pension. He was a Union soldier. He talked a lot but that is all I can tell straight. I don't know if he mustered out or not.

"I worked in the field, wash, iron, and cooked. We get $12 from the Welfare. My husband had two strokes. He has been sick three years.

"My parents' name Simpson Hatch and Jacob Hatch. They had thirteen children."

Interviewer: Mary D. Hudgins
Person Interviewed: Mrs. Anna Huggins
Home: Pleasant at John Street.

MRS. ANNA HUGGINS

"Miss Huggins? (pronounced hew–gins) Yes, ma'am she lives here. Oh Miss Huggins, Miss Huggins. They's somebody to see you."

The interviewer had approached an open door of an "L" kitchen attached to a "shot gun house". Thru the dining room and a bed room she was conducted to the front bedroom. This was furnished simply but with a good deal of elaboration. The bed was gay with brightly colored pillows. Most of them had petal pillow tops made from brilliant crepe paper touched with silver and guilt. The room was evidently not occupied by Mrs. Huggins herself for late in the interview a colored girl entered the room. "Do you want your room now?" Mrs. Huggins inquired. "No indeed, there's lots of time," the girl replied politely. But the interviewer managed to terminate the interview quickly.

"So you knew Fanny McCarty. Well, well, so you knew Fanny. I don't know when I've heard anybody speak about her. She's not so much on looks, but Fanny is a good little woman, a mighty good little woman. She's up in Michigan. You know she worked at one of the big hotels here—the Eastman it was. When they closed in the summer they sent her up to the big hotel on Mackinac. For a while she was here in the winter and up there for the summer season. Then she stayed on up there.

"You say she worked for you when you were a little girl? Before the fire of 1913? Now, I remember, you were just a little girl and you used to come over to my house sometimes with her. I remember." (A delighted smile.) "Now I remember.

"No, I don't remember very much about the war. It is mostly what I heard the older ones say. My grandmother used to tell me a lot about it. I was just a little thing in my mother's arms when the war was over. Guess I was about four years old. We lived in St. Francis County and as soon as we were free pappa sent for us. He sent for us to come by boat to where he was. We went to Helena. I remember they were all lined up—the colored soldiers were. But I knew pappa. They all wondered how, hadn't seen him in a long time. But I picked him out of all the line of men and I said, 'There's my pappa.' Yes, my pappa was a soldier in the war. He was gone from home most of the time. I only saw him once in a while.

"My grandmother told me lots of things about slavery. She was born a free girl. But when she was just a little girl somebody stole her and brought her to Arkansas and sold her. No, from the things they told me—especially grandmother—they weren't very good to them. Lots of times I've gone down on my knees to my grandmother to hear her tell about how mean they were to them.

"I'd say to her, 'Grandmother, why didn't you fight back?' 'You couldn't fight back,' she said, 'you just had to take it.' 'I wouldn't,' I said, 'I wouldn't take it.' Guess there's too much Indian blood in me. A white person never struck me but once. I was a girl—not so very big and I was taking care of a white lady's little girl. She and a friend of hers were talking and I sneaked up to the door and tried to listen to what they were saying. She caught me and she scolded me—she struck at me with her fan—it was just a light tap, but it made me mad. I fought her and I ran off home, she came to get me too. I never would have gone back otherways. She said she never did see a girl better with children.

"I remember my grandmother telling about once when she was cooking in the kitchen, her back was turned and an old hound dog got in and started to take the chicken which was on the table. He had even got part of it in his mouth. But she turned and saw him—she choked the dog—and choked him until she choked the chicken out of him. You can see she must have been pretty scared to be afraid to let them know the chicken had been tampered with. Then we always thought my mother's death was caused by her being beat by an overseer—she caused that overseer's death, she got him while he was beating her. They had to hide her out to save her life—but a long time afterwards she died—we always laid it to that hard beating.

"We lived in Helena after the war. My father was the marrying kind. He was a wild marrying man. He had lots of wives. But Mother and grandmother wouldn't let us call them Mother—she made us call them Aunt. It really was my grandmother who reared me. She was a good cook, had good jobs all the time.

"When I grew up I married. Mr. Huggins was a bar tender in a saloon. He made good money. We had a good home and I took care of the home. I had it mighty easy. Then one day he fell in the floor paralyzed. I brought him to Hot Springs. That was back in 1905. We stayed on and he lived for 18 years.

"I got a house there and I kept roomers. That was where Fanny stayed with me. It was at 311 Pleasant. You remember the place, tho. When I was young, I had it easy. But now I'm old and I don't have it so well. A few years ago I was out in California on a visit. There was a man shining up to me and I wrote my niece 'What would you think if your aunty married?' 'Law,' she wrote back to me, 'you've lived by yourself so long now, you couldn't stand a man.' Maybe she was right."

(At this point the girl passed into the room.) "Look Maggie! three pretty handkerchiefs. Miss Hudgins brought them. And I was just writing to my sister—my half sister today, I didn't even expect to much as a handkerchief for Christmas. And my initials embroidered on them two. One with A on it and two with H. I'm really proud of them.

"I'm going to write to Fanny to tell her about your coming to see me. She'll be so glad to know about you. I'll tell her about the handkerchiefs. You know, for a while Fanny had it pretty hard while she was here. She stayed at my house and I kept her for a long time without pay. I knew Fanny was a good girl and that when she got work she would pay me back. Do you know what Fanny has done? When she heard I was hard up she wrote me and told me to come up to Michigan to her and she would take care of me just as I had taken care of her. But I didn't want to go. Wasn't it nice of her, though?

"Yes, when I was young I had it easy. I had my home and took care of it. If I needed more money, I mortgaged my home and paid it back. Then I'd mortgage it and pay it back. But I mortgaged it once too often. That time I couldn't pay it back. I lost it.

"Well, I'm so glad you came to see me. I remember the pretty little girl who used to come to my house with Fanny. Be sure to write to her, she'll appreciate it, and thank you for the handkerchiefs."

United States. Work Projects Administration

Interviewer: Mrs. Annie L. LaCotts
Person interviewed: Margret Hulm, Humphrey, Arkansas
Age: 97

(Story of Abraham Lincoln as a spy)

MARGRET HULM

In the west edge of Humphrey in a small house beneath huge old trees lives an aged Negro woman with her boy (61 years old) and his wife. This woman is Margret Hulm who says she was born March 5, 1840 in Hardeman County, Tennessee. When asked if she remembered anything about the war and slavery days she said:

"Oh yes mam. I was 24 years old when the slaves were set free. My folks belonged to Master Jimmie Pruitt, who owned lots of other slaves. When they told him his niggers were free, he let them go or let them stay on with him and he'd give them a place to live and some of the crops. I guess that's what folks call a share crop now. I was what folks called a house girl. I didn't work in the field like some of the other slaves. I waited on my mistress and her chillun, answered the door, waited on de table and done things like that. I remember Mr. Lincoln. He came one day to our house (I mean my white folks' house). They told me to answer the door and when I opened it there stood a big man with a gray blanket around him for a cape. He had a string tied around his neck to hold it on. A part of it was turned down over the string like a ghost cape. How was he dressed beneath the blanket? Well, he had on jeans pants and big mud boots and a big black hat kinda like men wear now. He stayed all night. We treated him nice like we did everybody when they come to our house. We heard after he was gone that he was Abraham Lincoln and he was a spy. That was before the war. Oh, yes, I remember lots about the war. I remember dark days what we called the black days. It would be so dark you couldn't see the sun even. That was from the smoke from the fighting. You could just hear the big guns going b-o-o-m, boom, all day. Yes, I do remember seeing the Yankees. I saw 'em running fast one day past our house going back away from the fighting place. And once they hung our master. They told him they wanted his money. He said he didn't have but one dollar. They said 'we know better than that.' Then they took a big rope off of one de Yankee's saddle and took de master down in de horse lot and hung him to a big tree. The rope must a been old, for it broke. Our master was a big man though. Then they hung him again. He told 'em he didn't have but one dollar and they let him down and said 'Well, old man, maybe you haven't got any more money.' So they let him go when the mistress and her little chillun come down there. He didn't have but one dollar in his pockets but had lots buried about the place in two or three places."

While Margret was giving this information she was busily sewing together what looked like little square pads. When examined they proved to be tobacco sacks stuffed with cotton and then sewed together which would make a quilt already quilted when she got enough of them sewed together to cover a bed.

Interviewer: S. S. Taylor
Person interviewed: John Hunter
3200 W. 17th Street, Little Rock, Arkansas
Age: 74

JOHN HUNTER

Biographical

John Hunter claims to be only seventy-four years old, but when he is talking he has the manner of an eye-witness to the things he relates. In this connection, many of the ex-slaves seem to be sensitive concerning oldness.

Hunter is blind. He lives with Mrs. Alston, herself the widow of an old ex-slave. His relation to her is simply that of a renter, although where he gets the rent from I don't know.

His father fought in the Confederate army until disabled by disease.

Hunter was born in North Carolina but has lived in this state something like fifty years.

Houses

"Slave houses were old log huts. Some made log houses and some made tent harbors. Just any sort of way on dirt. Some of them didn't have any floors.

"One with a floor was built with one room. Cooked and et and everything in that one room. About 16 × 16. One window. No glass panes in it. Shutter window. Some niggers just built up a log house and dobbed it with dirt to keep the air from coming through.

"Food was kept in an old chest. There weren't no such things as trunks and cupboards. I brought one from North Carolina with me—old-fashioned chest. Bed was homemade and nailed to the side of the wall. Some of them had railings on both sides when they were trying to make it look nice. Mattress was made out of straw or shucks. You could hear it rattling like a hog getting in his bed at night. I have slept on 'em many a time. Those with floors and those without were made alike. A box or anything was used for a table. If his master would give him anything he would make it out of a plank. Make it at night. Boxes and homemade stools were used for chairs. No chairs like there is now. People are blessed now. Didn't go asking for no chairs then. They'd give you a chair—over your head.

"They et anything—any way they could get it,—in pans, old wooden trays, pots, anything. Fed you just like little pigs. Poured it all out in something and give them an old wooden spoon and telled them to get down and eat. Sometimes get down on your belly and eat. No dishes for niggers like now. No dishes till after freedom, and often none then."

Tent Harbors

"Sometimes they'd have a great long place with walls in it with logs and planks and divided into stalls just like a man would have a great long place for mules and divide it into stalls. They were called stockades. You can see them in Tensas Parish in Louisiana. Now, each man would take his family and live in his stall. No doors between the rooms. Each room had a door leading into the open. They called 'em 'tent harbors' because they were built more like a tent. Some of them were covered with boards. People would go into the woods and rive out boards with a fro. A fro is a piece of iron about a foot and a half long with an eye in it and a wooden handle in the eye. You would drive it into the log and then work it along until you rived out the board.

"Slave quarters were built right straight on down so that the master could look right down the avenue when he would walk out. Little houses one right after the other."

Food

"The niggers had anything to eat that the master give 'em. He would give plenty such as it was. Certain days they would go up and get it. Give it to 'em just like they go draw rations now. But they'd give it to you not you say what you wanted. So much meal and so much meat, and so on. Some of 'em raised flour. You had to take whatever you could get."

Father and Mother

"My father was a soldier (Confederate). He got sick with the scrofula and they sent him back to his old master, Dr. Harris, in Enfield, North Carolina. *He was a field hand at first, but after he come back with the scrofula, they just made him a carriage driver.* That's how I came to be born in 1864. My father married Betsy Judge right after he came back. They didn't marry then as they do now. Just jumped over the broom."

Patrollers

"A slave couldn't go nowhere without a pass. If they caught you out without a pass, they'd whip you. Jus' like if I wanted to go to a girl's house, my master would hand me a pass. If he didn't, they'd ketch me and whip me if I got out and wasn't able to run away from them."

What the Freedmen Expected

"When the slave was freed, he was looking to get a home. They were goin' to do this and goin' to do that but they didn't do nothin'. They let us stay on the place until we made the crop, told us we was free to go wherever we wanted to go. That is all they give us and all we got. Some said, 'You promised to give us a home', and they said to them, 'Well, you can stay here as long as you live.'"

How Freedom Came

"The old master called them together and told them they was free. 'Peace declared. You all have to go for yourselves. Won't whip no more now. You are all free.'"

Runaways and Mean Masters

"My father's master was right smart mean to him. It was partly my father's fault. He wouldn't take no whipping much. If they would get after him he would run off. Whenever there was anything they wanted him to do and he didn't go and do it just that minute, they wanted to whip him. Jus' like a child, you know. He had to move when he was told. If he didn't do it then he got a whipping. He would run away in the woods and stay a week or two before he'd come back. Sometimes some of the boys would see him and they would say to him, 'Old master says for you to come back home; he ain't goin' to do nothin' to you.' Nobody would go in the woods and hunt him. Some of them would go in there and get hurt.

"There was some masters that would go in the woods hunting their niggers. Sometimes they'd carry bloodhounds with them. They never did run my father with the bloodhounds though.

"My mother's master and mistress was good to her. They never drove her around. Old man Judge died and left her mistress and she lived a widow the balance of her life. But she never gave my mother no trouble."

Sales and Separations

"There was plenty of slaves being put up on the block and sold. My mother was sold. Her father was a Cooper and she was sold to Judge. He bought my mother's mother and her both, so that made her a Judge. He bought her and she had to go in his name. Her husband was left with the Coopers. She was put up on the block. 'Who will give me a bid on this woman?' The old man was bid back. The Coopers bid him back."

School

"My mother didn't get no schooling no more'n what I learned her after freedom. She never went to school in her life. Still she saw she could read the Bible, the hymn-book, and such things like that as she wanted to before she died."

What the Slaves Got

"They said that the President and the Governor was going to give land to the niggers—going to take it off the owners that they worked for. But they never did get it."

Ku Klux Klan

"I heered talk of the Ku Klux. I can remember once when they come through there (Enfield). That was eight or ten years after the War. They would ketch some of the niggers and whip them. The young niggers got their guns and rigged up a plan to kill them and laid out in a place for them, but they got wind of it and stopped coming."

Mother's Occupation

"My mother was a great weaver. She would weave cloth for the hands on the place. Some days she would work around the house and some other days she'd go out and weave. When they wasn't any weaving or spinning to be done, she'd go out in the field. The weaving and the spinning was right in the white folks' house."

Own Occupation

"I used to be a preacher. Don't do much of nothin' now. Ain't able. Get a little help from the Welfare—a little groceries sometimes. Don't get any pension. You see, I can't do much on account of my blindness."

Opinions of Young People

"I can't tell you what I think of the young people. Times have got to be so fast. It is just terrible to think how this life is. So much change from forty to fifty years ago. Just as much difference on both sides, white and colored, as there is between chalk and cheese."

Praying Under Pots

"When they'd go to have a church meeting, they turn up the pot so that the noise wouldn't come out. They could go to the white folks' church. But the spirit would come on them sometimes to have service themselves. Then they'd go down to the house at night and turn up those big old iron pots and master never would hear. They wouldn't put the washpot flat on the ground. They'd put sticks under it and raise it up about a foot from the ground. If they'd put it flat on the ground the ground would carry the sound."

Voting

"There weren't no voting at all in slavery times (in his locality—ed.) that is, far as the niggers were concerned. But after everybody was free you could vote up until they stopped the people from voting. They kept a Republican ticket in then. There wasn't no Democrat. None like they is now. I don't know how this thing got mixed up like it is now.

"I remember once in North Carolina a man named Bryant got away with a lot of votes in the boxes. He was seen to go out with two boxes under his arms. And when they counted up the votes, the Democrats was ahead. In them days, they counted up the votes before they left the polls. They wanted to kill him. They sent him to the penitentiary to stay five years. When he went in he was a young man, and when he came back he was gray.

"There was some fighting down there that night. My father was a constable. It was the white folks got to fighting each other. They got to 'resting them and they filled the calaboose full that night. Didn't have but one jail and that was in Halifax. The penitentiary was in Raleigh. Raleigh was about 85 miles from Halifax, and Halifax about 75 from Enfield. The jail was twelve miles from Enfield."

Mulattoes

"There were mixed bloods then just like there are now. Them came by the old master, you know. They treated the mulatto a little better than they did the other slaves. You know you would have more respect for your own blood. My Aunt Rena was half-sister to my father. They had the same mother but different fathers and they always gave her a little better treatment than they give him. They didn't sell her. When slavery broke she was still with her master, Old Tom Hollis. The old lady (her mother) was there too. They hadn't sold her neither. But they never give none of them nothin' when they was freed.

"My father was a field hand at first. But after he went to war and come back with the scrofula, they just made him a carriage driver. But he wasn't no mulatto though."

United States. Work Projects Administration

Interviewer: Miss Irene Robertson
Person interviewed: William Hunter, Brinkley, Arkansas
Age: 70

WILLIAM HUNTER

"John McBride was my mother's last owner. His wife died in slavery. I never heard her name called. My mother come from Abbeville, South Carolina, a Negro trading point. When she was put on the block my father went to McBride and asked him to buy that woman for him a wife. He said she was a mighty pretty young woman. McBride bought her. I don't know how they got to Carroll County, Mississippi but that is where I was born. My mother raised Walter and Johnny McBride (white). She nursed one of them along with my brother May—May McBride was his name. That was at Asme, Alabama before I was born. I heard my mother say she never worked in the field but two years in her whole life. It must have been just after the war, for I have seen a ditch she and another woman cut. When they cut it, it was 4 ft. × 4 ft. I don't know the length. When I seed it, it was a creek 100 ft. wide. I don't know how deep. I recollect hearing my father talk about clearing land before freedom but I don't know if he was in Alabama or Mississippi then.

"My mother was mixed with the white race. She was a bright woman. My father was a real dark man. He was a South Carolina gutchen—soft water folks, get mad and can't talk. He was crazy about yellow folks.

"McBride died fifty-one years ago. When I was a boy he carried me with him—right in the buggy or oxcart with him till I was up nineteen years old. He went to the saloon to get a dram. I got one too. When he went to a big hotel to eat something he sent out the kitchen door to me out to our buggy or wagon. We camped sometimes when we went to town. It took so long to go over the roads.

"When freedom was declared McBride called up all his slaves and told em they was free; they could go or stay on. My father moved off two years after freedom and then he moved back and we stayed till the old man died. Then my father went to Varden, Mississippi and worked peoples gardens. He was old then too.

"I never seen a 'white cap' (Ku Klux). I heard a heap of talk about em. The people in Mississippi had respect for colored worship.

"I farmed till we went to Varden, Mississippi. I started working on the section. I was brakeman on the train out from Water Valley. Then I come to Wheatley, Arkansas. I worked on the section. All told, I worked forty years on the section. I worked on a log wagon, with a tire company, at the oil mill and in the cotton mill. I had a home till it went in the Home Loan. I have to pay $2.70 a month payments. I get commodities, no money, from the Welfare. My wife is dead now."

MAY 11 1938
Interviewer: Samuel S. Taylor
Person interviewed: Ida Blackshear Hutchinson
2620 Orange Street, North Little Rock, Arkansas
Age: 73

IDA BLACKSHEAR HUTCHINSON

Birth

"I was born in 1865 in Alabama in Sumter County on Sam Scale's place near the little town called Brushville (?).

Parents and Grandparents

"My father's name was Isom Blackshear. Some people call it Blackshire, but we call it Blackshear. His master was named Uriah Blackshear. I have heard him say so many times the year he was born. He died (Isom) in 1905 and was in his eighty-first year then. That would make him born in 1824. His birth was on the fourth day of May. People back in them days lived longer than we do now. My grandfather, Jordan Martin, lived to be one hundred sixteen years old. Grandpa died about nine years ago in Sumter County, Alabama. He was my grandfather on my mother's side.

"My grandfather on my father's side was Luke Blackshear. He was born in Alabama too, and I suppose in Sumter County too. He died in Sumter County. He died about five years before the Civil War.

"My mother was born in North Carolina. Her name was Sylvia Martin before she married my father. She was a Blackshear when she died. She died in 1885. The white people went out in North Carolina and bought her, her mother, Nancy, and her father, Jordan, and brought them to Sumter County, Alabama. My mother's mother was an Indian; her hair came down to her waist."

Luke Blackshear (Breeder)

"My grandfather on my father's side, Luke Blackshear, was a 'stock' Negro.

"Isom Blackshear, his son, was a great talker. He said Luke was six feet four inches tall and near two hundred fifty pounds in weight. He was what they called a double-jointed man. He was a mechanic,—built houses, made keys, and did all other blacksmith work and shoemaking. He did anything in iron, wood or leather. Really he was an architect as well. He could take raw cowhide and make leather out of it and then make shoes out of the leather.

"Luke was the father of fifty-six children and was known as the GIANT BREEDER. He was bought and given to his young mistress in the same way you would give a mule or colt to a child.

"Although he was a stock Negro, he was whipped and drove just like the other Negroes. All of the other Negroes were driven on the farm. He had to labor but he didn't have to work with the other slaves on the farm unless there was no mechanical work to do. He was given better work because he was a skilled mechanic. He taught Isom blacksmithing, brickmaking and bricklaying, shoemaking, carpentry, and other things. The ordinary blacksmith has to order plow points and put than on, but Luke made the points themselves, and he taught Isom to do it. And he taught him to make mats, chairs, and other weaving work. He died sometime before the War."

Isom Blackshear

"Isom Blackshear, Luke's son and my father, farmed until he was eighteen years old, and was a general mechanic as mentioned when I was telling about my grandfather Luke, for sixty odd years. Up to within seven months of his death, he was making chairs and baskets and other things. He never was in bed in his life until his last sickness. That was his first and his last. Never did he have a doctor's bill to pay or for his master to pay,—until he died. He worked on the batteries at Vicksburg during the War.

"Isom ran away three times. He was a field hand up to eighteen years. The overseer wanted to whip him. Isom would help his wife in the field because she couldn't keep up with the others and he would help her to keep the overseer from whipping her. He'd take her beside him and row his row and hers too. He was the fastest worker on the place. The overseer told him to not do that. But

Isom just kept on doing it anyway. Then the overseer asked Isom for his shirt. When they whipped you them days they didn't whip you on your clothes because they didn't want to wear them out. Isom said he was not going to take off his shirt because his mistress gave it to him and he wasn't going to give it to anybody else. Then the overseer stepped 'round in front of him to stop him, because Isom had just kept on hoeing. Isom just caught the overseer's feet in his hoe and dumped him down on the ground and went on hoeing his own row and his wife's. He called his hoe 'One Eyed Aggie.'

"The overseer said, 'You think you done something smart' and he went for his master. The overseer was named Mack Hainey. His master came out the next morning and caught Isom. Isom has often told us about it.

"'First thing I knowed, he had his feet on my hoe and he said, "Isom, they tell me you can't be whipped." "I'd be willing to be whipped if I'd done anything." "Huh!" said my master, "Right or wrong, if my overseer asked you for your shirt give it to him."'

"He held a pistol on him. They made him pull off his shirt and tied him up to a gin post. The overseer hit him five times and kept him there till noon trying to get him to say that he would give his shirt to him the next time. Finally Isom promised and the overseer untied him. When the overseer untied him, Isom took his shirt in one hand and the overseer's whip in the other and whipped him almost all the way to the big house. Then he ran away and stayed in the woods for three or four days until his old master sent word for him to come on back and he wouldn't do nothing to him.

"When he went back, his master took him off the farm because he and my father was nursed together and he didn't want Isom killed. So from that time on, my father never worked as a field hand any more. And they put Isom's wife as a cook. She couldn't chop cotton fast enough and they couldn't handle Isom as long as she was in the field; so they put her to washing, and ironing, and cooking, and milking.

"The second time father ran away was once when they missed some groceries out of the storeroom. Master asked him if he took them because he made the keys to the place and not a person on the place but him could know anything about getting in there. He didn't own it, so they tied him up and whipped him two days. When night come they took him and tied him in his house and told his wife that if he got loose they would put the portion on her. He didn't try to get loose because he knowed if he did they would whip her, so he stayed. At noon time when they went to get the dinner they poured three buckets of water in his face and almost drowned him. Then after dinner they came back and whipped him again. Finally he said, 'I didn't do it but nothing will suit you but for me to say I did, so I will say I did it.' So he owned up to it.

"A few days later Mr. Horn who owned the adjoining plantation came over and asked him if he had missed anything,—any rations he said. Old master told him 'Yes' and went on to explain what had been taken and what he had done about it. Then Mr. Horn took Mr. Blackshear over to his house and showed him the rations and they were the one he had whipped my old father about. Then Blackshear came back and told my father that he was sorry, that he never had known him to steal anything.

He turned him loose and apologized to him but he made him work with the bloody shirt that they whipped him in sticking to his back.

"The third time he ran off he was in the army working on the batteries at Vicksburg. He worked there till he got to thinking about his wife and children, and then he ran off. He got tired and hungry and he went to Mopilis and give himself up. The jailer written to his master, that is to his mistress, about it, and she got her father to go and see about him and bring him home. They'd had a big storm. The houses were in bad shape. The fences was blown down. The plows was broken or dull and needed fixin'. And they were so glad to see Isom that they didn't whip him nor nothin' for runnin' away.

"Isom's mother was named Winnie Blackshear. She was Luke's wife. She was a light brownskin woman and weighed about one hundred fifty pounds. I have seen her, but Luke was dead before I was born. Grandmother Winnie has been dead about twenty years now. She labored in the field.

"My mother's mother was named Nancy Martin and her father was named Jordan Martin. We kept a Jordan in the family all the way down. Both of them farmed. They were slaves.

"There were fourteen children of us,—eleven sisters and three brothers. The brothers were Jordan, Prince, and John. The sisters were Margaret, Eliza, Nancy, Tempy, Bell, Abbie, Caroline, Frances, Dosia, Mattie, Lucy, Louisa, Ida."

Suicide

"They say Negroes won't commit suicide, but Isom told us of a girl that committed suicide. There was a girl named Lu who used to run off and go to the dances. The patrollers would try to catch her but they couldn't because she was too fast on her feet. One day they got after her in the daytime. She had always outran them at night. She ran to the cabin and got her quarter which she had hid. She put the quarter in her mouth. The white folks didn't allow the slaves to handle no money. The quarter got stuck in her throat, and she went on down to the slough and drowned herself rather than let them beat her, and mark her up. Then patrollers sure would get you and beat you up. If they couldn't catch you when you were running away from them, they would come on your master's place and get you and beat you. The master would allow them to do it. They didn't let the patrollers come on the Blackshear place, but this gal was so hard-headed 'bout goin' out that they made a 'ception to her. And they intended to make her an example to the rest of the slaves. But they didn't get Lucy."

Death of Sixty Babies

"Once on the Blackshear place, they took all the fine looking boys and girls that was thirteen years old or older and put them in a big barn after they had stripped them naked. They used to strip them naked and put them in a big barn every Sunday and leave them there until Monday morning. Out of that came sixty babies.

"They was too many babies to leave in the quarters for some one to take care of during the day. When the young mothers went to work Blackshear had them take their babies with them to the field, and it was two or three miles from the house to the field. He didn't want them to lose time walking backward and forward nursing. They built a long old trough like a great long old cradle and put all these babies in it every morning when the mother come out to the field. It was set at the end of the rows under a big old cottonwood tree.

"When they were at the other end of the row, all at once a cloud no bigger than a small spot came up, and it grew fast, and it thundered and lightened as if the world were coming to an end, and the rain just came down in great sheets. And when it got so they could go to the other end of the field, that trough was filled with water and every baby in it was floating 'round in the water drownded. They never got nary a lick of labor and nary a red penny for ary one of them babies."

Experiences just after the War

"Mother had been a cook and she just kept on cooking, for the same people. My father he went to farming."

Patrollers

"My father said that the patrollers would run you and ketch you and whip you if you didn't have a pass, when you was away from the pass. But they didn't bother you if you had a pass. The patrollers were mean white people who called themselves making the niggers stay home. I think they were hired. They called their selves making the niggers stay home. They went all through the community looking for people, and whipping them when they'd leave home without a pass. They said you wasn't submissive when you left home without a pass. They hounded Lucy to death. She wouldn't let 'em get her, and she wouldn't let 'em get her quarter."

Ku Klux Klan

"I have seen the Ku Klux. I have washed their regalia and ironed it for them. They wouldn't let just anybody wash and iron it because they couldn't do it right. My son's wife had a job washing and ironing for them and I used to go down and help her. I never did take a job of any kind myself because my husband didn't let me. The regalia was white. They were made near like these singing robes the church choirs have. But they were long—come way down to the shoe tops. That was along in the nineties,—about 1890. It was when they revived the Ku Klux the last time before the World War. In the old days the patrollers used to whip them for being out without a pass but the Ku Klux used to whip them for disorderly living.

"Way back yonder when I was in Alabama, too, I can remember the Ku Klux riding. I was a little child then. The Republicans and Democrats were at war with each other then and they was killing everybody. My brother was one of them they run. He could come out in the daytime, but in the night he would have to hide. They never got him. He dodged them. That was 'round in 1874. In 1875, him and my uncle left Alabama and went to Louisiana. They called him a stump speaker. They wanted to kill him. They killed Tom Ivory. He was the leader of the Republicans—he was a colored man. His father was white but his mother was a Negro. His father educated him in slavery time. He had been up North and was coming back. They knew he was coming back, so they went up the creek and waited for him—his train. They flagged it down, and some one on the train commenced hollering, 'Look yonder.' Ivory stepped out on the platform to see what they were hollering about, and all them guns started popping and Ivory fell over the end of the platform and down on the ground. He was already leaning over the gate when they fired. Then they come up and cut his tongue out before he died. They said if they got him that would stop all the rest of the niggers. You see, he was a leader.

"Niggers was voting the Republican ticket 'long about that time. They just went in gangs riding every night—the Ku Klux did. Ku Kluxing and killing them they got hold of.

"The police arrested all the men that had anything to do with Tom Ivory's killing. The leader of the killers was a white man they called Captain Hess. I never knowed how the trial came out because we left there while they was still in jail."

How Freedom Came

"I heard my mother say that when the Refugees came through Sumter County, Alabama, she wasn't free but was 'sot' free later. The refugees came through along in February. Then the papers was struck and it went out that the niggers all was free. Mother's master and my oldest brother who had stayed in the War with his master four years came home. The refugees was in there when he got home. They went on through. They didn't tarry long there. Then the papers came out and the next day, master called all the hands up to the big house and told them they was free. Mother was set free in the latter part of February and I was born June 5, 1865, so I was born free."

Leaving Alabama

"We left Alabama in the same year Tom Ivory got killed. More than fifty colored people left on the train and come off when we did. People was leaving Alabama something terrible. I never did know what happened to Tom's killers. I heard afterwards that Alabama got broke, they had to pay for so many men they killed."

Interviewer: Mrs. Bernice Bowden
Person interviewed: Cornelia Ishmon
3319 W. Second Avenue
Pine Bluff, Arkansas
Age: 78

CORNELIA ISHMON

"I was born in Mississippi and I can member seein' the Yankees goin' by. I was a little bit of a girl and Betsy Hardy, that was old Miss, she kep' the Yankees from gettin' me. She told me many a time if it hadn't been for her I'd a had my brains beat out against a tree. When I didn't do to suit her, she'd tell me bout dat. I stayed right in the house.

"I member when they was lookin' for Johnson's brigade and when they saw it was the Yankees they just flew. The Yankees was goin' through there doin' what they wanted.

"I never got no further than the third grade."

United States. Work Projects Administration

El Dorado District
Name of interviewer: Mildred Thompson & Carol Graham.
Subject: Uncle Jack Island—Ex-Slave.
Story—Information (If not enough space on this page add page)

JACK ISLAND

"Yas'm ah membuhs a lil'l bit bout slavery days. Ah wuz jes a chap den. Ah'm 73 now. Ah wuz such a chap dat ah didn' do much work. Day use tuh cook on de fiuh place an ah'd tote in bark an wood fuh em tuh cook wid an git up de aigs (eggs) an sich li'l things as dat.

"Mah ole marster was Marse Bullock an we lived in de Lisbon community.

"Mistress' baby chile wuz a boy an he wuz jes six months olduh dan ah wuz. Ah wuz de only boy chile in de whole business uv slaves. Evah evenin bout a hour by de sun dey would feed us an by sundown we bettuh be in baid. Dat wuz tuh git us outn de way when de grown fokes come in. Dey wuz six uv us chillun an dey would feed us in a big wooden tray. Dey'd po' hot pot liquor in de tray an crumble braid in hit. Den dey'd give us each a spoon an we would all git roun an eat. Dere wuz Lizzie, Nancy, Sistuh Julia, Sistuh Lu and Martha. Der wuz six uv us. Aftuh dey fed us we would go tuh baid an tuh sleep. Dey had ole fashion wheels. Some nights de women would spin. We wouldn' heah dem when dey come in but when dat ole wheel started tuh goin hit'd wake me up an ah'd lie der a while an watch em spin den ah'd go tuh sleep ergin, an leave em spinnin'. Sometimes we wouldn' see our mamas fum Sunday night till next Sunday mornin. Mah mistress wove cloth. Bout de biggest thing ah done wuz help huh wid huh weavin. Ah would pick up de shickle (shuttle) an run hit through fuh huh. Dat bout de biggest thing ah'd do sides feedin the chickens an bringin in bark. In dem days wuznt no buckets much. We used hand gourds dat would hold two or three gallons uv watuh. An ah'd carry one uv dem gourds uv watuh tuh de fiel' tuh em while day was pickin cotton. One yeah de cotton worms wuz so bad an ah hadn' nevah seen none. Ah'd started tuh de fiel' wid de gourd uv watuh an saw dem worms an oh, ah jes bawled. Mah mama had tuh come an git me. Ah didn' know nothin bout dem worms.

"De nearest battle in de wah was at Vicksburg. Ah membush one day hit got so smoky an ah could heah de guns. Ah thought hit wuz thunderin an said tuh ole missus dat hit wuz gointer rain soon but ole missus say: 'Oh Lawdy, dat aint thunder. Ah wish hit wuz. Dat's guns and dat, dat yo sees is smoke an not clouds.' Aftuh de wah wuz ovah we stayed on wid ole marster. Soon aftuh de wah wuz ovah marster died an missus mahried Ed Oakley, a spare built man. Dey lives in Arcadia, Louisiana now. Ah stayed on thar till ah wuz bout fo'teen an ah lef' dere. Wuz gone bout a yeah an ah learnt sumpin too. When ah got off ah had tuh go to work. Bout all ah had tuh do at home wuz tuh take keer uv de stock aftuh ah got big nough tuh but ah sho nuff worked den. Ah stayed way bout a year den ah went back an stayed dere too till ah was bout twenty-one. Ah been mahried three times. Ah had five chillun by mah fust wife an dem is all de chillun ah evah had. One uv dem lives in town, one in Texas, one

Dubach, La., one is daid an ah don' know de where-bouts uv de othuh one. De las' time ah heerd anything bout him he wuz in Hot Springs. Mah present wife's name is Talitha. We has one gran'chile livin wid us. He bout fifteen an is at school ovah dar crost de road wha yo sees dat house. Oh Missy dem times we been tawkin bout wuz de good times. Dese times are hard."

Circumstances of Interview

STATE—Arkansas
NAME OF WORKER—Mrs. Carol Graham
ADDRESS—El Dorado, Arkansas
DATE—December, 1938
SUBJECT—Ex-slave

1. Name and address of informant—Jack and Talitha Island, Route 1, El Dorado, Arkansas.

2. Date and time of interview—December, 1938

3. Place of interview—Route 1, El Dorado, Arkansas.

4. Name and address of person, if any, who put you in touch with informant—

5. Name and address of person, if any, accompanying you—

6. Description of room, house, surroundings, etc.—

Personal History of Informant

STATE—Arkansas
NAME OF WORKER—Mrs. Carol Graham
ADDRESS—EL Dorado, Arkansas

DATE—December, 1938
SUBJECT—Ex-slave
NAME AND ADDRESS OF INFORMANTS—Jack and Talitha Island, Route 1, El Dorado.

1. Ancestry—

2. Place and date of birth—Talitha was born April 14, 1864 in Arcadia, Louisiana. Jack was born in 1863.

3. Family—Talitha had three children and Jack had three children.

4. Places lived in, with dates—Talitha lived in Arcadia, Louisiana until freedom. Jack and Talitha now live in El Dorado.

5. Education, with dates—

6. Occupations and accomplishments, with dates—

7. Special skills and interests—

8. Community and religious activities—Goes to church in schoolhouse across the road.

9. Description of informant—

10. Other points gained in interview—They tell some of their childhood days.

Text of Interview (Unedited)

Talitha: "Howdy, chillun, come in. Naw suh, Jack ain't heah right now. He down tuh the thicket back uv de house gittin' some wood. Naw suh, he won't be gone long. He soon be back. You all come in and set on the gallery. Here's a cheer, missy. He be back in no time tall.

"You wants to know how old I am? I was born April 14, 1864 before the niggers was freed in '65.

"My mother was a field woman (worked in the field) and had seven chillun when set free. Her mistress raised her from three weeks old. Her mother burned to death in a house on the plantation. Our home was 'bout four miles east of Arcadia, Louisiana, or rather Miss Sarah Given's house was, and we stayed on wid her until I was a big girl, plowin' and hoeing.

"No ma'am, I never did go to no parties. I was never 'lowed to go. I been a member of the church since I was ten and now I'm seventy-three.

"I first married a man by the name of Williams and had three chillun by him, two boys and one girl. Then I was a widow fifteen years before I married Jack. We ain't never had no chillun, but Jack had three chillun and I helped to raise them and I've helped raise a bunch of his gran'chillun.

"I believes I hear Jack back there now."

Jack: "Howdy, howdy! So you is back for more tales 'bout long ago. I'se seventy-three and I been in this world a long time I tell you."

Talitha: "Now, Jack, you knows you is heap older 'n me and I'm seventy-three and I was born jes 'bout a year befo the War closed and you say you was a big chap then."

Jack: "Well, I guess I was around six years old when the War started. I was a good big chap. I 'member one evening 'bout three o'clock I was settin' out in the yard playin' with a mate of mine—Johnnie Cook. I guess you would call him my mate; he was my mistress's boy and 'bout my age and we played together all the time even if I was black. I was the only black boy on the place, all the other cullud chillun was gals. Us chaps was out in the yard making frog nesties with our bare feet in the sand. They was fightin' in Vicksburg then. They was doing a whole lot of shooting. You could hear it one right after the other and it got so smoky. I thought it was thunder and said something 'bout hit. Mistress was setting on the gallery sewing and when I said that she said, 'Aw Lawd, that ain't no thunder,' but she didn' tell us what hit wuz."

Talitha: "Course I wasn't old enough to know anything 'bout hit but I heard my mother say it got so smoky the chickens didn't get off the roost while they was bustin' all them big cannons."

Jack: "All us chillun was just as fat and healthy as hogs. Warn't never sick. They'd feed 'bout this time every evening (4 p.m.) and by sundown I was in bed. My mother worked in the field and I've heard her say that sometime she didn't see her chillun from Sunday to Sunday. Old lady Hannah Banks done the cooking for everybody and she cooked on a big fireplace. They didn't have no stove. Why, I got here before the stoves did. Ma and pa and all the grown ones would get up at four o'clock and eat breakfast and be in the field workin' by sunup. They had a box with shelves drove up on the side of the wall to the cabin where we slept and old lady Hannah Banks would put our breakfast in that and when we woke up we would get it and eat. One morning I woke up before the other chillun did and 'cided I'd git my breakfast first 'fore they did. I clem up, rech up and got holt of that box and I was so heavy I pulled it down and broke all the old blue edge plates. That woke the other chillun up all right, and I can jes see them old blue edge plates now. For dinner they would give us boiled greens or beans wid bread and for supper they would save the slop (liquor), cram it full of bread, pour it in a tray and give it to all the chilluns and me, sister Julia, Nancy, Lizzie, Marthy, and all the little nigger chillun."

Talitha: "Huh! Old man Givens had so many little nigger chillun couldn' feed 'em in no tray. Had to have troughs. They'd take a log and hollow it out and make three tubs in a row and put peg legs on it and a hole in the bottom of each one with a pin in it. They would use these tubs to wash the clothes in and pull the stem up to let all the water run out, clean 'em out real good, fill with bread and pot-licker or bread and milk, and feed the nigger chillun."

Jack: "You say our nephew wants to come out and bring a bunch of young folks and wants me to take them 'possum hunting some moonlight night? Sho, sho, I'll go."

Talitha: "I don't know how he'd go lessen we totes him. Why, he got the rheumatism so bad he can't hardly git 'round in the daytime much less at night. Why, the other day he was out in the field follerin' the boy that was plowin' up the potatoes and we was goin' on pickin' them up. First thing I know I hear somethin' behind me go 'plop' and I looked roun and there lay Jack jes stretched out. Fell down over his own feet. So what would he do out nights? And you sees that knot on his ankle. Hit was broke when he was a boy an' hit still gives him trouble when his rheumatism starts up."

Jack: "You say how did I do it? I was jumpin'. A bunch of us boys was jumpin' 'cross a ditch jes to see how far we could jump. I was a young chap 'bout seventeen or eighteen then. I was doin' purty well with my jumpin' when I made a misjump an' jumped crooked and hit my ankle on a big old iron rock. My but hit hurt bad. I didn' do no more jumpin' that day. The next day I was down in the woods getting a load of lider. Had put on a few pieces on the wagon when I started to turn aroun and down I went. I jes lay there and hollered till someone come an' got me. That was in the winter just before Christmas and I didn't get out no more till in the spring. The woods looked right purty to me when I got out. The leaves was great big. And that ain't all, I ain't jumped no more since. 'Sides that I ain't never been sick to 'mount to anything. Had the whooping cough at the same time that Joe and Tom Snyder had hit. Still got my natchel teeth, lost four up here and got one that bothers me some, 'sides that I have 'em all. Yas suh, that the schoolhouse 'cross the road there. We has preachin' there sometimes too. Does Ab preach there? He, he, he! sometime he do. Did I ever tell you 'bout the time Ab was preaching out here at _____ and got to stampin' roun wid that peg-leg of his'n an' hit went through the rotten floor and we had to pull him out? He, he, he!"

Talitha: "Now, Jack Island, you knows that is jes 'nother one uv yo tales. I is been to hear Ab preach lots of times and he does storm roun mighty bad and I ain't got no faith in his religion tall but I warn't there when he fell through the floo'."

United States. Work Projects Administration

Interviewer: Pernella M. Anderson
Person interviewed: Mary Island
626 Nelson Street, El Dorado, Arkansas
Age: 80

MARY ISLAND

"I was born in Union Parish, Louisiana in the year of 1857, so the white folks told me, and I am eighty years old. My mama died when I was two years old and my aunty raised me. She started me out washing dishes when I was four years old and when I was six she was learning me how to cook. While the other hands was working in the field I carried water. We had to cook out in the yard on an old skillet and lid, so you see I had to tote brush and bark and roll up little logs such as I could to keep the fire from one time of cooking to the other. I was not but six years old either. When I got to be seven years old I was cutting sprouts almost like a man and when I was eight I could pick one hundred pounds of cotton. When it rained and we could not go to the field my aunty had me spinning thread to make socks and cloth, then I had to card the bats and make the rolls to spin.

"My auntie was a slave and she lived in the edge of the field. Of course I was born a slave but didn't know much about it because my aunty did the bossing of me but I had a pretty hard time. Our wash tubs, water buckets, bread trays and such were made out of tupelo gum logs dug out with some kind of an axe and when aunty would wash I had to use the battling stick. I would carry the wet clothes to a stump and beat them with that battling stick and we hung the clothes out on bushes and on the fence. We used water from a spring.

"In my young days all we wore was homespun and lowel. We lived in a log house with a dirt floor and the cracks was chinked with mud and our bed was some poles nailed against the wall with two legs out on the dirt floor, and we pulled grass and put in a lowel bed tick. My aunty would get old dresses, old coats, and old pants and make quilts.

"I never went to school a day in my life. No, the back of my head has never rubbed against the walls of a schoolhouse and I never did go to Sunday School and I never did like it. And I didn't go to church until I was grown and the church that I did attend was called the Iron Jacket Church. Now they call it the Hard Shell Church. I believe in foot washing. I don't go to church now because there is no Hard Shell church close around here."

Interviewer: Miss Irene Robertson
Person interviewed: Henrietta Isom, Biscoe, Arkansas
Age: 81

HENRIETTA ISOM

"I was born in Mississippi. It wasn't far from Memphis, Tennessee. I heard em talking bout it then. When I first knowed anything we lived way down in Mississippi. It was on a big farm not close to no place much. My ma's and pa's master was named Thornton. Seems lack it was Jack and her name was Miss Lucretia. They show did have a big family, little ones on up. I have three sisters and a brother all dead—ma was a farm hand. She left us wid a real old woman—all the little children stayed right wid her. We minded her lack our ma's. She switch our legs if we didn't. She carded and sewed about all the time.

"I don't know much about master and mistress; their house was way over the field. They lived on a hill and had the finest well of water. It was so cold. They had two buckets on a chain to pull it up by. The cabins down closer to the creek. There was two springs one used mostly for washing and the other for house use.

"I don't know how many cabins they was scattered. He had a lot of hands about all I remembers—on Saturdays we get to go up to the house to fetch back something; some provisions. They tell us if we be good we could go. They done their own cooking. When they work their dinners was sent to the shade trees from white folks house and the childrens was sent too. We would all stand around Miss Rachel (white) when she bring it then we go sit on the steps and eat. We show did have plenty to eat. We wear the dresses new in cold weather then they wear thin for summer. They be lighter in color too when they fade.

"I remember when the white folks left an went to war. They worked on. They had a white man and a colored man boss. When freedom was declared nearly all of them walked off so glad they was free. I don't know where they all went. My folks went to another big place. We had a hard time. We all farmed. I don't know what they expected from freedom. Nobody didn't ask for nuthin. I remembers when some new hands was bought and put on the place. I think they sold em off in town.

"After de war at the church they talked bout if they didn't get freedom they would clang together for der rights but they never did do nuthin. Times was so hard they had to work harder than before.

"The Yankees nor none of the soldiers ever come to our cabins—I seen them along the roads. They show did clean up Miss Leucretia's calves and hogs. Took em all off at one time. Rations show did get mighty scarce.

"They sing, I recken they did sing, go off to work singin and the men whistlin. Mostly sung religious songs. Master Thornton had a white man preach sometimes. Down in front of the cabins in the shade. Sometimes somebody get to go to white church with the family. They held the baby. They didn't have no school.

"I seed the Ku Klux Klans in the road light nights—when they pass we all peep out the cracks. They didn't bother nobody I knowed. We was scared they would turn in an come to the house.

"I farmed all my life, hoed cotton and corn. No maam I aint never voted—I jess lives wid my children here and my son in Memphis and my other daughter at Helena. My daughter do farm work and my son railroads. He works in the yards.

"I don't know what to say bout the generations comin on. They is smarter in their books and sees more than older folks, but they ain't no better. You kaint depend on what they says. I don't know what to say would make the country better lessen the folks all be better.

"I never heard of no rebellions. I jess lived in Mississippi till I comes here and Memphis and stay around wid the children and grandchildren. They all do fairly well for the fast times I guess."

Transcriber's Note

The original of this text had some handwritten annotations. Where these corrected typographical errors, the correction has simply been made. Where they queried certain words or phrases, the phrase has been marked by red underlining and a mouse-hover. Larger handwritten insertions to the text have been rendered in italics. (The only other use of italics was on the title page, since the main text was typewritten.)

The date marked at the beginning of some of the accounts was a stamp mark. Where this was partially missing or illegible, the omissions are marked as —.

Page numbers in body text refer to the page of the current interview, unlike those in the table of contents which refer to the numbering of the whole document. They have been hyperlinked to the correct place.

Some typographical errors have been corrected; they are marked by grey underlining and a mouse-hover. In addition, punctuation and formatting have been made consistent, particularly the use of quotation marks.

Slave Narratives

www.ingramcontent.com/pod-product-compliance
Lightning Source LLC
Chambersburg PA
CBHW071618170426
43195CB00038B/1341